# White Man's Grave

## Europeans in West Africa
## in the 15th to 20th Centuries

## Jeff Andrew

Red Llama Books

ISBN: 978-1-8384476-0-1 (Paperback Edition)
ISBN: 978-1-8384476-1-8 (EPub Edition)

# CONTENTS

# PREFACE

The British Empire in West Africa endured for over 150 years, from the foundation of the first Crown Colony in Sierra Leone in 1808 to the Independence of the Republic of The Gambia in 1965. During the Victorian era, Britain expanded its territory throughout the world and became the largest, richest and most powerful empire in world history. At that time the majority of the British population believed that their government was doing nothing wrong. The prevailing opinion was that Britain was improving and developing the overseas territories that it conquered. Racist attitudes of the time even promoted the idea that the Empire was bringing order to *'backward'* regions of the world. British churchgoers also believed that their country had embarked on a holy mission to save *'heathen peoples'* and convert them to the Christian faith, which they considered to be the only true religion. Paradoxically, Victorians were also fascinated to know more about the distant lands, and eager to receive detailed anthropological, botanical and zoological information about them.

Today, we are more sensitive to the wrongs that imperial conquest inflicted on the indigenous peoples of West Africa, and the long-lasting damage it caused to the local economy. While the Empire made Britain richer, the colonised territories became poorer, as much of the local wealth was plundered and removed to Britain. There is no doubt that Britain profited hugely from its empire, and that the military campaigns were at times brutal. The colonial regime was also based on an ingrained assumption of racial superiority, the arrogant and prejudiced belief that the local inhabitants needed *'civilising'*.

Recently the Black Lives Matter movement has stimulated an active debate about the legacies of slavery and imperialism. Undoubtedly Britain should be deeply ashamed of its role in the Atlantic Slave Trade from the sixteenth to nineteenth centuries. But equally we should applaud the fact that it was William Wilberforce and the West African Squadron of the Royal Navy who were at the forefront of the suppression of the slave trade and its eventual abolition in 1833. This book does not attempt to take sides, but to seek a balanced equation that takes into account both past and present perspectives.

It is important to register just how long European engagement in West Africa lasted. The first European adventurers arrived at the West African coast as early as the middle of the fifteenth century, to be followed by a succession of invasions from Europe over the next five centuries. In the modern age of international air travel and a rapidly shrinking planet, it is difficult perhaps to stand back and appreciate the hardships and dangers that faced previous generations of Europeans who travelled similar long distances at substantially greater danger to themselves.

In the sixteenth to eighteenth centuries, what defined the early European travellers to West Africa was the single-mindedness and dedication with which they followed their star, whether it be in pursuit of geographical knowledge, religious conversion, national reputation, social status, or simply commercial profit. What was remarkable was that they were prepared to risk their own health and sometimes to sacrifice their own lives in the process. Later, during the colonial period of the nineteenth and early twentieth centuries, we can also perhaps admire the determination and doggedness which European recruits to West Africa applied to their military, business, or civil service careers. A study of the diaries of British colonial administrators reveals that for many it also involved dedicated service to their country.

It was precisely these strengths of character that enabled Europeans for five centuries to maintain their spirits and good humour in a hostile environment that the public opinion back home had damned as the *'White Man's Grave'*. This is what makes it intriguing and perhaps at times instructive to follow the trail of those pioneering Europeans from a bygone age who, to quote Rudyard Kipling, *"yearned beyond the skyline where the strange roads go down"*.

# HISTORICAL TIMELINE

**1445**

Portuguese sailors establish first European trading post at Arguim on the West African coast.

**1515**

Portuguese Christian missionaries are invited to attend the court of the Oba of Benin, Nigeria.

**1638**

The French build a trading station on the estuary of the Senegal River.

**1661**

The British establish their first permanent settlement when they build Fort James at the mouth of the Gambia River.

**1672**

The Royal African Company is granted a charter giving it the exclusive right to convey slaves to the Americas.

**1770s**

The triangular trade, controlled from Liverpool, ships millions of Africans across the Atlantic as slaves.

**1787**

Abolitionist John Clarkson leads an expedition from the Americas to resettle 1200 formerly enslaved people in Sierra Leone.

**1795**

Scottish Explorer Mungo Park leads an inland expedition that reaches the Niger River and solves one of the great unanswered questions Europeans had of African geography: the Niger flows east, not west.

**1807**

The British Parliament passes a Slave Trade Act that outlaws the trading of slaves in the British Empire, but does not abolish the practice of slavery itself.

**1808**
Sierra Leone becomes the first official British colony in West Africa.

**1821**
The Gold Coast (present-day Ghana) becomes a British Crown Colony.

**1824-1900**
A series of five conflicts take place between the British and the Ashanti Empire in the interior of the Gold Coast.

**1830**
Richard and John Lander become the first Europeans to follow the course of the Niger to the ocean, proving that the river was navigable. This discovery paved the way for the more 'legitimate' trading that was to replace the slave trade.

**1832**
Liverpool merchant Macgregor Laird pioneers the use of steamboat navigation on the Niger River.

**1833**
The British Parliament passes a Slavery Abolition Act to abolish the institution of slavery by making the purchase or ownership of slaves illegal within the British Empire.

**1841**
British missionaries mount a government-backed expedition up the Niger River to introduce Christianity and to promote trade.

**1854**
William Baikie pioneers the use of quinine to protect his crew on an expedition up the Niger, and returns to the coast without the loss of a single life.

**1861**
The British annex Lagos as a colony.

**1879**
George Goldie and British traders on the Niger consolidate their interests to create the United Africa Company (later the Royal Niger Company).

**1884 -1885**

The Berlin Conference divides Africa between European powers without consulting the African people.

**1897**

Richard Ross makes the breakthrough discovery that malaria is spread by the anopheles mosquito.

**1900**

The British Empire creates the Southern Nigeria and Northern Nigeria Protectorates. In 1906 the Colony of Lagos is merged with the Southern Protectorate.

**1906**

Frederick Lugard is appointed the Commissioner of the Northern Protectorate, and begins the consolidation of military conquest by British forces.

**1914**

A single unified Colony and Protectorate of Nigeria is created, with Lagos as its capital.

**1945 -1965**

The rise of Independence Movements in West Africa after World War II leads to Ghana becoming the first British colony to be declared an independent nation in 1957, and culminates in the Independence of The Gambia in 1965.

# HISTORICAL MAP OF
# WEST AFRICA (1729)

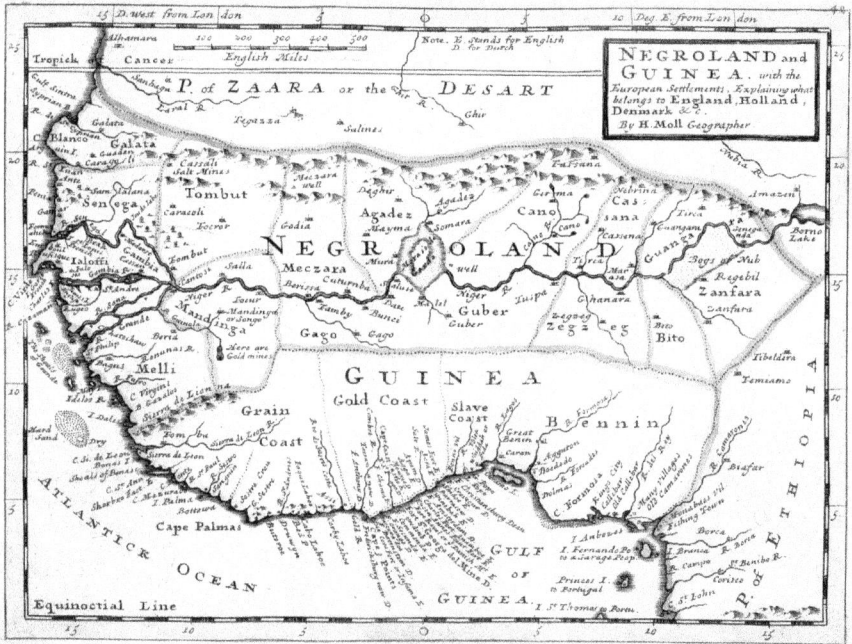

# CONTEMPORARY MAP
# OF WEST AFRICA

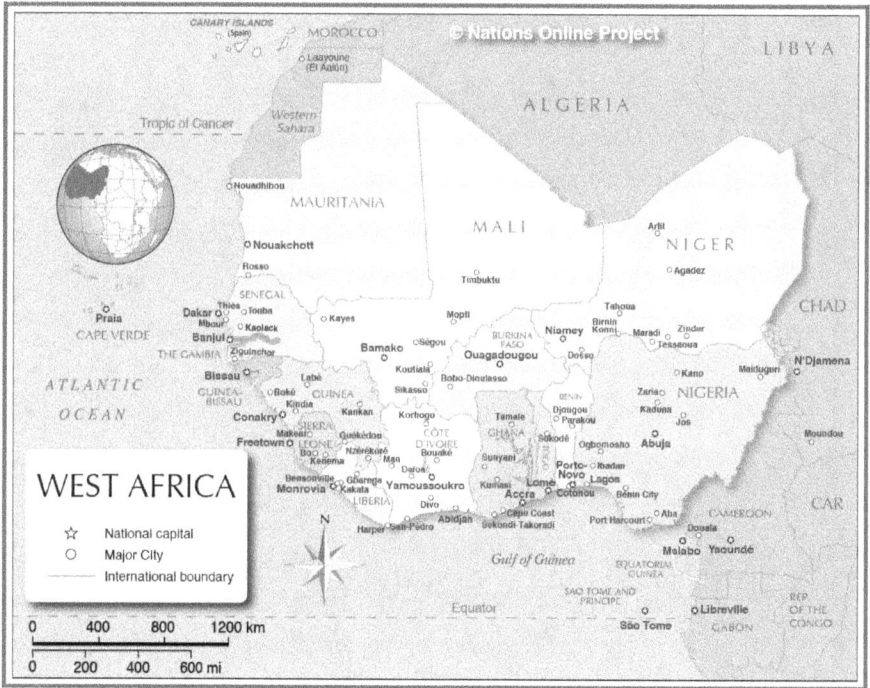

# 1  THE BIGHT OF BENIN

*"Beware and take care of the Bight of Benin.*
*There's one comes out for forty goes in."*

In 1553, Thomas Wyndham on a voyage to West Africa cast anchor to buy gold at the fort of Elmina on the Gold Coast (the coastal area of present-day Ghana). His Portuguese pilot became nervous and begged his captain to return home without delay. But Wyndham was determined to sail further along the West African coast to the city of Benin, where he wanted to load a cargo of black peppers. As he waited in the Benin River for the peppers to be delivered, he watched with increasing alarm as one by one his crew succumbed to some deadly fever. Sometimes up to five of his men died in a single day. Without an obvious cause for their sickness, he rebuked his sailors for their lack of restraint and excessive behaviour and accused them of:

*"eating without measure of the fruits of the country, and drinking of the wine of the Palme trees, and in such extreme heate running continually into the water."*

In his opinion, it was this overindulgence, coupled with rapid changes in their body temperature, which explained why they were dying like flies around him. But it was not long before Wyndham himself caught the fever and died. His Portuguese pilot was forced by the terrified survivors to put to sea, leaving stranded their poor colleagues who were still upriver buying peppers at Benin. The voyage had been an abject failure, and the death toll made a bleak record when the ship finally did limp back to its home port of Plymouth. Even then the misery was not over, as it was later reported:

*"Of seven score men, came home to Plimmouth scarcely forty and*

*of them many died."*

It is not surprising that for a while this melancholy episode put a dampener on British trade to the West African coast. Rumour spread, and the creeks and estuaries where the ships first anchored soon gained a sinister reputation. Other European nations were happy to leave West African trade to the Portuguese, who had first visited the coast in the fifteenth century, as part of a national effort to expand its empire by opening up ocean trading routes to Africa and Asia. Their main goals were in Asia, but to reach Asia it was necessary to circumnavigate Africa. In the process, they hoped to establish contact with the empire of Mali in the interior, and to divert some of the lucrative trans-Saharan gold trade from Muslim North Africa to Christian Europe.

For nearly a hundred years the Portuguese monopolised the West African gold trade, and to protect themselves they built a series of stone forts along the coast. In the seventeenth century, there was a revival of interest in the rest of Europe, and the Portuguese were rapidly supplanted by the Dutch, English, and Danes. They set up about thirty trading forts along the coast, which continually changed hands because of distant European wars, or local deals and skirmishes. In 1672, the Royal African Company was granted by the British government a legal monopoly of trade in West Africa, and it established its local headquarters at Cape Coast Castle on the Gold Coast. The company maintained forts or factories not only on the Gold Coast itself, but also to the west at the River Gambia and in Sierra Leone, and to the east on the Slave Coast (roughly the coastal area of present-day Benin and Nigeria). Its trade was mainly in gold and slaves, but other goods such as ivory, wax and dyewoods were also purchased. The company lost its monopoly of the West African trade in 1698, and thereafter went into decline.

During its short existence, the letters of Royal African Company employees posted to West Africa are punctuated by sad tales of the misery and loneliness of their existence, and especially of the harrowing and debilitating effect of disease. William Pley from James Fort in Accra starts one letter:

*"I bless God I have overcome a desperate and dangerous feavour (under which I have a long time languished) soe far as I am gaine upon my leggs, though soe weake I am scarce to stand."*

In fact, sickness was so common a fact of life and so regular a part of correspondence that one begins to wonder whether it became an excuse for negligence or tardiness on the part of some employees. In one letter from the same fort Ralph Hassell begins:

*"Yours of the 2nd instant received, and your honour indeed may wonder att my silence, which indeed hath been occasioned by sickness and aloes per a sting of scorpion on my right hand, which I could not till this day hold a penn in my hand, else had not been negligent in performing my duty."*

At around the same time, Jean Barbot, a French commercial agent on slave ships working for the Compagnie du Sénégal, made two voyages to the coast of West Africa, in 1678 and 1682. He observed that:

*"Fevers, above all other distempers, destroy the greatest number of people, especially newcomers from Europe, carrying them off in less than eight days sickness…Cholics are frequent and so terrible as to distract the sufferer for three or four days. The cause is mostly attributed to the excessive use of women or to the evening dews."*

He was not alone in condemning the disreputable behaviour of those unfortunate enough to be marooned in one of the forts along the coast.

In 1705, William Bosman, Governor of the Dutch fort at Elmina, published an account of trading life in West Africa. He suggested that the nearby English fort of Cape Coast was mainly garrisoned by drunks expelled from his own fort

Elmina, describing them as:

*"chiefly sottish wretches, yet they are very welcome to them: the English never better pleased than when the soldier spends his money on drink...it is incredible how many are consumed by this damnable Liquor."*

In his view excessive drinking was normal among all Europeans:

*"And to make quicker work, they are as zealous votaries to Venus as Bacchus, and so waste the small portion of strength left to them from tippling...and then adieu to Health and soon after to Life itself."*

But he consoled himself with the thought that:

*"If men lived here as long as in Europe, 'twould be less worth while to come Hither, and a man would be obliged to wait too long before he got a 'good post'."*

Bosman himself had survived fourteen sober years on the West African coast and was a somewhat unforgiving character. In his memoirs he wanted to insert some drawings of the forts, but was somewhat put out that:

*"Death, which spares no man, visited my draughtsman before he could complete the illustrations."*

It was in the nineteenth century, that West Africa was considered to be a *'White Man's Grave'* because of the extremely high mortality of Europeans there. In 1825, there were 108 European residents of the garrison at Jamestown at the mouth of the Gambia River: but within four months there were only 21 survivors. At Fernando Po, an island off the coast originally colonised by the Portuguese, the standing orders posted for the labour force were:

*"Gang No 1 to be employed digging graves as usual. Gang No 2 making coffins until further notice."*

A study of military mortality over the period 1817-1836 has revealed the comparative death rates of British troops serving in different parts of the world. Annual death rates from disease were 10 per 1000 soldiers for the Cape of Good Hope in South Africa and 75-85 per 1000 for India and the West Indies, but a staggering 480 per 1000 for Sierra Leone. In 1841, an expedition up the Niger River lost 48 out of 145 men on the river in only nine weeks. It is not surprising therefore that the Royal Navy ships, which patrolled the coast of West Africa after the abolition of slavery, became quickly known by their crews as the *'coffin squadron'*.

At the time, there was no known cure for the tropical diseases which new arrivals on the coast seemed to contract so readily. Indeed, for over five centuries Europeans on the coast of West Africa, whether would-be conquerors, traders, explorers or missionaries, successively succumbed to tropical fevers. Analysis of the records of the European employees of the English Royal African Company during their time in West Africa in 1683-1766 has revealed that the risk was highest for the men who had just arrived from Europe but remained high also after they had spent several years on the coast. The Europeans formed a virgin population for endemic local tropical diseases, and so the first encounter with them led to extremely high mortality rates. If the *'Black Vomit'* (yellow fever) did not carry them off, then the *'Ague'* (malaria) might.

The study of tropical medicine was largely neglected by the medical profession at home. And so, it was left to naval and army surgeons to make what observations they could. Sadly, the remedies that they prescribed all proved to be ineffective. It seems strange to reflect today that, while every European visitor to the coast would complain about being bothered and bitten by mosquitoes, not one of them connected the insects with the fevers they were suffering on a regular basis. Government authorities also poured scorn on any idea that the ubiquitous mosquito had any part to play in the spread of the disease.

Sailors' first impressions on reaching the West African coast were of a sickly breeze that came off the land, and then as the sun rose of a white mist that hung low over the dark, still waters. And so, suspicion grew that it was the very air they breathed that brought on the fever, and the sweats and the shakes that were the beginning of the end for many. Contemporary pathology was based on the theory that diseases such as cholera or the Black Death were caused by a *'miasma'*, a noxious form of *'bad air'*. Any strange new illness was therefore commonly attributed to bad air or bad smells, and so for new European arrivals on the West African coast the culprit had to be the bad air - the *'malaria'*. The land itself must be sick and releasing noxious vapours fatal to the unsuspecting visitor.

Suggested cures were very hit or miss. Patients recovered more from the body's inherent tendency to repair itself, than because of any remedies that doctors might prescribe. Bloodletting and various purgatives were often inflicted on the suffering to no avail. Indeed, they often weakened the patients and allowed the fever to take hold. Laxatives, emetics and liberal doses of calomel (which was the explorer Mungo Park's own favourite remedy) caused more problems than they cured.

There were other precautions taken on board ship to ward off the evil vapours. In 1834, Macgregor Laird, a Liverpool sea captain, recorded in the journal of his expedition the various measures taken to prevent sickness. These included covering the deck fore and aft with double awnings, raising the sides of the vessel with canvas to a height of eight feet, and sprinkling the cabin and deck areas daily with chloride of lime. He also urged future captains never to allow their white crew to work away from under the ship's awnings, or to sleep in the open exposed to the morning dew. Two of his more eccentric prescriptions for swampy areas were to triple the crew's usual allowance of spirits, and to have constant music played on board. Typical of his time, he attributed the causes of sickness to:

*"the sudden change from the open sea to a narrow and winding river, the want of the sea-breeze, and the prevalence of the deadly miasma to which we were nightly exposed from the surrounding swamps".*

Nevertheless, despite all the inherent dangers European traders continued to visit the West African coast in pursuit of the highly profitable trade in slaves and gold. They continued to operate at a distance, using African traders and chiefs as local intermediaries, and retained only a minimal presence on land. Indeed, until the end of the nineteenth century the British presence in West Africa was confined to a few small trading settlements on the coast. The frightening loss of life on these early trading ventures impeded and delayed further commercial exploitation of the interior. In 1854, however, some measure of protection against disease was achieved through the use of quinine as a prophylactic on an expedition up the Niger River led by William Baikie. All the crew returned safely from the voyage, which meant that malaria no longer needed to present an insurmountable barrier to European exploration of the interior.

Thereafter, quinine provided Europeans in West Africa with a limited form of protection against malaria. But its regular use was not widespread, since it was difficult to obtain supplies adequate in quality as well as in quantity. There was also as yet no general agreement on the precise dosage required. Quite apart from the unpleasant side effects quinine could produce, insufficient or inconsistent dosage could bring about an attack of blackwater fever. The root cause of the disease remained a mystery, and there was still no effective cure. And so, European traders, missionaries, and government officials in West Africa continued to die or fall seriously ill from unknown fevers.

It was only in 1897 that Richard Ross, an Indian Army surgeon, made the breakthrough discovery that malaria was spread by the anopheles mosquito. And so, the horrific death rate that had plagued European visitors to the West African coast for over four hundred years had been traced to the bite of a tiny insect. The mosquito had effectively delayed penetration of the interior, and so prevented European settlement of West Africa. In recognition of the part played by this powerful ally against colonisation, one of the early political parties in Independent Nigeria adopted the mosquito as its election symbol.

European mortality in West Africa began to decline steadily from the 1890s, although this was largely due to the improved sanitary measures that followed the discovery of the role of mosquitoes in malarial transmission. At the extreme, such measures included the segregation of European housing by maintaining an open space of a quarter of a mile from the rest of the population. It was not until the Second World War that a more effective treatment for malaria became widely available as a result of the development of synthetic drugs, such as chloroquine.

And so, well into the twentieth century the West African Coast retained its sinister reputation. Indeed, the coastline of West Africa between Freetown in Sierra Leone came to be known as 'The Boneyard'. And the Atlantic Ocean received into its depths the bodies of many homebound 'coasters' who had left it too late to book their return passage home after falling ill. For almost four hundred years of European contact with the West African coast, the threat of serious illness or death was an accepted part of the daily lives of a succession of traders, explorers, missionaries, empire builders and colonial administrators. Their collective story is by no means glorious, and it is particularly stained by the brutal early period of unrestricted slavery. For many the adventure ended in failure and disappointment, often worn down by the climate or debilitated by disease. But for others the experience was inspiring and rewarding, as they embraced the warmth, generosity of spirit and good humour of the inhabitants of the land in which they briefly trespassed.

# 2 ATLANTIC SLAVE TRADERS

*"Cape Coast to Bonny, who cares but for money?"*

Portuguese mariners sailed beyond Cape Bojador in Morocco for the first time in the 1430s. Like other European countries, Portugal was looking for a route to Asia. Instead of heading to Asia, they headed down to Western Africa. By 1445, a trading post was established on the small island of Arguim off the coast of present-day Mauritania. As Portuguese ships continued to explore African coastlines and rivers over the following decades, they established similar *'feitorias'* or trading *'factories'* with the goal of tapping into pre-existing local commercial networks. When their ships reached the coast of present-day Ghana, they found that the local Akan people had access to supplies of gold that were plentiful by contemporary European standards. The Portuguese named the coastline *'Mina' ('The Mine')*; and more generally in European languages it soon became known as the Gold Coast.

However, European interest in African gold was quickly overshadowed by the richer prospects for gold and silver in the Americas. Commercial opportunities for European traders were also more attractive in India and China. And so, the Portuguese monopoly of West African trade went largely unchallenged for well over 100 years But at the beginning of the seventeenth century their dominance of the coastline started to collapse, as ships from almost every European nation set sail for the Gold Coast. They were intent on a new and more sinister mission: the export of slaves which were increasingly in demand for the new plantations in the Americas.

# Origins Of The Slave Trade

In the early years of the seventeenth century over 300,000 white servants and prisoners were shipped to work in England's tobacco colonies, lured by the promise of their own plot of land after four years of service. On their outward voyage they were packed tightly in the holds of cargo ships, as slaves would be later. Even after their arrival many were badly housed, beaten and starved. Some did manage to set themselves up with a small farm. But many died before their term was up, and others sank into abject poverty. When the Caribbean tobacco boom faded in the 1630s, landowners switched their attention to sugar.

However, sugar production was backbreaking work and needed a much larger work force than tobacco. This was because the production process combined not only agriculture, as the cane was cultivated, but also manufacture, as the cane juice was reduced into semi-refined sugar. The landowners simply could not import enough servants from Britain to do this work, nor could the Americas provide the pool of labour required. But just across the Atlantic in West Africa there seemed to be an inexhaustible supply, and so the landowners turned instead to Africa and to slave labour.

The low cost of purchasing a slave on the West African coast was another crucial factor in the development of the slave trade. Plantation owners in the Caribbean in the eighteenth century ruthlessly calculated that it was cheaper to buy a newly imported field labourer than to raise a slave child from birth to the working age of fourteen. The price on the heads of imported slaves was kept artificially low because very few of the people sold into the slave trade were working slaves sold by their African masters. Many were prisoners captured in local wars, and others were condemned criminals, kidnap victims or political prisoners. Some were even relatives sold to clear a debt, or in exchange for food in time of famine. Even though the selling price of a landed slave had to be divided between the African intermediaries, who purchased the slaves from local rulers and brought them to the coast for sale, and the European traders who shipped them across the ocean, there was still considerable margin for profit.

As far back as the middle of the fifteenth century Portuguese traders had imported some African slaves to supplement the meagre labour resources of their own country. The Portuguese plantations on Madeira, the Cape Verde Islands and the islands in the Gulf of Guinea also came to depend on African slave labour. In the early sixteenth century Spanish landowners in the Americas followed suit, and a slave trade to the Caribbean commenced on a small scale.

This trade accelerated at the beginning of the seventeenth century when the Dutch West India Company became heavily engaged, since it urgently needed African slaves for its plantations in Brazil. But the company also had an eye for the main chance and realised that a handsome profit could be made from the supply of slaves to European colonies elsewhere in the Americas. And so, it embarked on the conquest of the Portuguese forts on the Gold Coast to secure its source of supply. By the middle of the seventeenth century the Dutch West India Company was firmly in control of most of the former Portuguese bases and was able to dominate trading along the whole of the West Africa coast.

However, the Dutch West India Company's activities in the Atlantic Slave Trade soon caught the attention of the other main seafaring nations of Europe. Soon traders from France, Britain, Germany, and Scandinavia were providing stiff competition. The French and British governments were particularly keen that their colonies should not have to depend on a

Dutch trading company for the supply of slave labour. They encouraged their own merchants to set up companies strong enough to challenge the dominant position of the Dutch West India Company, by offering them national monopolies of trade with West Africa or the Caribbean. They also backed these new enterprises with the promise of naval support. The ever increasing demand for slaves led to a relentless rise in European commercial activity on the West African coast. By the beginning of the eighteenth century there were also few parts of the coastline where African rulers and their agents were not prepared and organised to sell slaves to the foreign intruders.

During the second half of the seventeenth century and in the early eighteenth century there was a succession of wars involving France, Britain and the Netherlands. Although the main battles were fought far away from West Africa, throughout this period traders of each nation jockeyed to increase the number of their trading posts on the West African coast and to deny trading opportunities to their rivals. During this period of intense competition, the number of major European forts on the coastline increased to thirty. The Dutch West India Company had the greatest number of forts and the strongest defensive structures.

But their headquarters at Elmina on the Gold Coast were soon rivalled by a large British fort at Cape Coast only a short distance away. Indeed, almost every Dutch fort had a neighbouring British establishment in competition with it. Although the Dutch West India Company remained a major force throughout the eighteenth century and into the nineteenth century, it steadily lost trade to its British rival trading companies. The two main reasons for this were that Britain had displaced the Netherlands as the major European naval and sea-trading power, and that the burgeoning industrial revolution in Britain made it better equipped to supply overseas traders with cheap goods for the world market.

The British were also more successful than their rivals in adapting their operations to meet changing market conditions. The Dutch and French governments held fast to the principle that African trade was best handled by large single companies, which were granted monopoly rights in return for shouldering military, administrative and commercial responsibilities. The British government calculated that such cumbersome corporations were counter-productive. The practice of first building or capturing coastal forts, and then maintaining and defending them, was also considered to be unnecessarily expensive. It decided that it was more efficient and cost-effective to operate through a variety of small traders, who would not need to be tied to any onshore installation. Instead, they would be free to roam the coast, and so be able to negotiate the best terms of trade they could find at any point. This type of small and more mobile European trader was also welcomed by local African rulers, who were naturally not keen for European traders to set up permanent bases on their land.

Soon Britain came to dominate the slave trade, carrying more *'black ivory'* than all the other countries combined. The human freight transported across the Atlantic became a vital component in a commercial network which spanned the globe. For, in addition to selling domestic manufactures such as guns, cloth, glass and paper, the slave traders traded in foreign goods, such as textiles from India, wines from France, tobacco from America, and cowrie shells from the Maldives for use as currency. By the time of its abolition in 1807, half of Britain's long distance shipping was engaged in the slave trade.

In addition, slaves in the West Indies produced sugar, which was the largest single British import until the 1820s. A luxury in the eighteenth century, it became a necessity in the nineteenth century, as Britain developed a sweet tooth. It was an essential additive to tea, coffee, and chocolate. It transformed puddings from savoury to sweet and promoted them to a special place at the end of meals. The profits from sugar also helped to fuel Britain's phenomenal growth as an industrial powerhouse.

Between the sixteenth and nineteenth centuries over 10 million Africans were forcibly taken to the Americas, and it is estimated that as many as 20 per cent of them were to die on route. In the decade after the American War of Independence, the British alone carried nearly 40,000 slaves to the West Indies to work on the sugar plantations. Up to a quarter of them are thought to have died within eighteen months of arrival. By the end of the century, it is estimated that twenty tons of Caribbean sugar cost the life of a single slave. No wonder Dr Samuel Johnson condemned Jamaica to be:

*"a place of great wealth and dreadful wickedness, a den of tyrants and a dungeon of slaves."*

The barbarities of the trade are well documented and remain stark even after allowing for the exaggerated rhetoric and propaganda in the accounts of nineteenth century Abolitionists. But at the time it was also viewed as a business enterprise, conducted openly and on relatively level terms with experienced dealers in well-organised African states. Latterly also the slaves were transported in custom-made ships, specially adapted to accommodate the captured slaves and so deliver the maximum cargo to their destination. Profit was the primary consideration for a ship's captain, particularly as slaves became an increasingly expensive commodity. It is even said that some captains placed a higher value on the life of their human cargo of slaves than their white crews, nearly a quarter of whom are estimated to have died during each slaving voyage.

## The Slave Ships

The Royal African Company had the monopoly of the British slave trade from 1642-1698, and most of their ships sailed from the port of London. Later, the ports of Bristol and Liverpool made the biggest profits from slavery, and their local economies began to depend on it. The following is a typical letter of instruction of the day, from a group of Liverpool businessmen to Captain Earle of the slave ship Chesterfield, dated 22nd May 1751:

*Captain Earle*

*You being commander of our snow the Chesterfield we give you the following instructions which you are to observe.*

*The first favourable opportunity you are to sail hence for Douglas, Isle of Man. There, take on board from Mr. Paul Bridson sundry goods as per list enclosed, from thence proceed for Old Callabar where you are to barter our cargo as per invoice annexed for slaves and elephants teeth.*

*As you are experienced in the custom there, we need not dictate to you how to act. Therefore we depend on your prudent management with the natives and ships in the river in your trade for our best interest. Should the purchase be very tedious and slaves scarce, we think it advisable that you leave the river when you have got 350 slaves rather than risk your own lives by such long detention, and what goods remain lay over for teeth of any size if possible and then proceed to Barbados and apply to Mr. Samuel Carter, merchant there who will advise you the state of prices for slaves at the other islands, from which you will judge whether to proceed farther or stop there.*

*If you go to Antigua apply to Messrs. George and Ralph Walker and Mr. Andrew Lesley. If to St. Kitts, Messrs. Guichard and Scerett and Messrs. Payne and Leigh, any of which will make the most in sales given the earliest dispatch and best remittance. If none of our islands offer to encourage your calling, proceed directly from Barbados to St. Eustatia and if you can, obtain £17 per head there with full remittance in good bills at thirty, forty or sixty days sight. If not, proceed to Jamaica. There apply to Messrs. Hibbert, Woodcock and Sprigg and Mr. Peter Furnall, either of which will take you on the best terms and load the ship with the island produce, provided the prices are not so extravagant as heretofore. In that case get a freight if possible, to London or Bristol and bring the remittance in bills of exchange. Be always on your guard against insurrections and strictly charge your people to act cautiously that no accident happen by fire or otherwise and see that nothing be wanting that's necessary for your hands.*

*You are to have for your privilege, two slaves, Mr. Bankes your mate one slave, your doctor Mr. Black one slave and one boy slave. Pay your doctor his head money, your coast commission one dollar in ten and pay what seamen's wages they'll take in the West Indies. In case of your mortality, (which the Almighty prevent), your mate Mr. Bankes is to succeed you in command and observe there our directions, and when he arrives in the West Indies, that he be entirely directed by Mr. Carter of Barbados whether to stay there or proceed farther and to what place.*

*We hope what letters we write to meet you will come in due time and may perhaps think of some other mention which we have therein omitted. Advise us by every opportunity of your proceedings. We wish you health success and safe return to.*

*Your assured friends*
*Wm Whaley   Rob Hallhead   John Williamson   Peers Legh*
*Edward Lowndes   John Clayton   Willm Davenport*

*P.S. You are to make choice of your privilege slaves in the river or when you leave Callabar. We would have you purchase all the elephants teeth you possibly can at all events. Rather choose to have them to depend upon even if your cargo should not purchase your full compliment of slaves. But as your cargo is so large, we hope that will not be the case.*

The greed of those involved is all too apparent, as is their indifference to the condition or treatment of the human cargo, which appears to be only of marginally more value to them than ivory. The overriding concern is to reap the greatest possible return on their financial investment in the ship's cargo, which is to be used for barter when the ship reaches West Africa. Even the wages of the captain and his senior officers are defrayed by allowing them to select and trade some slaves on their own account when they reach the Caribbean. This, of course, has the additional bonus of tying in the captain to the enterprise, thus ensuring his commitment and determination to see the hazardous assignment through to a successful conclusion. Just in case the captain should be unfortunate or inconvenient enough to die on the journey, a clause is built into the contract for his mate to take over command of the ship.

Few ships were specially constructed for the slave trade, and they ranged in size from small sloops and schooners to larger ships measuring hundreds of tonnes. However, most slave vessels were small and relatively inexpensive vessels, rigged for speed. The typical *'Guineaman'* was a fast, lightly-armed, copper-bottomed, square-rigged ship of about 200 tonnes, 68 feet long, 24 feet across and 12 feet deep. She was manned by about forty sailors, who were often kidnapped or *'crimped'* in the ports of Liverpool and Bristol. The crews also included surgeons, carpenters, coopers, cooks, and others hired to guard slaves on the West African coast and on the voyage across the Atlantic.

They embarked on a journey lasting several weeks to the Guinea Coast of West Africa, which stretched from modern Senegal to Angola. This was divided somewhat arbitrarily into the Slave Coast, the Gold Coast, the Ivory Coast, and the Grain (or Pepper) Coast. It was an alien and intimidating landscape, with a steamy coastal strip fringed by jungle and swamp. Grim tales were told of cannibalism and human sacrifice practised by fearsome *'natives'* of the interior. So, the early slavers clung to the shore like barnacles, building fortified trading posts from which to barter their cargo.

A typical ship's cargo is illustrated by the following list of a ship going to Africa from Bristol in the 18th century:

*An estimate for a cargo to purchase 250 Negroes at Bonny*

*80 rolls of blue chintz cloth*
*100 rolls of cotton cloth with fine small stripes (small)*
*100 rolls of cotton cloth with fine small stripes (large)*
*100 cotton rolls with red and blue mixed stripes.*
*30 cloths blue and white checked*
*300 muskets bright barrels*
*300 muskets black barrels*
*40 pair common large pistols*
*2 tons lead in small bars*
*14 tons iron*
*1000 copper rods*
*80 cases bottles of brandy*
*5 cases pipe beads*

It would be interesting to know the criteria used for selecting the different striped cloths, and the relative merits of muskets with bright or black barrels. Presumably over time the African chiefs, who traded in their fellow human beings for such luxury goods, also dictated their fashion and style. The brandy, of course, could have had a variety of uses.

Because the harsh and foul working conditions of slave ships and the risks attached to their voyages were well known, few sailors volunteered to serve on them if any other work was available. Many were tricked into signing up for the voyage. The slave ship captains often resorted to *'crimps'* to recruit their crews, which were the equivalent of the press gangs used to enforce military or naval service. Crimps, however, were not government controlled, and so they often resorted to trickery, usually involving alcohol or prostitutes, or both. The common ploy was to get the sailor into debt to a local pub which was under the influence and in the pay of the slave traders. In the ports of Liverpool or Bristol, it seemed that *"there was always plenty of liquor to be had and painted girls enough to go round"*. Most sailors joined slave ships to escape financial ruin, or because they were from seafaring families and knew no other life. Although the slave trade was dreaded, in hard times any job was better than none.

Recruitment of slave ship captains and ship's doctors was an altogether different affair. They applied for their positions and were able to negotiate their terms and conditions with the ship's owner directly. Polite letters of enquiry were written to slave merchants offering their services. In 1764, Joseph Wanton applied for the position of Master of the *'Sally'*, stating that he was *"well aquainted and well experienced in the Ginea Trade all Down the Coasts"* and was ready to *"come up to…fit her with what Dispatch will Sute you."* In 1788, a law was passed requiring each ship to have its own surgeon on board. Like the captains, medical doctors too would negotiate their own wages. When a merchant James Rogers was desperate to find a surgeon for his ship, the *'Trelawney'*, he had to give in to the wage demands of James Burton, as well as pay three guineas for his medical certificate, since he had never been a ship's surgeon before. Some medical doctors, however, were less mercenary and worked on slave ships as a practical learning experience before attaining their qualifications at university. They used their time treating enslaved people, before studying medicine formally.

Unlike the sailors below decks, there was a considerable financial incentive for men to serve on a slaving voyage as a Captain, Surgeon or Senior Officer. The profits to be gained could be large, particularly as they were usually granted a few *'privilege'* slaves which they could sell on their own account at the end of a successful voyage, freight free. Unsurprisingly, these would generally be the higher priced adult males. The number of slaves an officer could take varied but could amount to a substantial profit for the seller if they arrived in top condition. The potential reward also grew during the late eighteenth and early nineteenth centuries, as the gross sales value of a slave more than doubled over the period.

Captains were paid commission by some owners, as an alternative to privilege slaves. In 1798, Captain John Lawrence of the *'Perseverance'* was paid £1,500 at the end of a voyage to Tobago lasting 249 days, while the Chief Mate and Surgeon received an additional £150 each in privileges. These were substantial sums, considering that the the ship had been purchased second-hand for £1,700, and the total wage bill for the rest of the crew of 56 ordinary seamen was only £2,650. In the 1750s, Captain Lewis of the *'Racehorse'*, who died off the West African coast, left a ring worth 5 guineas and £150 for each of his sisters.

But this was small beer compared with the riches which the Captains were able to acquire at the peak of the slave trade. The real prize was to squirrel away sufficient sums from several voyages, to be able to purchase your own vessel and set up business in your own right. For, by far and away the main winners of the slave trade were the ships' owners. Slave merchants were the self-made millionaires of their days, and some of their fortunes were immense. Liverpool merchants Thomas Leyland and John Earle both left around £100,000 in their wills. Some were able to become substantial landowners of country estates, or to set up their own banks. As a result, they were able to rise up the social ladder and to exercise considerable power within their communities. The risks were considerable, and only a few would make it rich. Nevertheless, it was the dream of every ship's captain to retire from the sea, to become a merchant, and so to enter the ranks of the wealthy elite in society.

The position of slave ship captain was amost an exclusive club. Many used their family or other connections to advance their career prospects. Others followed in their father's footsteps and inherited their promotion prospects. Some captains had their own sons on board ship, grooming them for future command. More commonly, captains would apprentice their sons to their contemporaries. Ambrose Lace, who captained seven slave ships in the 1750s and 1760s, later became wealthy enough to establish himself as a Liverpool merchant. His son William followed him into the family business and took command of nine voyages to West Africa. The only other way to become a slave captain was to qualify through years of experience as a ship's doctor.

Such opportunities simply did not exist for the ordinary seaman, who could only realistically hope to rise to one of the junior mate positions. At the same time as the career prospects and financial rewards for ship's captains and their senior officers were expanding in the late eighteenth and early nineteenth centuries, wages for sailors remained remarkably constant. The common average wage for the period was about 25 shillings per month in peacetime, rising to 60-70 shillings in times of war. In general, sailors earned roughly one-fifth of their captain's monthly wage, before considering privileges and commissions. For them, the chances of earning vast riches from the slave trade were almost non-existent. Even if they survived the journeys, few would escape the poverty they had left behind. And, despite the high mortality of sailors, there were few opportunities to move up the ranks.

A typical example of the career of a sailor on a slave ship is provided by James Morley, who sailed on the *'Eagle'* to Angola in 1760 when only ten years old as a servant boy. Three years later he was back at sea on board the *'Amelia'*, and again in 1767 on the *'Marcus'*, both ships bound for the slave port of Calabar in Nigeria. He made three more trips to the West African coast in the 1770s, and by then had graduated to the posts of junior mate and gunner. Even after surviving this high number of voyages for a young man, James was not able to rise above these junior ranks and to earn the higher wages of his senior officers. He would only have counted himself lucky that he had not succumbed to disease, an accident, or some other premature end, like so many of his colleagues whose bones littered the ocean floor.

There was therefore for the ordinary seaman no reason to relish the prospect of a voyage on a slave ship. Once on board and far from shore, conditions on ship quickly deteriorated, and provisions were cut back to the limit. The food was as monotonous as it was grim. Drinking water, rank at the best of times, could be in dreadfully short supply for a tropical climate. As the ship sailed south, men on board became dehydrated and increasingly desperate. A sailor on one ship was even reported to have resorted to licking the heavy dew off the roofs of the hen coops on board. This acute shortage of water was doubtless due in part to the fact that the hold was crammed to the brim with the goods to be traded for slaves at the other end of the journey.

The ships' captains were also an unprincipled and hard bitten lot, who never for a moment questioned the legality or the morality of their trade. Discipline on board was severe, and slave captains were renowned for their vindictiveness and brutality towards their crews. Sailors were flogged at the slightest pretext. Alexander Falconbridge, a surgeon on several slave ships, regularly witnessed and recorded such acts of cruelty:

*"Another seaman…had a long chain fixed around his neck, at the end of which was fastened a log of wood. In this situation he performed his duty (from which he was not in the least spared) for several weeks, till at length he was nearly exhausted with fatigue; and after his release from the log, he was frequently beaten for trivial faults."*

The same man and another sailor were flogged until their backs were raw, at which point pepper was mixed in a bucket of salt water and applied to the wounds as an additional torture.

Another surgeon, on board a Bristol slave ship, testified before a parliamentary commission that the ship's cook:

*"was the common butt on which the captain and mates daily exercised their cruelty. The former, indeed, appeared to enjoy a particular pleasure in flogging and tormenting him. Among other instances of wanton and unnecessary barbarity, he often amused himself with making the man swallow cockroaches alive, on pain of being most severely flogged, and having beef brine rubbed into his wounds."*

Even more horrifically, Captain John Steele of the Elizabeth used the instruments of torture meant for the slaves on his cabin boy, Thomas Watson. While on the coast of Africa, he put Watson in the thumbscrews:

*"which he screwed till the blood flowed from the ends of his thumbs and kept him in that pain & torture for about ten minutes at same time flogging him naked with a horse whip till his back was raw".*

He then ordered another boy to *"rub him raw and naked with a hard brush such as they clean decks with, and also salt water".* Later, other crew members were ordered to beat Watson, *"one with a cat with nine tails and the other with a horse whip".* His final humiliation was to have to sing before the captain.

Such was the breed of men who came to do business on the West African coast. The brutality on board ship was contagious. The cruelty routinely meted out by captains on the captive Africans created an atmosphere in which stark violence seemed to have no consequence on the perpetrator, and where human life had little value. As a result, not only did captains feel free to exercise their arbitrary authority over the ship's crew as well its cargo, but also the crew took out their grievances on the slaves in their charge. Sailors were not just permitted to be use violence against the slaves but were also actively encouraged to do so. As a result, a general atmosphere of fear and suspicion prevailed on board ship. Ignorant of African languages and customs, captains and crew kept a wary eye out for any sign of insubordination, or for secret signs that might signal an imminent insurrection. Some slave ships carried crews fifty per cent greater than needed, to guard against slave rebellions.

The sailors fared no better when their ships lay at anchor off the West African coast. The trading posts were guarded by heavy guns and equipped with slave pens. At Cape Coast Castle, the British headquarters on the Gold Coast, an enormous underground dungeon was even hewn out of the bare rock to house the slaves. These forts were not only hotbeds of debauchery and corruption, but they were also incubators of disease. Dysentery, sleeping sickness, malaria and yellow fever were rife and took a terrible toll. White crews went down like flies, since at the time there was no medical treatment available. With grim humour, therefore, the area around the trading post at Ouidah on the Slave Coast soon became known popularly as the 'hog yard'.

Some seamen spent more time incarcerated inside forts such as Cape Coast than the African slaves did. Sailors accused of mutiny, piracy or some other misdemeanour were detained there until they could be sent back to Britain to stand trial. Royal Navy ships, which would return the temporary captives back home, were less frequent visitors to the coast than the ships that came to plunder for slaves. And so, the European sailors' confinement would last longer than that of the African slaves. Other seamen seized the opportunity to desert and preferred to take their chances in a strange land than to endure more cruelty on board ship. So many sailors deserted in Sierra Leone that the Governor John Clarkson felt compelled to post a notice warning sailors that they would not be given shelter. Many sailors absconded only temporarily, either in search of food or other items they had been deprived of, or in pursuit of local women. Sailors who extended their stay on shore often formed long term relationships with African women.

But, although desertion was commonplace, abandonment on shore was sometimes used as a punishment, to put the fear of God into the wrong-doer. Rumours abounded of the alleged savagery of local inhabitants and of their cannibalism. The fear of disease was also intense, and dysentery could strike anywhere. Captains would also abandon on shore any sailors who during a voyage had fallen ill from the effects of scurvy, poor diet, or floggings. They were judged to be too sick to continue the voyage and left to survive as best they could.

James Colen was *"left at a factory in Africa"* by the captain of the *'Jemmy'* after having *"lost his leg by a Shark 12th April"*. Another seaman was forced to leave his ship because he had *"frequent eruptions breaking out on his Legs and Thighs"*. Rather unfortunately, Francis Myers of the *'Fanny'* was *"left on the Coast Oct.18 1800 by accident"*. Other seamen were left on the African coast in a group if pirates or *'privateers'* had captured their ship. The French abandoned many men from captured ships at Sierra Leone in the 1790s. More routinely, sailors were abandoned because of shipwreck or because their ship had become so rotten that it could not sail any further. The *'Lumbey'* was found to be so eaten by worms in 1793 that it was riddled with *"holes so large as to receive your finger"*.

But these hardships were nothing compared with the squalor they would face on the journey across the Atlantic. They would be required to clean up after their human cargo, force feed those who had lost the will to eat and subdue the slaves while they were washed and exercised. Merchants in their instructions made a special point that captains should regularly clean the slaves' quarters below decks, not through any philanthropy but with an eye on their profits at the end of the journey. While at sea, sailors were employed in:

*"scraping the slave rooms, smoking with tar, tobacco and brimstone for two hours, afterwards washed with vinegar"*.

During this work they briefly shared the degrading conditions in which the slaves were held captive. One sailor recalled that:

*"the floor of their rooms, was so covered with blood and mucus which had proceeded from them having flux, that it resembled a slaughter-house"*.

Slave ships were notorious for stinking so badly that other ships could smell them before they even clapped eyes on them. Apart from the filth and disease, sailors had to contend with slave revolts on board, as well as the usual dangers of the sea. Sailors often had to sleep on deck after their human cargo had been loaded, so exposing them to the heat, humidity and rainfall of the African coast. Mortality rates on the West African route were extremely high, and it was not unusual for a ship to lose all its original crew, as happened with the *'Depsey'* in the late 1750s and the *'Virginia'* in the 1760s.

Such cumulative hardships led to frequent complaints from seamen to their employers about their conditions. Increasingly, they came to compare their lot with that of the slaves. A common grievance of seamen was that their food and accommodation were as appalling as those of the African captives. On a daily basis they bore witness to the obscenity of the slave trade and considered that they in many ways they were not much better off. Their complaints eventually reached the ears of the politicians in London. When the movement for the abolition of the slave trade gained momentum towards the end of the eighteenth century, the plight of the ordinary white sailor on board slave ships captured almost as much attention as the fate of the ships' black human cargo. Thomas Clarkson, the leading Abolitionist, made as many impassioned speeches based on the suffering and dying of the ships' crews in the slave trade as on its victims. He rightly judged that this injustice would be of greater concern to a British parliament than the fate of the slaves.

## Customs On Arrival At The Coast

When a slave vessel arrived on the coast, trade was *'broken'* by a variety of customs payments made to local African rulers or traders. Captains also paid fees to African canoe man who piloted slave ships across sandbars to safe anchorages. Among the captain's first tasks were purchasing or gathering wood, water, and other provisions from shore. The wood was brought on board for fuel, but also so that a carpenter could construct a large box-shaped barricade in the space above the upper deck. Slaves were led through a small doorway in the barricade to the hatches and decks below. Sometimes sons or daughters of the local chiefs were given temporarily to the slave ship captains as a form of credit, known as *'pawnship'*. If any captain dared to kidnap a *'pawn'*, the local African chief would cease immediately all slave trading activity in the area. Or, as a reprisal, the captain and crew of the next slave ship to arrive from the same port would be killed or taken hostage.

The ships employed a variety of African support workers to supplement the crew. Porters, cooks, washerwomen, canoe men, pilots and translators were regularly hired, setting up a cadre of Africans who came in part to rely on the visiting Europeans for employment. Some of these men were slaves, but they were paid wages and could only be sold in exceptional circumstances. By the end of the eighteenth century, they had adopted some of the European culture and customs, and they spoke a hybrid creole language. The extent to which they were controlled by the Europeans varied along the coast. The largest group, the Kru, used their seafaring skills to retain a relative independence, as well as to escape the ordeal of transportation to the Americas.

Translators or linguists were also crucial to ships employed in the slave trade. Some made the Atlantic crossing with the ship, but most were employed by the ship only for the duration of its stay at the coast. Those who made the voyage could become more important than ordinary seamen, as they could help the captain control the slaves, or at least alert him to any potential uprising. Peter Green a steward on the *'Alfred'*, was savagely beaten to death by his captain after he argued with the ship's translator, *"a black African woman, of the name of Rodney"*.

An even more essential cog in the slavery machine was the canoe man. By 1790 on the Gold Coast there were between 800 and 1,000 men engaged on working for visiting ships. They were particularly needed on the Gold Coast as incoming vessels could not cross the pounding surf of the Atlantic Ocean. Canoe men were essential to ensure safe passage of people and merchandise to and from the shore. Some were employed by the coastal forts, but most were free agents. Many of them spoke English, and they formed a unique element of the trading network as they travelled up and down the coast aboard slave ships. Their elevated status encouraged them to be rebellious, and they frequently withheld their labour to win improved wages and conditions.

Slave ships remained on the coast of West Africa for a period of four to six months, depending on the trading location, availability of slaves and provisions, as well as the state of health of the slaves and the crew. On the Gold Coast there were no large river outlets or safe harbours, and so slave ships anchored several miles offshore where they were met by large trading canoes. In the major slave trading sites of Ouidah (in present-day Benin), Bonny and Calabar (in present-day Nigeria) slave ships anchored in lagoons or bays close to African villages and small towns. Some slave ships would load their cargoes in a few weeks, from the smaller wooden factories or the larger stone trading forts along the coast. At other trading sites, such as Calabar and Bonny, African traders acting as agents and intermediaries created complex road and river networks for transporting slaves from the interior to the coast. Slave supplies on that stretch of the coastline were regular. Sometimes as many as twenty slaves were purchased and loaded on board ship every day.

Certain patterns of trade became fixed, including the convention that the European traders would stay at the coast and not venture into the interior. The African chiefs and their agents insisted on this arrangement to protect their position as middlemen. The Europeans were happy to cooperate, since they had enough trouble keeping the coastal posts fully manned in the face of the alarmingly high death rate of new arrivals. These shore side establishments were called 'slave factories', and it was the job of the 'factor' to negotiate with the local African traders, and to induce them to step up their slave hunting expeditions into the interior. When the slaves were brought down to the coast, they were purchased by a system of barter. They were then housed and guarded in sheds or warehouses, known as 'barracoons', until the arrival of the slave ships.

On the Gold Coast substantial stone forts were constructed along the shore, and located near the mouths of important rivers, or on islands offshore. They were designed for defence against Europeans rather than Africans. The locals had the simple option of cutting off supply if the slave dealers became too greedy or demanding. Under the command of a governor, the staff of the forts included an assortment of soldiers, clerks, and mechanics, all employed in the service of the company. There were also junior factors, who oversaw the traffic with the interior. These unfortunates were tasked with the perilous job of ascending the rivers in small sailing vessels or armed boats to exchange European goods for slaves, gold dust or ivory. Braver souls would open up a trading post in an inland village and remain there for several months as guests of local rulers.

The greatest opportunities for trade, however, lay to the east on the Slave Coast, where populations were denser and much better organised, not only politically but also commercially. These advanced communities had access to developed trading routes which linked them with large inland centres of population. Initially the company-fort pattern of trading was applied here, but it never took root to the extent that it had done on the Gold Coast. This was mainly because on the Slave Coast the river estuaries provided safe natural harbours for the slave ships. But it was also because the local rulers demanded that any forts should be built in their own inland towns, and not on the coast.

For reasons of health and security, the European traders were not prepared to make such a commitment. Instead, they adapted themselves to a new form of trade and set up their bases along the margins of the coast or at the entrances to the major rivers. Rather than large corporations, trading was typically conducted by individual European traders or small partnerships, who acknowledged the authority of the local rulers and paid the fees and duties demanded of them. The slaves were delivered to them at the coast by African agents or intermediaries, who sourced their human merchandise either directly from local chiefs, or through an inland network of Arab slavers.

When a ship first entered a river, the captain would make an opening gift to the local chief to secure the right of trade. When that formality was completed, the crew would construct an awning of matting and thatch from bow to stern to provide shade from the sun for both the African slaves and European traders. This was very necessary, as a ship might have to remain for several months in the river waiting until it had its full cargo of slaves. The quicker that crews got their business transacted, the sooner they could get away, and the greater chance they had of survival. So, when two or three ships were anchored side by side, there would be fierce competition to get away first. Fights between rival crews were frequent, and sabotage became a way of life.

Not only did the high European mortality rate and the inhospitable climate make ships' crews desperate to depart, but it also made it increasingly difficult to recruit staff to man the bases on shore. As a result, as the eighteenth century progressed more and more of the trading posts became Euro-African than European. Whereas the typical European numbers might vary from a dozen to a few hundred, the associated African population was always much larger, including many descendants of European fathers and African mothers. These Afro-Europeans, and others of purely African descent, occasionally went to Europe to be educated, such as Philip Quaque the Anglican chaplain of Cape Coast fort on the Gold Coast. On his return, he and others like him helped to found schools which taught the rudiments of European languages and commercial arithmetic. These schools were often short lived, but by the end of the eighteenth century a scattered, partly European population of permanent residents could be found along the coast.

The composition of the population of Saint Louis in Senegal in 1810 was typical: there were 10 Europeans, 500 Afro-Europeans, 500 partly Europeanised free Africans, and 2,200 African slaves. By the beginning of the nineteenth century, Afro-Europeans were amongst the most important members of local 'European' society, partly because the Afro-Europeans stayed on, while Europeans typically came for a few years only. Thomas Joiner had been a slave in Virginia and returned to Banjul after the Napoleonic Wars to become the largest ship owner and one of the most prosperous traders in the Gambia. On the Gold Coast, the Brew family, descendants of an Irish trader, founded a dynasty of Anglo-African merchants and officials which flourished for more than a century. Only in the 1880s and later were Afro-Europeans pushed aside by Europeans fresh from Europe. By that time, colonial regimes with exclusive, racist policies had replaced the more democratic mix of the early trading communities.

## Trading Practices

The pattern of trade between the sea-based Europeans and the land-based African traders was remarkably uniform over long stretches of the West African coastline. Bargains were struck along the coast in a currency that was neither a conventional European nor African one, but a local invention. One such currency was the *'bar'*, originally an iron bar weighing about twelve kilograms. These bars were about three metres long and were usually notched for sub-division into smaller units of 25-30 centimetres each. Bars became the currency from the Senegal River south and east to the area of present-day Ivory Coast.

On the Gold Coast the unit of exchange was the *'trade ounce'*, which somewhat curiously was half the value of a measured ounce of gold dust. This currency spread further east along the coast to the Slave Coast, displacing earlier currencies of brass and copper and a currency of account that represented the value of a slave. The area of the Niger delta used a variety of different currencies that changed over time, including a horseshoe-shaped brass object called a *'manila'*, cowrie shells from the Indian Ocean and a form of cloth currency based on the value of a standard piece of woven African cotton. Two or more currencies were sometimes used in the same place, and cowrie shells were often used for minor purchases.

The system was biased heavily in favour of the European trader. The prices for African exported goods varied according to market conditions, whereas prices for imported goods tended to be set by custom at an early date and could remain fixed for a century or longer. Thus, a *'bar'* of slaves depended on the bargain struck between buyer and seller at the time, whereas a bar of guns or textiles was a fixed quantity. Originally the bar values of imported goods had been based on their actual cost in Europe. But by the eighteenth century this was far from the case. As a result, no single exchange rate expressed the relationship between bars and any European currency.

Each commodity had in effect its own exchange rate: for example, a bar of *'blue bafts'*, a prized Indian textile, was worth considerably more than a bar of brandy. This system of multiple exchange rates complicated the process of striking a bargain. First buyers and seller had to agree on the price to be paid for the slaves, gold, or ivory to be exported. Then they had to repeat the bargaining process over the *'sorting'* of the contents of the goods to be exchanged in payment. The African trader would naturally try his utmost to be paid in *'heavy bars'* such as blue bafts, while the European trader endeavoured to pay as much as possible in *'light bars'* such as brandy.

To complicate negotiations yet further, European visitors to the coast had to pay out a variety of fees, duties, and other charges. The African state where the trade took place normally charged for the privilege, and imposed additional fees for anchorage, wood, and water. Local African chiefs also required ceremonial gifts at the opening and closing of a bargaining session, and a variety of brokers and interpreters and other intermediaries had to be paid. As the power of the chiefs increased, so did their demands on the European slave dealers. The custom of making presents to the chiefs endured long after the disappearance of the slave trade. These presents or 'dashes' were known by different names and varied in amount, but they were always required before any trading could begin. They also served as a form of protection payment for the traders and guaranteed their security while they conducted their business on the chiefs' lands. In some places a gift known as 'shake hands' had to be made, in other areas a 'topping' proportionate to the amount of trade was paid, and in other areas a 'comey' was levied on every slave or ton of cargo exported.

As a rule, European traders were serial cheats, falsifying the number, weight, measure, and quantity of whatever goods the Africans purchased. Sadly, it was common practice that hardly any article was delivered to the Africans in mint condition. Bottles of spirits would be diluted by water, false heads placed inside gunpowder kegs so that the powder inside was less than it appeared, and a couple of yards would be cut out of the middle of bales of cloth where hopefully they would not be missed. In time, the black traders grew wise to these practices, and came up with some tricks of their own to turn the tables on the European traders. On the Gold Coast gold was adulterated with copper, on the Ivory Coast tusks were plugged with lead and heavy clay, and palm oil was ingeniously mixed with sand so that every drop had to be boiled down before the factors dare send it back to their employers.

Authorities, both African and European, tried to regulate the trade, but they rarely succeeded in the face of opposition from private traders, both African and European. Each European government thought it had a paramount duty to keep its colonies supplied with slaves and feared that a rival supplier might cut off its trade at any time. And so, some countries granted a monopoly to a single, chartered joint-stock company, which was expected to use some of its profits to subsidise the cost of maintaining the fortified trading posts and naval patrols. In practice, it was impossible to enforce any such monopoly, as plantation owners in the Americas were always prepared to buy slaves at knockdown prices from private shippers, or *'interlopers'* as they became known. With over 16,000 kilometres of open coastline to be patrolled, all the interlopers had to do was to stay out of the reach or the eyeshot of the forts and garrisons on the shore.

In the face of such competition, the chartered companies found their profits fell well short of what was needed to maintain their forts. This problem was certainly not helped by the fact that the companies' employees were often dishonest, and hell-bent on cheating the company out of anything that they could get away with. They were perfectly aware that they had a less than fifty-fifty chance of returning home and few were willing to accept such risks for the sake of their small company salary alone. In the end, all the monopoly companies went out of business, and the bulk of the slave trade at its peak was carried out by independent shippers, who were in fierce competition with one another.

## Life On The Coast

The era of the slave trade was a lawless period, when a man owned only what he was able to defend. Life was cheap, and the garrisons of the forts and the crews of the slave ships were decimated by disease. As a result, the slave trade attracted the dregs of humanity. Many were outcasts from their society, often on the run from their creditors or the law, and with few home ties. They feared that the deadly climate would claim them in the end. Indeed, for much of the time they were unwell and physically unfit for service. The soldiers were seldom pressed into active service, and so spent most of their time drinking, gambling, and womanising.

Jean Barbot, who spent some time at the fort at Cape Coast on the Gold Coast, was incensed by the behaviour of his fellow residents. He made representations to the directors of all the main African trading companies of the time:

*"to employ ...men of known candour, probity, understanding, true courage, and experience; attended with modest behaviour."*

He complained that he had:

*"often represented to some of the principal men how to live more regularly, viz., to abstain from the black women, whose natural hot and lewd temper soon wastes their bodies, to drink modestly, especially of brandy, rum and the punch; and to avoid sleeping in the open air at night, as many when heated with debauchery, do, having nothing on but a shirt, thinking thus to cool, but, on the contrary, they murder themselves."*

Barbot himself was tucked up safely in bed offshore and took the further precaution of wearing a hare's skin over his stomach night and day for protection, apparently without change for two years.

Life in the forts and trading posts for the Europeans was one of utter tedium and loneliness. This placed a mental and physical strain on individuals, and frequently led to disputes and arguments between them. Contact with the local African communities was sporadic and was generally restricted to the peoples who lived near the coast. It was the African middlemen who travelled inland to seek out the next batches of slaves. There was some travel by Europeans along the shoreline, but communication between forts was usually done by letter. Only officers made regular journeys away from the confines of the forts. They jumped at the chance of going visiting a neighbouring establishment, normally a journey of several hours by canoe or in a hammock carried by one or two pairs of bearers.

The different companies along the coast made a play of entertaining each other, and relations were superficially amicable. But business rivalry also meant that there were regular spying missions and constant plotting between them. Apart from the local rivalries between forts, there were constant raids from pirates operating off the West African coast. Many were *'buccaneers'* from the Caribbean, who had been forced to close their operations and to seek new pirate pastures. Their ships, usually hunting in packs of two or three, roamed up and down the coastline, and were a constant menace to trade. Normally they would waylay any slave ships that they came across, transfer the human cargoes to their own vessels, and then sell them for their own profit in the Caribbean. At other times they would simply burn ships and confiscate their contents. Some bands of pirates were so formidable that they even raided and captured some of the Gold Coast forts.

The slave factors' job was to accumulate slaves and other African goods to await the incoming ships. No other form of initiative was expected of them. There was also no fixed pattern to their work, as slaves would often reach the coast in dribs and drabs, and the arrival of ships was equally unpredictable. They therefore frequently had time on their hands, and there were few local opportunities for recreation. Senior officers might arrange for Africans to drum and dance in the garden for their entertainment. The English also allowed men to spend the night in the town and to bring women into the fort. But the main pastime seemed to be drinking, usually to excess. The favourite English drink was a cocktail of brandy mixed with lime juice, sugar, and water.

The arrival of a ship was a welcome interruption to this routine. When the fort's lookout sighted approaching sails, the national flag would be raised, and preparations made to receive the vessel. Canon would be made ready just in case it was a pirate ship. A friendly ship with a dignitary on board would be honoured with a gun salute. Cargo would then be brought ashore by canoes or small boats belonging to the fort. The goods were transported from the beach to storerooms by slaves carrying their loads on their heads. Clerical staff would then be hard at work, making an inventory of the goods and calculating prices. Meanwhile the ship's captain would be fretting anxiously on board ship, as he wanted to spend the minimum time possible at anchor to avoid his crew catching any nasty diseases.

The Europeans based on shore were just as keen to find a way home and out of their miserable existence. Quite apart from the discomfort of the climate and the living conditions, the constant illness and the inevitable deaths, commercial life on the coast was a permanent struggle. The forts needed frequent and great repairs, as the humidity, torrential rains and fierce heat corroded the buildings. In their steamy lodgings traders, soldiers and clerks lived out their unpleasant and often all too brief existence in Africa. The death rate of Europeans was horrendous, and there was a regular procession of corpses to the local burying grounds.

A British surgeon called Atkins, who visited Cape Coast Castle in 1721, observed that the officers were both wretchedly paid and badly abused. They were subject to heavy fines for drunkenness, swearing, sleeping outside the fort, and even for not going to church. According to Atkins, these fines were so frequently inflicted that many of the men saw their whole pay swallowed up. As a result, they found themselves in hock to their company, which thereafter had a complete hold over them and was able to prevent them from resigning their posts. Even senior officers were desperate to leave, and while Atkins was at Cape Coast the captain of the garrison escaped by night to a ship that was leaving the coast. However, his escape was soon discovered, and the ship was pursued and caught. The ship's captain was *"fined seventy ounces and flogged for good measure"*, and the captain of the garrison was restored to the tender mercies of his company.

Conditions for white settlers on the coast continued to prove problematic, as the sorry tale of the Royal Sierra Leone Company illustrates. This was a valiant attempt at the end of the eighteenth century to establish a permanent settlement on the coast of Sierra Leone, in the area which later came to be known as Freetown. The ambitious plan was to found the first African American colony in Africa through the resettlement of ex-slaves who had initially been settled in Nova Scotia after the American Revolutionary War. The Sierra Leone Company was the brainchild of the anti-slavery activist Granville Sharp, who published a prospectus for the proposed company in 1790 entitled *"Free English Territory in AFRICA"*. The prospectus made clear its abolitionist view and stated that several respectable gentlemen who had already agreed to sponsor the new company had done so:

*"not with a view of any present profit to themselves, but merely, through benevolence and public spirit, to promote a charitable measure, which may hereafter prove of great national importance to the Manufactories, and other Trading Interests of this Kingdom".*

To prepare the site for the prospective colony, the leading Abolitionist Alexander Falconbridge volunteered to lead an advance party of 119 men and women from England. Falconbridge had served as a surgeon on slaving ships from Bristol but had left the trade on grounds of principle. He accompanied Thomas Clarkson, a leading campaigner, on his travels collecting evidence from sailors. After the failure of a previous expedition in 1787, Falconbridge was selected by the Anti-Slavery Society to try and restart the failing Sierra Leone community. He seemed eminently qualified for the job.

But when Thomas's brother, John Clarkson, arrived with 15

ships carrying around 1200 freed slaves from Nova Scotia, he found that no progress had been made. The whites had remained obdurately on board ship, as they thought it beneath their dignity to do work more fit for Africans, such as felling trees, clearing the ground, erecting tents, or building huts. Clarkson wrote that as a group they showed:

*"nothing but extravagance, idleness, quarrelling, waste, irregularity in accounts, insubordination and everything that is contrary to what is good and right."*

The whites also behaved as if they were the masters of some commercial or military colony and did not sympathise either with the lofty ideals of the mission or with the returned black slaves themselves. Whites abused and insulted the returned slaves and were contemptuous of their complaints at not having received their promised plots of land. Some whites even usurped their properties. They were also a debauched and disreputable bunch - drunken, promiscuous, and syphilitic. Worse still, from the perspective of the religious Clarkson, they failed even to turn up at church. Both he and the African community felt betrayed.

The whole venture was dogged by disaster from the beginning. Supplies ran down quickly and settlers, both black and white, had to subsist on worm-ridden biscuits, supplemented by a little salted meat and fish. Local villagers brought cassava and groundnuts, but the settlers were clueless as how to cook them. Medical care, including cinchona bark to help combat malaria, was in short supply and the timber intended for the hospital had not arrived. To make matters worse, the company surgeon, Dr Bell, promptly fell ill and died from alcoholic poisoning. The rainy season brought infestations of ferocious red ants that frequently drove families from their homes. In the first few weeks and months around forty of the freed slaves died. But it was the European population sent out to establish the colony, with little or no immunity to disease, that perished fastest and in the greatest numbers.

Anna Maria Falconbridge, Alexander's wife, lay gravely ill for three weeks, *"stone-blind"* for four days and *"expecting every moment to be her last."* She wrote later of five, six or seven deaths a day in the white community at the height of the epidemic, the victims buried *"with as little ceremony as dogs or cats."* By the time the catalogue of deaths reduced, barely 30 of the original 119 whites remained. The deaths included Alexander, her husband. He had failed to establish trading links with the local peoples, was therefore dismissed from company service, and died of drink shortly afterwards. Anna remained in Sierra Leone and remarried three weeks later. She returned to England via the Caribbean on a slaving ship, abandoning the *"foolish experiment"* in Sierra Leone.

After she arrived back in England, she wrote down her experiences in a series of letters. In them she makes it quite clear that she did not share her husband's idealistic views about the settlement, and that like many of her contemporaries she thought that slavery was an economic necessity and, in some way, virtuous:

*"I now think of it in no shape objectionable either to morality or religion, but on the contrary consistent with both, while neither are to be found in unhappy Africa."*

Her writings also paint a graphic picture of the European settler community that she and her husband had joined so optimistically, and that had become brutalised by the appalling living conditions and the ever-present threat of disease and an early grave.

## Treatment Of Slaves

The raw and sometimes brutal experience of the few Europeans who dared to settle on the West African coast pales in comparison with the treatment meted out to the slaves in their charge. The slave trade was conducted in a manner that was utterly inhumane and degrading, from the very start to the end of the slaves' miserable journey. Guns and alcohol were given to the African rulers in exchange for slaves, and they were then encouraged by the slave dealers to raid their neighbours, and even to hand over people from their own tribe. The chiefs could accumulate more wealth and power through the traffic in human flesh and blood than by any other means.

Local populations were decimated by the constant raids and inter-tribal wars that were waged, simply for the purpose of capturing slaves. Villages were sometimes surrounded at night and set on fire, so that the inhabitants could be seized as they escaped the flames. Anyone who could not be sold into slavery would be butchered on the spot. Jean Barbot was particularly scathing about the role played by African traders:

*"Those sold by the Blacks are for the most part prisoners of war, taken either in fight, or pursuit, or in the incursions they make into their enemies territories; others stolen away by their own countrymen; and some there are, who will sell their own children, kindred, or neighbours. This has been often seen, and to compass it, they desire the person they intend to sell, to help them in carrying something to the factory by way of trade, and when there, the person so deluded, not understanding the language, is old and deliver'd up as a slave, notwithstanding all his resistance, and exclaiming against the treachery."*

Many of the slaves exported were prisoners of war, of both sexes, and of all ages. Others were already slaves in their own community or had been condemned to slavery because of their debts or crimes. Many young men were also tricked into slavery. Unprincipled local men of rank would instruct their wives to form private liaisons, and then to denounce their new partners in public. Under local law such an offence required the accused to make payment of a large sum of money to the injured husband, in proportion to his standing in the community. The alternative was slavery. And, since the young victims were usually unable to pay, that would generally be their fate.

The maltreatment and abuse of slaves began on the journey down to the coast, and their suffering only increased while they waited to board ship. They arrived at the slave factories on the coast in *'coffles'*, a string of 30-40 men and women tied to each other at the neck with leather thongs, at about a yard distance from each other. After a long painful march to the coast, weighed down with chains and driven on by their captors, they were crowded into the slave factory barracoons until they could be sold. Slave ships also offered alternative storage space for the slowly accumulating cargo. Since it was often difficult for European traders to distinguish a young from a middle-aged slave, except perhaps by the decay of their teeth, various ruses were adopted by African slave dealers to give an appearance of youth and health to slaves of an inferior quality. A common practice was for slaves to be close-shaven and rubbed with palm oil to give the skin a glossy appearance.

There was as much chicanery brought into play over the sale and purchase of slaves as there is in modern day car dealing. Slave traders did not want unhealthy or diseased Africans, and so experience was important in spotting sick slaves. Worst of all was to have contagious slaves since their ailments could cause devastation in the squalid confines of the ships. Consequently, all slaves bought for export were carefully examined by a surgeon to see if they were in good condition and of *'sound wind and limb'*, in the same way as a butcher would inspect animals at a slaughterhouse. The surgeons looked for slaves who had a good physique and complexions, possessed a sound set of teeth, were flexible in their limbs and joints, and betrayed no signs of venereal disease.

William Bosman graphically described the degrading way in

which the slaves were handled by the slave factors:

*"When these Slaves come...they are put in Prison all together, and when we treat buying them, they are brought out together into a large Plain; where by our Chirurgeons... they are thoroughly examined...and that too naked both Men and Women...In the mean while a burning Iron, with the Arms or Names of the Companies, lyes in the Fire; with which ours are marked on the Breast. This is done that we may distinguish them from the Slaves of the English, French or others... I doubt not that this Trade seems barbarous to you... ...but yet we take all possible care that they are not burned too hard, especially the Women."*

For the women that would have seemed a small mercy at the time.

Alexander Falconbridge was rather more perturbed by what he saw:

*"When the negroes whom the black traders have to dispose of are shown to the European purchasers, they first examine them relative to age. They then minutely inspect their persons and inquire into their state of health; if they are afflicted with any infirmity, or are deformed, or have bad eyes or teeth; if they are lame, or weak in the joints, or distorted in the back, or of a slender make, or are narrow in the chest; in short, if they have been afflicted in any manner so as to render them incapable of such labour they are rejected. The traders frequently beat those negroes which are objected to by the captains. Instances have happened that the traders, when any of their negroes have been objected to, have instantly beheaded them in the sight of the captain."*

To make matters worse, the procedure for buying slaves was exceedingly slow and painstaking, as the custom was that each sale had to be negotiated individually. In 1789, John Goodwin, captain of the Bristol ship *'Sarah'*, carefully recorded that he had bartered a single slave boy for 28 yards of cloth, 5 guns, 8 kegs of gunpowder, 1 iron bar, 2 brass rods, 6 knives, 6 flints, 1 hat, 1 cap, 1 kettle, 1 basin, 1 lead bar and 1 mug. This protracted process meant that the slaves could spend many months imprisoned in a dungeon or a ship's filthy hold before they sailed across the Atlantic. In some forts the slaves were kept in massive airless cellars called *'slave holes'*. Light and air filtered into the slaves' prisons from grilles set in overhead walkways; and the enslaved Africans could see free people walking above their heads, just as later they would watch the crews of slave ships pacing the decks above.

In Cape Coast Castle on the Gold Coast slaves were often captive for anything up to two months. At any one time there were up to 1,000 men and 600 women confined within the walls of the fort. The dark airless dungeons can still be visited today and are a testament to the appalling conditions that the slaves were forced to endure. There were two female dungeons and one male dungeon. The sanitation was extremely poor, and the only sources of light were tiny portholes high up on the walls. During the day, the slaves were allowed out into the small courtyard to cook. Disease was rife, and some slaves rebelled against their captors. Their punishment was to be shackled to the walls, whipped, and tortured. Some were left to die from starvation and suffocation in a tiny vault, as the penalty for anything the British deemed to be a misdemeanour. When the ships finally arrived to load their cargo, the slaves were taken through a slit in the castle wall known as the *'Door of No Re-turn'*, so named because the slaves would never see their homeland again.

Most slaves were in a state of shock as they were herded on to the waiting ships. Olaudah Equiano, one of the few African slaves to record his experiences, was *"quite overpowered with horror and anguish"*. Many were so terrified of leaving their native land that they preferred suicide to a life of unknown terrors in a foreign land. As a result, the slave factors had to ensure that their captives were securely held and supervised round the clock. Otherwise, some would leap overboard from a canoe or ship and stay under water until they drowned, and others would simply starve themselves to death. Death apparently held no terrors for them, as they believed that they would be transported to a spirit world, where they could continue their old life among their own people. A large number were cut down as they made their one last-ditch attempt to escape. Those that remained would be herded on to the waiting slave ships, only to suffer an even more barbaric confinement on what became known as the *'Middle Passage'* to the Americas.

## The Middle Passage

Once a ship was loaded, the journey was usually to Brazil or an island in the Caribbean and could last a matter of a few weeks or several months. Between the beginning of the fifteenth and the middle of the nineteenth century the time of the voyage shortened considerably. This change was important, because death rates, which ranged from around 10 to more than 20 per cent on the Middle Passage, were directly proportional to the length of the voyage. The ship captains had every interest in the health of their cargo, for they were paid only for slaves delivered alive. The death rates among the European captains and crew engaged in the slave trade were at least as high as those among their cargo on the Middle Passage. Of the slave ship crews that embarked from Liverpool in the year of 1787, less than half returned alive.

During the Middle Passage male slaves were kept constantly shackled to each other or to the deck to prevent mutiny. The two sexes were kept apart by a wooden partition. So that the largest possible cargo might be carried, the captives were wedged horizontally, chained to low platforms stacked in tiers, with an average individual space of 6 feet by 16 inches wide. Unable to stand up straight or to turn over, many slaves died in this position.

If the journey took longer because of tropical storms or equatorial calms, the captain would have to conserve the remaining stocks of food. The meagre twice daily ration of water and food would be cut, resulting in near starvation and frequent illness. The worst killer was *'bloody flux'* or amoebic dysentery, which was spread by the distribution of food in communal buckets. The diet included such delicacies as ground corn or *'dabbadabb'*, *'slabber sauce'* (palm oil, flour, water, and pepper) and boiled horse beans, which were supposed to induce constipation.

Weather permitting, during the day the slaves were allowed temporary respite on deck for exercise or for *'dancing the slaves'* (forced jumping up and down). At this time, conscientious captains would order that the lower decks should be swabbed clean with vinegar and lime juice and fumigated with burning tar or brimstone in fire pans. But in bad weather, the oppressive heat and noxious fumes in the unventilated holds caused fevers and dysentery, leading to an inevitably high mortality rate. The heat in the hold could rise to over 30 degrees centigrade, and the slaves had no access to toilets or washing facilities. So foul was the smell of slave ships that other vessels took care to steer far away from them. In such unsanitary conditions disease spread, and many slaves died. It was not rare for hundreds to die in an epidemic, and occasionally every African on board was dead by the time the ship entered Caribbean waters.

Deaths also occurred from suicide, a condition called *'fixed melancholy'*, and from mutiny and insurrection. Slaves who resisted captivity sometimes died from flogging or other forms of punishment. Other slaves took their own lives by jumping overboard or by hanging themselves. Many refused to eat and, when clapped into irons, would descend into fear and a deep melancholy on board. The resistance to eating was so common that ships carried metal devices to force feed slaves. Shovels filled with hot coals were also placed near their lips to scorch and burn them. So many bodies of dead or dying Africans were jettisoned into the ocean that sharks regularly followed the slave ships on their westward journey.

Slave uprisings aboard ship were not uncommon, partly because of the small numbers of crew and the frequent disabling of the seamen from sickness, especially when the voyages were extended. Extreme brutality to individuals was the common form of deterrent. One slave ship captain claimed that he himself *"could not be perswaded...to cut off the legs and arms of the most wilful"*, but on another voyage a mutinous woman slave was *"slashed with knives till she died"*. Jean Barbot, an otherwise apparently sane and reasonable individual, advised other slave captains that:

*"the form of punishment that scares Africans most is by chopping parts off a living man with blows from an axe and presenting the separated parts to the others".*

This illustrates only too graphically the brutal nature of the slave trade and the callousness of those involved.

Equally shocking was the open encouragement given by both ship owners and captains to their crews to have forced sex with the female slaves. Their appalling motive was that a pregnant slave commanded a higher price tag at auction, by tempting clients with a bargain offer of two slaves for the price of one. The transaction was particularly profitable, if it was obvious that the child had been conceived at sea. For, a mulatto baby would command an even higher price than a dark skinned one. Lighter skinned slaves were prized by plantation owners as house servants, and so fetched higher prices than field hands.

What drove slave ship captains and their crews to such merciless acts, as well as to endanger their own lives and health, were the financial rewards that they believed they could grab for themselves and for their sponsors, the ship owners. The slave trade was essentially conducted for profit, and the captains of slave ships therefore tried to deliver as many healthy slaves for as little cost as possible. Some captains used a system called *'loose packing'* to deliver slaves. Under that system, captains transported fewer slaves than their ships could carry in the hope of reducing sickness and death among them. Other captains preferred *'tight packing'*. They believed that many Africans would die on the voyages anyway, and so carried as many slaves as their ships could hold. Their minds were always finely tuned to the margin of profit they expected to make for themselves and their financial backers, and they were not afraid at sea to make the most ruthless and calculated decisions to preserve the bottom line.

In 1781, the British slave ship *'Zong'* was crossing the Atlantic when it was discovered that water supply was short and would prove insufficient for the numbers on board. If slaves died a natural death, the loss would fall on the owners. But if they were thrown overboard the loss would be covered by insurance. So, without further ado, 132 slaves were cast into the sea to drown, and the underwriters were duly obliged by the courts to pay the owners £30 for each slave lost. The full horror of this atrocity was later captured in Turner's painting *"Slave Ship"*. However, at the time there was no public outcry. Appeals in parliament that the captain of the *'Zong'* should be tried for murder went unheard. And when the insurers took their claim to court, their claim was dismissed on the apparently perfectly legitimate grounds that *"the blacks were property"*. The presiding judge ruled that in law the killing of slaves was no different from killing horses.

In 1812, on another slave ship *'La Rodeur'* there was an outbreak of ophthalmia, a disease that causes temporary blindness, which afflicted both slaves and crew. The captain, fearing that the blindness was permanent and knowing that blind slaves would be difficult to sell, sent 39 slaves over the side to their death. As with the captain of the *'Zong'*, he hoped that the insurance would cover the loss.

In the last quarter of the seventeenth century, the average annual export of slaves to the Americas was in the region of 25,000, and the total number of African slaves exported during the century has been calculated to have been around 1.5 million. In the eighteenth century, the Atlantic Slave Trade operated on a vastly greater scale, and even the most conservative estimate is that over 5 million Africans were exported to the New World. The peak of the trade seems to have been reached in the 1780s, when on average some 80,000 slaves were brought to the Americas each year.

However, these estimates for the volume of the Atlantic Slave Trade are for the number of slaves who were landed at their destination in the Americas. A high percentage of slaves never reached the other side of the Atlantic because of death from disease, maltreatment, or shipwreck. Evidence from the eighteenth and nineteenth centuries, when the vast majority of the slaves were transported, suggests that the average loss of African lives on the Middle Passage may have been around fifteen per cent. In earlier times losses are likely to have been higher, perhaps averaging as much as twenty per cent.

## Abolition Of Slavery

Many levels of British society profited from the Atlantic Slave Trade, not only shipbuilders and slavers but also merchants, tradespeople and manufacturers. Moreover, even small-scale investors could buy a share in a slaving voyage, and profits could be made at every point of the 'triangular trade' between England, the West African coast and the Caribbean. The slave trade was generally viewed as a good investment and condoned throughout Europe by intellectuals, politicians and churchmen. Many, from the monarchy downwards, invested heavily. Robert Walpole, the Britain's first prime minister, made about £9,000 (over £1 million in today's money) by investing in the Royal African and South Sea Companies. The composer Handel's name also appears in the list of investors of the Royal African Company in 1720, together with a third of the Board of the Royal Academy of Music. Indeed, the forthcoming Dictionary of British Slave Traders will provide data on over 6,500 members of society who took part in the trade over a period covering more than two centuries. It will show how deeply the slave trade percolated British society.

However, in the middle of the eighteenth century public opinion began to shift quickly. After centuries of broad acceptance of the slave trade and its practices, leading figures in Britain led by William Wilberforce and by others, in what became known as the Clapham Sect, started to question the morality of enslaving and owning humans. They began a campaign to abolish slavery and determined that the first step should be to end the transatlantic trade. Attacking the British slave trade was crucial, since Britain had by then become the largest slave trading nation.

John Newton's first-hand experience as a slave trader proved to be a powerful testimony. Newton belonged to no political faction but was a national figure and lionised for his preaching. His attack on the slave trade was an unimpeachable document from an unimpeachable source. His *"Thoughts upon the Slave Trade"* published in 1788 was both a denunciation and a public confession. It led to Newton being called to speak again about his career when Parliament chose to investigate the slave trade. His evidence was stark and unembellished in its detail. But it was his frank admission that he had only quit the trade through ill-health and only recently repented that had the most impact. It painted in the public mind the image of a sinner saved, and perhaps of an example to the nation of the possibility for redemption. His full story is outlined in the next chapter.

More powerful testimony was supplied by ex-slaves themselves who gave their own personal experiences. Olaudah Equiano was enslaved as a child and was taken to the Caribbean and sold as a slave to a Royal Navy officer. He was sold twice more but purchased his freedom in 1766. As a freedman in London, Equiano supported the British abolitionist movement, and in 1789 he published an autobiography that depicted the horrors of slavery and was reprinted nine times in his lifetime. In the 1830s and 1840s the focus moved from the Caribbean to slavery in North America, and a number of African American abolitionists crossed the Atlantic to educate the British public on American slavery. Most notable among them was an escaped slave Frederick Douglass, who in 1845-1847 travelled all over Britain to deliver lectures to enthusiastic audiences crammed into church halls, town halls, or other local venues.

However, faced with the overwhelming opposition of business groups, the abolition of the British trade was a slow process, which dragged on for over twenty years. Parliament first regulated the trade, limiting the number of slaves British vessels could carry from Africa. It then moved to ban the importation of slaves in a number of colonies and in 1807 it abolished the trade altogether. However, the new law did not stop the British slave trade overnight. For many years slave ships tried to run the gauntlet of the British naval ships that patrolled the coast. British captains who were caught continuing the trade were fined £100 for every slave found on board. As a result, if slave ships were in danger of being captured by the navy, their captains would try to reduce the fines they had to pay by ordering the slaves to be thrown into the sea. Even when slave boats were captured and their cargoes liberated, what the patrol officers did not know was that as soon as the poor unfortunates reached shore, they became slaves again.

It was not until the passing of the Slavery Abolition Act in

1833, which made slavery itself illegal, that the trade could be stamped out altogether. The sheer extent of the British trade at that time highlights how significant the triumph of the Abolitionists was. For, during the previous decade a total of 150 British slave ships had sailed each year to West Africa and between them purchased more than 40,000 African slaves. And in 1841 the British Government, under pressure from the newly formed Society for the Extinction of the Slave Trade and the Civilization of Africa, sent out an expedition to negotiate agreements with local chiefs to abolish the traffic in human lives. In the following year Commander Raymond of '*HMS Spy*' made treaties with the Calabar chiefs, King Eyamba of Duke Town and King Eyo Honesty of Creek Town. At the end of the negotiations, the two kings wrote the following letters, which demonstrate at the same time their statesmanship, their appetite for education and their basic trading instincts:

*Old Calabar, Dec 4, 1842*

*Dear Commander Raymond,*

*Now we settle treaty for not sell slaves, I must tell you something. I want your queen to do for we. Now we can't sell slaves again, we must have too much man for country, and we want something for make work and trade, and if we could get seed for cotton and coffee we could trade. Plenty sugar cane live here, and if some man come teach we way for do it we get plenty sugar too, and then some man must come for teach book proper, and make all men saby God like white man, and then we go on for some fashion. We thank you too much for what thing you come do for keep thing right. Long time we no look man-of-war as Blount promise, and one Frenchman come make plenty palaver for slave when he can't get them. You can do very proper for we, and now we want to keep proper mouth. I hope some man-of-war come some time with proper captain all same you look out and help we keep word when French man-of-war come. What I want for dollar side is fine coat and sword all same I tell you and the rest in copper rods. I hope Queen Victoria and young prince will live long time and we get good friend. Also I want bomb and shell.*

*I am, your best friend.*
*King Eyamba V, King of all Black Man*


*To Commander Raymond Man-Of-War Ship Spy,*

*I am very glad you come and settle treaty proper and thank you for doing every-thing right for me yesterday. Long time I look for some Man-of-war, and when French man come I think we want war, and send one canoe to let you know, but too much wind live for him catch Fernando Po, and no one come help me keep treaty as Mr Blount promise, and when I give no slaves French Man-of-war come make plenty palaver. But I no will. One thing I want for beg your Queen, I have too much man now, I can't sell slaves and don't know what to do for them. But if I can get some cotton and coffee to grow, and man for teach me, and make sugar cane for we country come up proper, and sell for trade side very glad. Mr Blyth tell me England glad for send man teach book. And we make understand God all same white man do. If Queen do so I glad too much, and we must try do good for England always. What I want for dollar side is proper India Romall and copper rods, I want no fool thing. I want thing for trade side, and must try do good for Queen Victoria and all English women.*

*I hope Queen and young King can live long time proper, and I am, sir, your friend.*

*King Eyo Honesty*

In retrospect, the Atlantic Slave Trade seems to us to have been as irrational as it was immoral. It is hard to understand why Europeans for four centuries were willing to send a succession of young men to the West African coast, knowing full well that the average life expectancy on those shores was barely more than a year. In addition, about a quarter of the crew of each slave ship would die on the voyage across the ocean to the Americas. The explanation may lie in the fact that the triangular trade, and the plantation system that drove it, were not driven by society as a whole, but rather by individuals fulfilling their own limited roles in the overall operation and fuelled by their own individual desire for profit at the time.

There is no doubt that those who engaged in the slave trade had a great deal to gain from it, and that human greed was a more powerful sentiment than sympathy for the slaves in their charge, and even concern for their own well-being in a deadly environment. Only the promise of riches could have persuaded so many to risk their lives on shore or at sea, on such a pernicious trade, with its inherent dangers and sufferings, and in an environment that was literally life threatening.

Strangely, some African leaders actually regretted the ending of the Atlantic Slave Trade. When in the 1840s the British government put pressure on him to put an end to the trade in his area, King Gezo of Dahomey (the present-day Republic of Benin) is said to have responded:

*"The slave trade has been the ruling principle of my people. It is the source of their glory and wealth. Their songs celebrate their victories and the mother lulls the child to sleep with notes of triumph over an enemy reduced to slavery."*

But the vast majority of the long suffering peoples of West Africa would have breathed a collective sigh of relief to see the back of the slave factories with their degenerate staff, and of the slave ships with their unprincipled crews. Yet, although new visitors would arrive on the coast apparently on more legitimate business or with a nobler mission, the legacy of the slave days would survive. Not only would the horror of the slave trade endure in peoples' minds and national cultures, but the commercial system developed by the slave traders and their African counterparts would form the basis of the new endeavours and the new enterprises that would replace it.

# 3 JOHN NEWTON

## (1725-1807)

John Newton is best known for the hymn *"Amazing Grace"*, which he composed in 1772 when he was the charismatic vicar of the small parish of Olney in Buckinghamshire. His congregation was composed mainly of local farm workers, whom he liked to call his *'plain people'*. To inspire his humble audience of local farm workers he would write a new hymn to accompany each sermon. His output was prolific, and he joined forces with his close friend and neighbour, the poet William Cowper, to publish in 1779 the *"Olney Hymns"*, a prodigious collection of 348 hymns. Many of these became among the most popular hymns in the English language. But one hymn in particular, *"Amazing Grace"*, has become a universal anthem. Its enduring appeal lies in the simplicity of the verse and its message:

> *Amazing grace! (how sweet the sound)*
> *That saved a wretch like me!*
> *I once was lost, but now am found,*
> *Was blind, but now can see.*

However, few if any of his congregation would have been aware that the opening lines were also a recollection of their preacher's early life. The young Newton had been a slave trader and an active participant in the Atlantic Slave Trade. Only late in life did he have a life-changing experience which converted him into an evangelical Christian. Although in his sermons Newton would confess openly to his past sins and misdemeanours, their true nature was kept a dark secret. Only later in 1787, when he had become a committed Abolitionist, did he publish the detailed diaries he had kept of his voyages as *"An*

*Authentic Narrative."*

This is the source of much of our information about the life and times of a slave ship captain. The book's popularity at the time was more because it was an inspiring story of redemption for Newton's religious followers, as well as a compelling adventure story with added love interest for the general public. But underneath there lay another story that shows Newton in an altogether different light, as a harsh slave trader willing to dole out the most savage punishments, in order to make a profit for himself and his employers.

Newton's early history was typical of the social misfits and delinquents who became embroiled in the slave trade. He was born in London in 1725, the son of a ship's captain involved in the Mediterranean trade for the East India Company. At 11 years old he first went to sea with his father with whom he sailed on a total of six voyages until his father retired in 1742. Newton was then unemployed and seemed to be making little effort to find work for himself. So, his father first contacted an old friend, John Manesty, who was a Liverpool merchant, and persuaded him as a favour to offer his son a job. Newton was due to depart from Liverpool at the end of 1742 to take up a lucrative five year contract as an overseer on a Jamaican plantation, but he failed to turn up for the boat leaving for the Caribbean. On a visit to see family friends at Chatham in Kent, he had fallen in love with Mary (Polly) Catlett, who later became his wife.

When the time came to travel to Liverpool, he could not bear to leave his beloved Polly behind. Three weeks after missing his ship, Newton had to go cap in hand to his father. Surprisingly, his father forgave him, and asked Manesty to find him another position. But his father's punishment was that he should sail to the Mediterranean below decks as an able seaman, rather than in the relative comfort of the captain's cabin. If this was meant to be a learning experience, it seemed to have no effect on the wayward Newton. On his return, he ignored his father and immediately took off to see Polly in Chatham. At the time Chatham was a major naval base for the building, repairing, and equipping of British warships. Finding crews to serve in those ships was a constant headache for the navy, and press gangs were employed to trawl the docksides and lure the unsuspecting into forced service. Whilst visiting Polly, either Newton strayed into the wrong area or got into a brawl. One way or another he caught the attention of a press gang, and duly became another of their victims.

This time his father could not get him out of trouble, and so in 1743 Newton was pressed into naval service, initially as an able seaman on board the 'HMS Harwich' bound for the East Indies. Newton in desperation sent a letter begging his father to intercede on his behalf. His father by then was an employee of the Royal African Company, and as a final favour to his son persuaded the captain to promote Newton to the rank of a midshipman. This gave him not only the chance to serve his country with honour as a warrant officer, but also enabled him to escape the appalling living and working conditions below decks.

But true to form, far from showing his gratitude to the captain, Newton overstayed his leave on several occasions. And then when the ship was anchored off Plymouth in bad weather, and Newton was asked to go ashore for fresh supplies, he ran away for one last chance to see Polly. His freedom lasted two days until he ran into a party of marines, who arrested him and frogmarched him all 24 miles back to Plymouth. Newton was publicly stripped and flogged, and when fit for duty again was demoted to the rank of able seaman. Life on board ship at the time was brutal. One of his shipmates was flogged for "striving to commit sodomy" with a carpenter. The same man was punished by the whole crew two days later for the same offence with a black man. He had to run three times around the lower deck. Peter de Cruse, a black Portuguese sailor, had the same punishment for committing sodomy with a sheep.

The captain understandably lost patience with Newton after his desertion. It was common practice at the time for captains of merchant vessels to transfer undisciplined sailors to an accompanying warship in the hope that the Royal Navy might be able to beat some discipline into them. So, when the convoy of ships in which 'HMS Harwich' was travelling docked at Madeira to take on supplies on the last leg of the voyage, the captain took the opportunity of exchanging Newton for another seaman on a passing merchant ship, the 'Pegasus', which was engaged on the triangular slave trade and heading for the West African coast.

Newton had become suicidal and was only too glad to jump ship. The feeling must have been mutual, as it took only thirty minutes for his officers to negotiate his transfer. For Newton there was the added incentive that he could expect to be back home in a year, and not after five years' service in the Far East that service on the 'HMS Harwich' would have required. He may also have calculated that it was a lucrative opportunity, and one that would enable him to raise funds quickly. Throughout his early career his only motivation appeared to be to raise the funds he needed to marry his beloved Polly.

For six months Newton remained on board the 'Pegasus', sailing from river mouth to river mouth collecting slaves from the factories on shore. But he had again made himself unpopular with the ship's crew. In 1745, just before the ship was about to depart on the Middle Passage to the Americas, the captain took ill and died. Newton seized the opportunity to ask the ship's part-owner, Amos Clow, who was going on land to continue trading, if he could join his service. He was naively unaware of the risks and hardships involved in spending a lengthy time on shore. He could only see the financial reward.

Clow took him to the largest of three islands called *'Platanes'* at the mouth of the Sierra Leone River, a bleak inhospitable spot but close to the supply routes for transporting slaves from the mainland and ferrying them to the waiting Atlantic slave ships. Newton, his employers, and local workers set about the construction of a new factory for storing and trading slaves. Newton seemed to enjoy his first few weeks, but it was not to last. He soon fell ill with fever. To make matters worse, he also began to quarrel with his employers.

Clow had a partner in his local enterprise, Princess Peye of the local Sherbro people. It was common practice on the West African coast for Europeans and Africans to join forces to create trading dynasties, whose common endeavour was to fill the inbound merchant ships with African slaves destined for the Americas. With a mastery of the local language and English (or other European language), and with children born of African mothers and European fathers, such commercial families were wired into the African trade systems along the coast and into the interior, and with the foreign shipping companies. They reigned supreme and brooked no resistance or dissent from their employees.

Newton was a born troublemaker and soon got under the skin of Clow and his African partner, who developed an intense dislike for him. And so, when Clow was away from the slave factory, she moved Newton out of his comfortable hut into empty slave quarters and cut his daily rations to a handful of boiled rice. Half-starved, Newton had to survive on roots pulled up and eaten raw, and occasionally on food brought by African slaves.

On Clow's return, Newton complained about his treatment but was not believed. When he accompanied his employer on his next trip, matters went from bad to worse. Another trader accused Newton of cheating Clow, and Clow believed his side of the story. From that point, whenever Clow left the ship, Newton was locked on board deck, with a pint of rice for his daily rations. The rainy season was at its height, and Newton had no protection from the storms to which he was exposed for up to forty hours at a stretch. His condition was now little different from that of the slaves in the factory pens.

Not surprisingly, as these wretched conditions continued for over a year, the miserable Newton wrote in desperation to his father for help. Help was not immediately forthcoming, but meanwhile Newton's conditions took a turn for the better, when he was given permission by Clow to live and work for another trader called Williams. Soon Newton was involved in the management of the business, as he gained Williams's approval and trust. He was beginning to think that the slave trade suited him and that he had found a vocation in life, when news came of the arrival on the coast of a ship called the 'Greyhound'. The captain of the ship had been asked by Newton's father to bring his wayward son home. After some initial reluctance, Newton was persuaded to board the ship. What made up his mind was the lure of an inheritance of £400, a story which the captain had fabricated.

The 'Greyhound' spent nearly a year working her way south, trading for gold, ivory, beeswax and wood for the dying industry. When her holds were full up, the ship set sail for home. The journey involved heading first to Brazil, then north to Newfoundland before the final easterly leg back to Britain. It had already been a long and demanding trip along the West African coast putting a strain on an already ageing vessel. It was in no fit state to navigate safely the approximately 15,000 kilometres round trip. It was no surprise therefore that the ship was severely damaged when it was engulfed by a huge storm just after leaving Newfoundland, with all livestock and provisions lost overboard or ruined. The ship limped slowly back to Britain but was hit again by a storm off the Irish coast, forcing it on a detour around the Scottish islands before eventually docking at Lough Swilly in Ireland.

Newton survived the ordeal, but it had been a life changing experience for him. He had a spiritual conversion to Christianity, but he did not yet question the morality of the slave trade. Indeed, in 1748 he set sail again for the West African coast, this time as first mate on the 'Brownlow', a slave ship. He had embarked on a new career as a slave trader. On arriving in Sierra Leone his job was to go by open boat along the river estuaries buying slaves, and his behaviour seems to have been no different from that of the other European traders on the coast. He was a quick learner and soon became well-versed in the usual tricks of the trade. European traders routinely cheated their African counterparts in the number, weight, measurement, and quantity of the goods they traded. So much deception took place that, if the tables were turned and a local African trader was accused of dishonesty, he would answer Newton back in contempt: *"What? Am I a white man?"*.

When bartering for slaves with the local African traders or their European middlemen, it never seemed to occur to Newton that there was anything wrong in this cruel commercial trading in human beings. In his logbook he merely recorded the number of slaves he took on board, with often a complaint about any high price or inadequate physique:

*"In the morning Yellow Will brought me of a boy slave three feet ten inches, which I was obliged to take or get nothing".*

His moral conduct was no better. On shore he followed the other trader custom of taking a local African girl as his mistress, and on board ship he also condoned the rape by the officers and crew of their female cargo. Newton himself raped one of the slave women in the hold. As he recorded in his diary:

*"The enemy prepared a train of temptations, and I became his easy prey."*

Newton would have been aware of the risks to his health of travelling along the West African coast, as he had to bury seven members of his crew, and he himself suffered another bout of fever. The voyage to the Americas was also an arduous as well as dangerous experience with many human casualties. Given the appalling and demeaning living conditions endured by the slaves in the hold, mutinies were a constant threat. On the outward journey of the *'Brownlow'* to the Caribbean a group of slaves broke free, and a crew member was killed by a marlin spike. The rest of the crew fired their guns from the rigging, killing four of the unarmed Africans. The surviving mutineers were severely beaten and flogged without mercy.

The captain then took the decision not to dock in Antigua but to sail on to South Carolina. The longer time at sea led to a rapid rise in the mortality rate among the slaves. By the time the ship docked, the *'Brownlow'* had lost 62 out of the 218 slaves on board. Newton's reaction was to remark that he was glad to see the survivors leave for the slave market, since he felt *"shut up with almost as many unclean creatures as Noah was and in a much smaller Ark."* And yet the recently converted Christian had just disembarked from a ship where every Sunday he had held divine services for the crew, an unheard of event for a slave ship at the time.

Newton may have found God, but he did not immediately display any charity towards his fellow human beings. When he later reflected on his career in his diaries, his concerns always seem to be more about his own spiritual and moral struggles, and less about the plight of his human cargo. It is therefore with some irony that the town of Newton in Sierra Leone is named after him, a magnanimous tribute in view of his days as an unscrupulous slave trader on the Sierra Leone coast.

On his return to England, Newton obtained employment as a slave ship captain and made three more trips to the West African coast. In total he spent ten years at the heart of the Atlantic Slave Trade. He was to prove himself as brutal and severe master as any, never hesitating to inflict pain and misery on his human cargo, if he felt it necessary to maintain discipline on board. Like other slave ship captains, he was lured into the trade purely for financial gain and was equally determined to maximise the profits of the slave ship owners. In his diaries he reveals the attitude of even the most enlightened slave ship captain of the time. He observes:

*"During the time I was engaged in the slave trade I never had the least scruple as to its lawfulness. It is, indeed, accounted a genteel employment and is usually very profitable".*

When he bought African slaves, he was constantly worried about the escalating cost, and concerned that he was being outbid by his competitors.

Newton also kept meticulous accounts and maintained careful financial management. On one voyage his budget was so tight that he decided to cut back on the slaves' food rations:

*"Give the slaves bread now for their breakfast for cannot afford them 2 hot meals per day."*

He also thought that as a general principle it was important to have as many slaves as possible on board a slave ship:

*"With our ships, the great object is, to be full. When the ship is there, it is thought desirable, she should take as many as possible. The cargo vessel of a hundred tons, or little more, is calculated to purchase from two hundred and twenty to two hundred and fifty slaves."*

He was fully aware of what the cramped conditions would mean for the slaves below decks: in rooms no more than five feet high, lying in two rows one above the other *"like books on a shelf"*, and shackled together in irons at both hands and feet:

*"which makes it difficult for them to turn or move, to attempt either to rise or to lie down, without hurting themselves, or each other."*

However, despite his awareness of the brutal regime on his ship, throughout his long career Newton only made modest improvements to the welfare of the African slaves in his charge. What seemed to trouble him more was the appalling death toll of the white crews engaged in the trade at the time:

*"This loss, in the African trade, is truly alarming…In fact, the boats seldom return, without bringing some of the people ill of dangerous fevers or fluxes, occasioned either by unwholesome diet, such as the crude fruits and palm wine, with which they are plentifully supplied by the natives."*

Newton himself was twice struck down by fever and recorded in his diary in 1756 how he was obliged to leave the slave trade on account of ill health:

*"Thus I was brought out of a way of life, disagreeable to my temper and inconvenient to my profession (of the Christian faith)."*

He later tried to argue in public that he had been a humane slave trader:

*"I will treat them with humanity while under my power and not render their confinement unnecessarily grievous."*

But his diaries reveal a different story. He thought nothing of using thumbscrews on the African slaves, not merely to extract information about potential plots, but also as a form of punishment. After the discovery of a plot among the slaves on the *'Argyle'* in 1751 he wrote:

*"Put the boys in irons and slightly in the thumbscrew to urge them to a full confession."*

But Newton had at least begun to recognise how appalling and inhumane the conditions on board a slave ship were, and the hygiene on board was an improvement on previous voyages under his command. The hold was routinely cleansed and at times individual slaves were given a wash on deck. When the *'Argyle'* reached Antigua in the Caribbean in July 1751, 174 of the two hundred slaves on board had survived. This was a low death toll compared with the norm for such journeys, and was more than half the number of slaves who had died during Newton's previous Middle Passage journey as first mate on the 'Brownlow' three years earlier in 1748.

Newton was not exceptional in his views and attitudes towards his chosen profession. European public opinion at the time accepted slavery as a necessary evil and considered it to be an inevitable human condition. Individuals like Newton directly involved in the slave trade had few moral scruples or religious qualms about their behaviour. The trade was widely accepted as a morally neutral business enterprise which yielded both profit for his employers and a higher standard of living for most of the British population. That it caused misery on an epic scale for untold millions of innocent African victims barely registered among the people who ran and worked in the pernicious system. Moreover, many prided themselves on their sophistication and civility. Newton's own letters home to his wife, written every two or three days, were extravagant displays of noble virtue and righteous faith, and were littered with pretentious classical references.

Nevertheless, although slaves were pagan and thought to be inferior and stupid, they were to be treated as kindly as possible. This was not just because they were unfortunate fellow human beings (*"tho' of a different colour"*), but because it was economically unwise to do otherwise. Moreover, some slave ship captains, while far from being Abolitionists, felt compassion towards their slaves, and did not regard them in any way as sub-human. Jean Barbot recorded in his journal in 1679 his joy at seeing a family of five, whom he had bought at different times and places, reunited after being separated when they were first enslaved. Similarly, in 1732 Thomas Phillips wrote that he did not *"think there is any intrinsick value in one colour more than another"*. Moreover, Newton on his final voyages did at length show some compassion towards the slaves in his charge.

In 1750 Newton at last married Polly Cartlett, but he continued to work as a slave captain for a few more years, until he was finally forced to retire through ill health in 1754 after suffering a stroke. Thereafter he led a much less hazardous life, first as the surveyor of tides in Liverpool, and then as curate of the parish of Olney in Buckinghamshire. He became a respected evangelical preacher and well-known writer of popular hymns, gaining national celebrity with the publication of *"Authentic Narrative"* in 1764 and the hymn *"Amazing Grace"* in 1779. In 1780 at the age of 55 he moved to London to become Rector of St Mary Woolnoth Church, where he officiated until his death.

He had by then begun to reflect on the horrors of the slave trade and to express public regret for his part in it. He joined William Wilberforce in the campaign for its abolition and became one of its most prominent supporters. Newtons' pamphlet *"Thoughts Upon the African Slave Trade"* was published in 1787, and it became an immediate bestseller. Remorse was one of the motives behind its publication, but his testimony as an ex slave trader had a significant impact on public opinion and parliamentary debate. It was of vital importance on converting public opinion to the abolitionist cause.

Newton admitted that this:

*"was a confession, which…comes too late…It will always be a subject of humiliating reflection to me, that I was once an active instrument in a business at which my heart now shudders."*

He went on to explain why he had become involved in the campaign against the slave trade:

*"The nature and effects of that unhappy and disgraceful branch of commerce, which has long been maintained on the Coast of Africa, with the sole, and professed design of purchasing our fellow- creatures, in order to supply our West-India islands and the American*

*colonies, when they were ours, with slaves; is now generally under-*
*stood. So much light has been thrown on the subject, by many able*
*pens; and so many respectable persons have already engaged to*
*use their utmost influence, for the suppression of a traffic, which*
*contradicts the feelings of humanity; that it is hoped, this stain on*
*our National character will soon be wiped out."*

On 25 March 1807, the Abolition of the Slave Trade Act received its royal assent, abolishing the slave trade in the British
colonies and making it illegal to carry enslaved people in British ships. On 21st December of the same year John Newton
died.

# 4  RIVER NIGER EXPLORERS

*"I had now before me a boundless forest, and a country,
the inhabitants of which were strangers to civilised life."*

The trade in slaves dominated European and West African relations for over two centuries; and it was the slaves who brought the few scraps of knowledge about the interior which were gained during this time. Because the coast was so unhealthy, most ventures inland by Europeans in the seventeenth and eighteenth centuries were excursions rather than journeys, confined to the major slaving rivers of the Senegal, Gambia and Calabar. These trips added little to Europe's knowledge of Africa. They shed no light on one of the most puzzling questions of African geography - the course of the Niger River. The existence of the Niger had been known since ancient times. But where it came from and where it went remained one of Europe's great geographical mysteries. Did the Niger flow from the east or from the west? If it flowed from the west, did it join up with the Nile, or did it disappear instead into a great lake in the interior? If neither was true, what exactly was the river's course? At the end of the eighteenth century a complex web of strategic, commercial, scientific, and humanitarian factors made the solution of the problem an urgent necessity.

## The African Association

In 1788, a group of twelve senior establishment figures, who met regularly at a fashionable dining club in London's West End called the Saturday Club, decided to set up a new organisation dedicated to the exploration of the African continent. They grandly called their organisation the *"Association for Promoting the Discovery of the Interior Parts of Africa"*, but happily this title was later shortened to the *"African Association"*. As the founding members included Josiah Wedgwood and other leading figures of the Industrial Revolution, it was obvious that the aims of the Association were commercial as well as scientific. They hoped that the explorations that the African Association sponsored would succeed in opening new markets for the rising output of British manufacturing. Although humanitarian concerns were not explicitly mentioned in the African Association's manifesto, the list of early subscribers included William Wilberforce and other members of the Clapham Sect. They could see a golden opportunity to advance their crusade to abolish the traffic in slaves.

Within days of the founding of the African Association, two men were recruited to travel from North Africa into the interior, and to penetrate as far as they could towards the great river. The first to leave was John Ledyard, a restless American adventurer, who had already circumnavigated the world with Captain Cook, as well as made a rather hapless and unsuccessful attempt to walk round it on foot. His brief from the Association was to start in Egypt and to travel directly south down the Nile, before making a sharp right turn to the west, which it was hopedwould take him across the continent to the Niger. Unfortunately, this cunning plan never got across the starting line in Cairo, since on arrival Ledyard rather inconveniently died after muddling up his medicines and taking an accidental overdose.

The African Association, however, was not easily put off, and they had another plan up their sleeves. At about the same time as Ledyard was poisoning himself in Egypt, Simon Lucas was marching off with high hopes at the head of a second expedition from Libya. The Association's plan was that Lucas would travel due south from Tripoli and then join up with an Arab caravan, which would guide him across the Sahara to reach the Niger. Lucas's main qualification for the job was that as a young man he had been captured by Arabs in Morocco and kept as a slave, but managed to secure his freedom and to spend the next 16 years acting as Vice-Consul for the area. Suitably impressed by Lucas's resourcefulness and by the extent of his local knowledge, the African Association immediately engaged him as the expedition leader. Sadly, their judgement was misplaced. Not far into his route, Lucas found his way blocked by local tribes in open rebellion against the Pasha of Tripoli. Concerned for his safety and that he would also run out of supplies, Lucas turned on his heels and smartly returned to Tripoli, bringing a second expedition to a rather ignominious conclusion.

Undaunted, the African Association despatched a third investigator to West Africa by yet another route. The plan this time was based on the premise that the Niger entered the sea at the mouth of either the Senegal or the Gambia Rivers on the West Coast. This theory was fuelled by the records of the last traveller known to have reached the banks of the Niger, the sixteenth century Arab traveller known as Leo Africanus. He had stated that in the area around the inland city of Timbuktu the Niger flowed from east to west. If this was true, then the river's course must take it to the coast.

And so, Major Daniel Houghton was appointed to pursue a third entry strategy, starting from the trading posts along the Gambia River. On route he sent back a sensational report on his findings, which were in direct contradiction to what for centuries Leo Africanus had led the world to believe. His information was that the river flowed from the west, and that decked sailing ships had been observed carrying goods downstream past Timbuktu in an easterly direction. Houghton sent a message back to the African Association, saying that he was pressing on by a northerly route in the general direction of Timbuktu. This was rather foolhardy since he had already been robbed on route of all his possessions, and it was the last that was heard of the bold major.

On receiving Houghton's information, the African Association approached the British government with the suggestion that a Consul be appointed to reside at the mouth of the Gambia River for the purpose of developing a more extensive trade with the interior. James Willis was duly appointed Consul-General in 1794, and arrangements were put in hand to send him out with fifty soldiers and a small armed ship. Willis, however, would be tied to his base on the Gambia River, and the African Association needed another brave adventurer to volunteer to follow in Houghton's footsteps. Sir Joseph Banks, one of the leading members of the association, was the patron of a young Scottish doctor called Mungo Park, and he put his name forward for selection. The fact that all three of the earlier expeditions had ended in failure and in the death of two previous jobholders may have had something to do with Park's appointment, since he seemed to be the only volunteer. But he was destined to  become one of the most celebrated explorers of the Victorian age. His full story is told in the next chapter, but his two pioneering  expeditions are sumarised below.

Park's first expedition in 1795 made substantial progress, but ultimately it too ended in failure. He began by retracing Houghton's route along the Gambia River. After great hardship on route and surviving near-fatal encounters in Muslim territory, he reached the land of the friendly Bambara people who helped guide him to the Niger. He was the first European to lay eyes on the Niger and the first to record that it did in fact flow inland to the east. However, his attempt to follow the river until it led him to Timbuktu was thwarted by the intense heat and constant harassment by thieves. Park had become physically and mentally exhausted by the effort. Reluctantly he was forced to accept defeat and make his way back to the coast. By the time he reached the trading post at Pisania he had been travelling for nearly two years.

The indefatigable armchair explorers of the African Association continued to send their men out to Africa. Clearly undeterred by the earlier failure of Lucas and the deaths of Ledyard and Houghton, they commissioned two further expeditions in search for the Niger from a northerly direction. In 1797, they engaged a German, Frederick Hornemann, to make another attempt to explore Africa westward from Cairo. Like so many before him he vanished into rumour and a long silence. Only nineteen years later did the Association learn that Hornemann had, like so many European travellers in West Africa before him, died a miserable death through dysentery. It appears that he had reached the Niger and followed the river downstream some distance to a town called Nupe. But sadly, he took any revelations he had with him to the grave.

Nor did a second expedition from the south shed any additional light on the course of the river. This was led by Henry Nicholls whose objective was to travel north from one of the trading stations on the Atlantic shoreline. He arrived on the coast near Calabar in January 1805 and wrote the first of his reports for the African Association, in which he described the conditions at the trading post. But he then promptly caught a fever and was dead by April.

The torch of African exploration was therefore passed back to Mungo Park. In March 1805 he set off for West Africa, this time in charge of a much better equipped and government sponsored expedition. Park had been invited to draft his own version of the expedition's aims and requirements. He shrewdly placed emphasis on the commercial advantages that might result from the expedition, and even on the possibility of future colonisation, rather than on purely geographical concerns. This was exactly the approach that the government had in mind. And so, it was officially endorsed as a *"Journey of Discovery and of Enquiry for Commercial Purposes"*.

After Park's first expedition, there had been general agreement that the Niger flowed from west to east. What remained in dispute was the direction it took after passing Timbuktu. All theories agreed that it flowed towards the east for a considerable distance. One theory was that the Niger emptied itself into a great lake roughly in the position of Lake Chad. Others still held to the view that the Niger eventually joined the Nile. The two remaining theories suggested that after flowing east, the Niger either turned due south, or to the south and west. The first of these alternatives was advanced by George Maxwell, a trader who had spent some time around the mouth of the Congo, an exceptionally long river with no known source. The second theory was advocated by Christian Reichard, a German geographer, who suggested that the Niger eventually discharged its waters into the Bights of Benin and Biafra through a vast delta. But this theory was rejected because of the prevailing belief in the existence of the Mountains of Kong, which were assumed to stretch right across West Africa, thus blocking the exit of the river into the Atlantic Ocean.

Park arrived back at the mouth of the Gambia in June 1805 to embark on his second expedition. He headed off upriver from the coast in command of a force of 45 Europeans. But sadly, after a series of msadventures, only 12 survivors reached Bamako on the Niger River. Undaunted, pressed on with his voyage down the unexplored river, hoping to reach the coast at the end of January 1806. But their boat was shipwrecked on the rapids at Bussa after it had been attacked by local inhabitants. Park and his remaining European companions were all drowned. Only Isaaco, a local guide on the journey from the Gambia, survived and was able to carry Park's journal and other personal papers back to the coast. They were later published as *"The Journal of a Mission to the Interior of Africa in the Year 1805"*.

Despite Park's best endeavours, the mystery of the Niger remained unsolved. His own theory, that the Niger and Congo were in fact the same river, became the general opinion in the years after his death. In 1809, the African Association commissioned Johann Burckhardt, a Swiss explorer of the Middle East and Africa to make the overland journey across the Sahara from Tripoli to Timbuktu, but his travels shed no additional light on the course of the Niger. To prepare for the journey, he attended Cambridge University and studied Arabic, Science and Medicine. At this time, he also began to adopt Arabian costume. In 1809 he left England and travelled to Aleppo, Syria to perfect his Arabic and Muslim customs. But, despite years of meticulous preparation, he never did make his intended journey to the Niger. In 1817, while waiting in Cairo for a caravan to take him across the Sahara, he was stricken with dysentery and died.

The Napoleonic wars put paid to any further expeditions, except for the abortive trip of the eccentric German, Heinrich Roentgen. His plan was to travel disguised as a Muslim trader, and he made meticulous advance preparations for his expedition. He trained on a diet of spiders, grasshoppers, and roots: leaving nothing to chance, he even arranged to have himself circumcised. But he was tricked into recruiting a well-known local criminal as his servant and only travelling companion. This rogue murdered Roentgen early in the journey, thus ending the life of yet another enthusiastic but gullible volunteer.

Following the end of the Napoleonic Wars, the first attempt in a renewed outburst of Niger exploration was based on Park's theory that the Congo was actually one and the same river as the Niger. Captain Tuckey, a renowned Arctic explorer, was instructed to sail up the Congo, whilst two army officers, Peddie and Campbell, were to follow Park's trail inland from the Gambia on the Niger. It was hoped that the two parties would meet up somewhere in the middle. Tuckey was unable to penetrate further than the first great Congo cataract 250 kilometres from the coast, and he and most of his crew died of yellow fever on the return journey. The army fared no better, since they too were forced back to the coast in the face of hostility by the rulers of states on the Upper Senegal River, with the loss of over 100 soldiers. Peddie himself died shortly after the expedition's departure and his second-in-command died a little later. A surgeon called Dochard led the rump of the expedition back to the coast, where he also succumbed to fever, leaving only seven men standing. Yet another subsequent expedition, led by a Major Grey, fared little better and suffered a similar loss of life.

## The Mystery Solved

The Niger had been found and its direction recorded, but its final termination had not been discovered. This was fast becoming a major embarrassment to the British government and led to a change in policy. In future, large-scale expeditions were to be replaced by smaller groups travelling in tandem with Arab caravans. The less hostile and difficult trans-Saharan routes were also to be used. In 1820, an expedition was sent out over the Sahara, led by a retired naval surgeon called Oudney, Major Dixon Denham and Lieutenant Hugh Clapperton. Oudney died shortly after crossing the desert. Shortly after, Denham and Clapperton fell out with each other, and decided to go their separate ways, with Denham opting to explore the area around Lake Chad. Although the two men were later reunited and returned safely to England, they were never to speak again and only communicated by passing notes to each other.

Clapperton pressed on alone towards the Niger, and after much deprivation reached Kano in the north of Nigeria in January 1824. There he was warmly received by the local Emir, and later by the Emir of neighbouring Sokoto, who drew for him a map of the Niger and pointed out how easy it would be to reach his own territory from the sea. The European explorers had needed only to ask for directions. But, of course, that would have spoiled the adventure, or rather eliminated the potential for glory. They wanted to discover the course of the Niger for themselves. Clapperton returned to England with a mass of other information about the onward course of the river, but much of what he presented was contradictory.

And so, despite the relative success of Clapperton's expedition, as far as the expert geographers and seasoned travellers back in London were concerned, the question of the Niger was just as perplexing as ever. Nevertheless, a breakthrough had been achieved because the local rulers promised to put an end to the slave traffic to the coast in return for trade. At last, the dreams of the Abolitionists seemed to be coming true. Clapperton had found large, prosperous towns inland, ruled by friendly and enlightened leaders, who appeared to appreciate the advantages of legitimate trade over the slave trade.

Clapperton, therefore, returned to Africa in the following year to open up a river route for such trade from the south. Unfortunately, he landed at Badagry near Lagos, a long distance along the coast from the Niger Delta, and proceeded north through hostile Yoruba country. His companions died, and Clapperton and his servant, Richard Lander, fell desperately ill. After many trials and tribulations, the two explorers eventually reached Kano in the North. Clapperton rested for a month and then travelled west to Sokoto. There he was disillusioned to find that Arab traders, fearful that a river route from the south would cut out their lucrative caravans across the Sahara, had turned the Emir's head. Worn out by ill health and disappointment, Clapperton died soon afterwards.

Destitute and sick, Richard Lander nevertheless decided to make his own way down the Niger. He managed to reach Lokoja, where the Niger and Benue Rivers join each other. There he was forced to abandon the river and to make his way overland to the coast and then to England. But like so many Niger explorers before him, Lander would not easily give up the quest and was determined to solve the enigma of the river. And so, he set off once more for West Africa, this time in the company of his brother, John. They reached Bussa in 1830 and made their way without incident to the confluence of the Niger and Benue Rivers. After a brief period in captivity, the two escaped and set off by boat down the river, finally reaching the sea in November 1830.

At last, the puzzle of the Niger's route to the Atlantic Ocean had been solved, and the quest of the Niger explorers was at an end. However, the solution was not the one they expected, and not perhaps in keeping with their grand obsession. For the Landers discovered to their surprise that, at the end of its 4,000 kilometre journey across West Africa from the Fouta Djallon plateau in Guinea in the west, the mighty river does not enter the Atlantic Ocean in a mighty flood through a vast estuary. Instead, it oozed slowly through an intricate network of mangrove swamps, lagoons and narrow creeks that became known as the Niger Delta.

And so, the story of the long search to trace the Niger's course ended in almost an anti-climax. The great river had claimed many lives, ruined the health of many others, and made no one his fortune. Richard Lander himself received only £100 from the government for his troubles. When, because of continuing ill health, he asked for a pension, he received only another £100. Fortunately, he was paid 1,000 guineas for the book he published of his journeys.

The financial rewards for explorers were therefore meagre, and the real lure was the glory and national reputation that could be enjoyed on their return. In an age obsessed by status and class, the world of exploration offered an unaccustomed freedom and an opportunity to move up the social ladder. It was, however, a perilous career, and ruthless ambition had to be matched by a reckless bravery. West Africa was for a European the most hostile of environments, coupling a debilitating climate with an ever-present threat of deadly disease. The eighteenth century explorers may have been free spirits, but one after another they would make the ultimate sacrifice for that freedom. Their families at home would also pay a terrible financial price for their obsession.

It is ironic that the Niger Delta was the area of the coast most frequented by the slave traders, and where for centuries in some trepidation they had moored their ships, fearful of what they considered a hostile and deadly environment. They had made no effort to explore the interior, nervous of venturing beyond what seemed like an impenetrable forest wall. If the slaves were delivered safely to their ships, and they could make their profit from transporting them across the Atlantic, they were content to remain at the shoreline. They were bewildered rather than impressed by the strange infatuation of the Niger explorers, and indeed it was some time before the Landers' discovery would lead to commercial exploitation of the river. Another twenty-seven years were to pass before any serious attempt was made to maintain permanent trading stations on its banks above the delta. In the meantime, the slave trade had been replaced by a new so-called *'legitimate trade'* in palm oil, and the Niger Delta had become the den of a new breed of equally unscrupulous and disreputable traders.

# 5 MUNGO PARK

## *(1771-1806)*

Mungo Park was born in 1771 in Foulshiels near Selkirk in the Scottish Borders. He was the seventh child in a family of thirteen. Although only tenant farmers, the Parks were relatively well off and were able to pay for Mungo to receive a good education. His parents had originally intended him to become a Minister in the Secession Church, a strict Calvinist sect that had split from the Church of Scotland in 1733. But that idea did not inspire young Mungo, and so, at the age of fourteen, he was apprenticed to Thomas Anderson, a local surgeon.

In 1788 he enrolled at Edinburgh University to study medicine and competed his studies four years later, although he did not qualify with a degree. He had no fixed career in mind, but at university he had developed an interest in botany. His brother-in-law in London, James Dickson, happened to be a well-known botanist and a founding member of the Linnaean Society, set up in 1788 and named after the celebrated Swedish naturalist, Carl Linnaeus. Park accompanied Dickson on a botanical expedition to the Scottish Highlands in 1792, and the following year Dickson introduced him to Sir Joseph Banks, a co-founder of the Linnaean Society and President of the Royal Society. The meeting set in motion a train of events that led Park to becoming an African explorer, since Banks happened also to be the driving force behind the African Association.

In the following year, on Banks's recommendation, Park obtained the position of Assistant Surgeon on board the East India Company's ship *'Worcester'* bound for Sumatra. It was presumably Banks's notion that on the voyage Park could find time to carry out some botanical and zoological research for him. And shortly after Park's return in 1794 he presented

Banks with some plant specimens and some anatomical water-colours of rare fish species. After his discharge from the *'Worcester'* Park had no immediate professional prospects, so perhaps at Banks's bidding he offered his services as an explorer to the African Association. Park had the barest knowledge of surveying or cartography and knew no more than anyone else at the time about the geography or peoples of the interior of the continent. But, as he was the only volunteer available, the Association accepted Park's offer.

Park's assignment was to search for the source of the River Niger, a task that had already killed two other men. It was not the African Association's practice to get involved in the detailed planning of expeditions, and so the inexperienced Park was left largely to use his own initiative. His brief was as indeterminate as it was ambitious:

*"To proceed to the Niger by the nearest and most convenient route, and to endeavour to trace its course, from its rise to its termination; and also to visit, if possible, all the principal towns and cities on its banks, particularly Timbuctoo and Houssa, and afterwards return to Europe by the river Gambia, or any other way he thought advisable."*

For his trouble, Park was to receive the princely sum of 14 shillings a day and £200 to cover his expenses. The African Association cannily, although perhaps a little insensitively, insured themselves against the failure of a fourth Niger expedition by stipulating that Park's salary would only be payable on his return.

## First Niger Expedition

In May 1795, Park lost patience waiting for a baldly organised naval convoy that the African Association had intended him to join Instead, he left Portsmouth on a merchant ship that was travelling to Gambia to trade for beeswax and ivory, appropriately named the *'Endeavour'*. By June, Park had reached the mouth of the Gambia River, where a long journey into the interior awaited him. He boldly set off on a 300 kilometre journey upriver to a British trading station called Pisania. The early days of the expedition were not auspicious, as the boat struggled to make any progress up the river through tangled mangrove thickets and across insect-ridden mudflats and swamps. The journey was made almost unendurable by the regular stoppages when the ship had to be towed.

Then one evening Park stayed out late to record an eclipse of the moon and promptly went down with a severe bout of fever, having as he later recorded, *"imprudently exposed myself to the night dew."* Recovering slowly from what was almost certainly a bout of malaria, Park was struck down by fever again in September. As a result, he gained a certain degree of resistance to and immunity from future attacks. Without this *'seasoning'*, as it had become known to the few Europeans resident on the West African coast, he would have been at much greater risk. He certainly suffered several more attacks of fever over the next two years of travel, but somehow managed to survive them all.

When he was fully recovered, Park set off again on horseback to the Niger, in the company of only two African porters. The meagre supplies he took with him were:

*"provisions for two days; a small assortment of beads, amber and tobacco, for the purchase of a fresh supply as I proceeded; a few changes of linen, and other necessary apparel, an umbrella, a pocket sextant, a magnetic compass, and a thermometer; together with two fowling pieces, two pairs of pistols, and some other small articles."*

This was hardly a list of the essential equipment for someone venturing into the West African interior and uncharted territory, let alone into a war zone and a land unsettled by the collapse of local empires.

It is small wonder that Park's thoughts were full of gloom and trepidation:

*"I had now before me a boundless forest, and a country, the inhabitants of which were strangers to civilised life, and to most of whom a white man was the object of curiosity and plunder."*

Few of the people he would meet on his journey would not have been bewildered by the sight of someone suffering such hardship for nothing more than a glimpse of a river.

The African servants did not share Park's enthusiasm for the journey, which must have seemed pointless to them. They would not have been able to comprehend Park's inexplicable ambition, and his strange European passion to see something for the first time. They had nothing to gain by making their stumbling and hazardous way to the banks of yet another watercourse. What enraged them even more was that Park, as a Christian, was putting their lives at risk by entering Muslim dominated territory.

The journey was a catalogue of misfortune and was fraught with danger at every turn. What made it so dangerous was that the peoples who lived in the interior simply could not fathom out what Park's purpose was. They were well accustomed to travellers as traders in slaves, ivory, gold, or salt. Their assumption was that anyone who was not obviously engaged in trade, especially if he was an infidel and a white man, must be some sort of spy. In which case, he should either be killed on the spot, as previous Niger explorers had been, or at least captured and humiliated. As Park was not carrying anything worth stealing and was utterly defenceless, his presence in the fanatical Muslim lands further east was almost a provocation to murder.

Sometimes Park's whiteness was merely the object of benign curiosity and wonder. People who had never seen a white man before would gather round and gawp as he entered their towns and villages. One group of Muslim women wanted to count his toes to see if he was real. They declared that he must have been dipped in milk at birth, and that his slender pointed nose must be the result of constant pinching.

On another occasion he was descended upon by a party of Arab women eager *"to ascertain, by actual inspection, whether the rite of circumcision extended to Nazarenes, as well as to followers of Mahomet"*. Park showed his dry sense of Scottish humour by offering:

*"to give ocular demonstration...if all of them would retire except the young lady to whom I pointed (selecting the youngest and handsomest) ...she did not avail herself of the privilege...but the ladies enjoyed the jest"*.

But mostly Park's whiteness was a sign of his Christianity, and this made him vulnerable. The fact that he was a Christian was enough to justify robbery. And so, as he travelled eastward, at every town his baggage was searched and rifled, either by Arabs or by the local tribesmen. He survived only because at each place he was helped by Africans who took pity on him.

Park endured every humiliation and pressed relentlessly on, without the slightest regard for his own or his fellow travellers' safety. When he reached a town called Dina, he was abused, shouted at, and spat upon. He recorded in his diary that *"they accordingly opened my bundles, and robbed me of everything they fancied"*. To those with him it was clearly time to call it a day, but for Park it was simply time to move on. His narrative of events ends abruptly with the terse statement: *"I resolved to proceed alone."* True to his words, at two o'clock the next morning he marched off across the moonlit plain, *"the howling of distant beasts making it necessary to proceed with caution"*. If no one would go with him, the bold Mungo was prepared to strike out on his own, alone in a hostile and unfamiliar environment and hundreds of miles from anyone he knew. In his mind's eye, he must have cut a heroic figure, taking on the continent single-handed, determined to overcome distance, wild animals and the combined fanaticism of all Islam.

To everyone else he would have seemed stark, staring mad.

At the next town of Benown the local Arab leader asked Park as a Christian to kill and eat a wild pig. When Park refused, the Arab released the wild pig, expecting that it would savage Park, on the basis that pigs hated Christians for eating them so much. As it turned out, the pig went berserk, and ran around in circles biting everyone else in sight but leaving Park alone. Although spared by the pig, Park was bullied and tortured as a prisoner for two months. At one point, suffering from thirst, he was compelled to kneel with the cattle to drink out of their trough.

He was regularly humiliated for his Christian religion, but never once lost his temper, which would have been fatal. The intense heat, the acute pangs of hunger and thirst, and the continuous insults would have broken a lesser man, but Park was oblivious to pain and suffering. His was a grand obsession, and he was a driven man, wholly consumed by the quest to solve the mystery of the Niger River.

Park's European clothing was another object of curiosity to locals. Previous Niger explorers had adopted local clothes, for comfort as much as to conceal their identity. But despite all the heat and humidity Park never changed from his European clothing, and always maintained an impeccable military bearing, sitting bolt upright on his horse. He must have seemed a very odd spectacle dressed in a beaver top hat, a blue cloak with brass buttons, pale yellow trousers, and a pair of silk stockings. He certainly turned heads and became an object of much amusement and speculation wherever he went.

At one of his first stops he recorded that the ladies of the village *"tore my cloak, cut the buttons from my boy's clothes, and were proceeding to other outrages"*, with the result that he was forced to flee. At another town he had to give up his best blue coat to secure his safe onward passage. Then before he could secure his release from imprisonment in Benown, the local leader and his wife demanded that he showed them how he put on his European clothes, including his stockings, a performance which had them falling off their seats with laughter. The glamour and novelty of his clothing seems to save Park on several occasions. When only a week's journey short of the river, he was captured by a party of Arab slave traders who viewed him with suspicion and intense curiosity. The brass buttons on his uniform were objects of great interest. He was soon relieved of most of them, but fortunately he was left with a few that he had concealed about his person, And so he was able to continue with his journey and to hawk his way towards his destination.

Finally, *"at the moderate price of a button"*, he was directed to the object of his quest:

*"The majestic Niger, glittering in the morning sun, as broad as the Thames near Westminster, and flowing slowly to the <u>eastward</u>".*

This was for Park a priceless revelation. Yet the locals must surely have observed the phenomenon for themselves, and could have saved him a lot of time, trouble and expense.

Park's troubles were far from over. Once more, he was captured and this time stripped of all his remaining possessions, except his papers. Travelling through mosquito infested swamps, Park then was again struck down by fever. His diary records that he slumped exhausted against a tree to take a breather:

*"Worn down by sickness, exhausted by hunger and fatigue, half naked, and without any article of value by which I might buy provisions, clothing and lodgings, I began to reflect seriously on my situation."*

The last phrase is somewhat of an understatement, given his predicament. He was totally isolated, dependent on charity, and in a country where he and his kind were hated. Nature seemed to have turned against him as well, as the seasonal rains were beginning to lash down. He gloomily noted that:

*"the rice grounds and swamps were everywhere overflowed; and in*

*a few days more travelling of every kind, unless by water, would be completely obstructed."*

And so, on the following morning Park stepped down into the narrow length of a canoe and took the first step of his return journey. It is difficult not to be sorry for him at this moment, the gaunt stranger afloat on the river that he had come so far to find, but now heading in the wrong direction. The locals watching from the bank would surely have been baffled by this lonely traveller, so immersed in his incomprehensible and apparently meaningless pursuit. They would have been hard put to explain the purposes of this apparently deranged voyager. For European exploration was based on the single, monstrous assumption that whatever black Africans may have observed for generations, as natives of their own country, counted for absolutely nothing. A white European explorer was needed, a stranger to those lands and not necessarily someone skilled in scientific observation, to bear witness to the rest of humanity that a phenomenon did truly exist.

Park literally had to beg his way back to the Gambia, and on his return journey he was yet again struck down with fever. He was in bed for five long weeks, followed by a lengthy period of convalescence. So preoccupied was Park with his own noble cause, and so indifferent to the ignoble plight of others, that he was happy to seek refuge in a slave trading post and, when he had recovered fully, to join a slave caravan down to the coast. By this stage of his travels Park had developed a note-taking passion. He recorded events faithfully, but in a terse and detached style. Park did describe in his diary the treatment meted out to the slaves, but his commentary has an air of almost indifference.

The slave caravan travelled at some speed, with Park and the head slavers at the front setting the pace. Behind them the shackled slaves staggered forwards, sweating under their burdens, and lashed relentlessly by the whips of other slavers who brought up the rear. At one point in the heat of the afternoon, the slaves fell forward and began vomiting clay. This event is noted in Park's diary as a matter of scientific interest, in that it demonstrated that the slaves must have been eating large quantities of clay out of hunger. In another incident a slave girl was stung head to toe by bees, and then suffered further injuries on the journey because of her weakness. As she was therefore slowing down the caravan, some slavers shouted for her throat to be cut immediately. Instead, their leader had her stripped and chained and left to die, which Park seemed to regard as an act of compassion on his part.

The only time that Park displayed any emotion was when one of the slaves reminded him of a favour he had received on his outward journey. The memory touched Park, but not so much out of sympathy, but rather because it reminded him of his own great mission. When eventually Park reached the coast, he also had no qualms in boarding a slave ship for the Caribbean, despite witnessing the most appalling conditions for both sailors and slaves before it set sail.

Mungo Park's narrative of his first expedition was documented in *"Travels in the Interior of Africa Performed under Direction and Patronage of the African Association in the Years 1795, 1796 and 1797"*. This early account of European exploration highlighted the dangers and risks involved in such an enterprise, as well as perhaps its folly. The book was a great success with the reading public and was immediately translated into several European languages. His contemporary audience had an appetite for tales of adventure and derring-do, especially if they were based on first-hand accounts.

Park had some literary assistance in the composition of the book from Bryan Edwards, the Secretary of the African Association, who was consulted on every part of the work, and revised and corrected the whole manuscript before it went to press. Edwards was a retired Caribbean planter, who was a notorious anti-Abolitionist, and who approved of slavery. It is not known to what extent he might have interpolated his own views on slavery as he edited the text. However, overall Park's account is based on the copious and detailed notes that he took at every step of his journey, and his authentic voice remains.

The book appeared at a time when the debate in Britain between those who supported slavery and the slave trade, and those who argued for its abolition, had entered a critical phase. Park had seen the slave trade at first hand and commented at length about it, but he signally failed either to approve or condemn it. This led to the paradoxical situation where Abolitionists on the one hand used his material to illustrate the horrors of the slave trade, whereas on the other hand Anti-Abolitionists pointed to the absence of any outright condemnation of it in Park's writings. Certainly, at the end of a detailed chapter on domestic slavery among the Mandingo people, he refrains from making any comment on the extent to which this practice was being sustained by the Atlantic Slave Trade. He writes instead that it was *"neither within my province, nor in my power, to explain."* And he later offers his opinion that the ending of the slave trade might not be as *"beneficial as many wise and worthy persons fondly expect."*

In Park's judgement, abolishing the Atlantic Slave Trade would have done little to affect slavery in Africa. The prime focus of his narrative is instead on how entrenched human bondage was in the local African economy and society, with slaves outnumbering the free by three to one. Moreover, throughout his journey he seems to have had no qualms about associating with the slave traders operating in the region. He starts and ends his journey indebted to one called Ledley, who provides him with the necessary credit to finance his inland expedition. He also owes his life to another called Karfa Taura, who befriends him when he is sick and destitute, and cares for him for seven months. Indeed, Park is only able to return to the coast by joining Karfa and a coffle of slaves who were destined to be sold there.

At no time does Park question or challenge the evils of the Atlantic Slave Trade. However, he does observe that domestic slaves enjoyed certain rights denied to slaves who had been captured in war or purchased on the slave markets. He also shows some appreciation of the fact that commercial slavery and social violence had created a vicious circle in the region. Park's views perhaps reflect his own moral ambiguity over slavery. He may also have felt that he did not have the authority to make a political statement on the issue. Or he may simply have not wanted to offend his employers, since any statement from him against the trade would have split the African Association down the middle.

Park's writings also illuminate another obsession of the age in which he lived: a pseudo-scientific curiosity in the lives of distant peoples. Explorers were specifically tasked to make observations of the customs and beliefs by which the peoples they came across in their travels lived out their lives. Park was no exception, and his book gives a detailed description of the tribes in the regions of the River Gambia: their environment, appearance, values, morals, living arrangements and customs. He presents the local people through the eyes of a typical eighteenth century Europeans, with an inherent bias and constant reference back to his own culture. In line with the economic purpose of his mission, he concentrates on the opportunities for trade and commerce. Africans in his narrative are observed and recorded with the same interest as the local flora and fauna. Their existence is ratified, but there is no recognition of the fact that across West Africa at the time there were empires of great power and wealth, with complex social organisations, advanced political institutions, developed economies, sophisticated religious and political institutions, and a variety of art forms - music, dance, poetry and sculpture. They existed, but their lives had little significance.

Some of Park's more patronising observations were:

*"...but they are commonly very noisy and very troublesome, begging for everything they fancy with such earnestness and importunity, that traders, in order to get quit of them, are frequently obliged to grant their requests."*

*"Of the Feloops, I have little to add to what has been observed concerning them in the former chapter. They are of a gloomy disposition, and are supposed never to forgive an injury."*

*"The Mandingoes, generally speaking, are of a mild, sociable, and obliging disposition. The men are commonly above the middle size, well-shaped, strong, and capable of enduring great labour. The women are good-natured, sprightly, and agreeable."*

## Second Niger Expedition

In the autumn of 1803, Park was invited by the British government to lead another expedition to the Niger from the Gambia River. but the expedition was delayed until January 1805. His plan was to carry boat building materials overland from the coast, with a view to construct boats when they reached the Niger and then sail them down the river to its mouth. Previous explorations had been conducted by lone Europeans travelling alone or in company with slave caravans. But in Park's expedition there were 45 Europeans, including his brother-in law, Dr Alexander Anderson. There were also five naval engineers to build the boats on reaching the Niger, and two seamen to supervise the engineers. Park recruited Isaaco, a Mandingo, as a guide. He was the only African to accompany the expedition, as well as the only person to survive it.

For whatever reason, Park did not hire any African porters for the journey. Protection was provided by 35 soldiers from the Royal African Corps under the command of a Lieutenant Martyn. Sadly, the Royal African Corps at the time of the Napoleonic War contained the very dregs of military life. It appears to have consisted largely of men whom the other regiments did not want. Many were men who had faced a flogging for breach of discipline and had been offered the Royal African Corps as an alternative. This would have been an easy choice to have made, since a flogging in the army at that time could have led to serious injury, permanent disablement or even death. Service at the British forts along the West African coast was therefore regarded throughout the British army more as a punishment than as a duty, and for many unfortunates it turned out to be a death sentence. Lieutenant Martyn himself proved to be a quite insane and brutal leader, whose favourite pastime was taking pot shots at any Africans whom the expedition encountered on route.

As if to seal its fate, the expedition also set out from the coast with impeccably bad timing, a few weeks before the rainy season began in earnest in June. Park had been ready to leave London in October 1804. Had he done so, he could have been on the Gambia River by the beginning of the following year, with the best travelling months ahead of him. As it was, official vacillation kept him in London until January 1805, and it was only at the end of April that his expedition force was ready to leave the Gambia and head off inland. They marched proudly off, dressed absurdly for the climate in full military uniform. With over 500 miles of the roughest terrain to cross there was little chance of reaching the Niger and taking to boats before the rainy season began.

When in early June the rains broke, the expedition was still toiling in the upper reaches of the Senegal River. Within a week of the start of the rains, nearly all members of the expedition were suffering from malaria, dysentery, or jaundice. Park's journal from mid-June is largely a record of struggle with the elements, and of sickness and death. And yet at no time did he give thought to the possibility of halting the caravan. By the the middle of July, a total of twelve casualties had been recorded: five were dead, four had been abandoned and three were missing. As the caravan lost strength, with men falling out almost daily, it began to disintegrate and became an easy prey for thieves and wild animals. Men had only to turn their backs for an instant and a thief would pounce to seize a musket or a greatcoat, or to drive away an ass. Those who were sick or weak were even stripped of their clothes.

The expedition finally reached the Niger at Bamako in mid-August, having taken 115 days to cover a distance that Park had hoped to cover in less than half that time. A further 19 casualties had been suffered on the journey: four were dead, six had been left behind and nine had failed to reach camp after a day's travelling. Now three quarters of his soldiers had died, and there was only one carpenter left to build the boats Park needed to sail downstream. No wonder he felt that *"the prospect appeared somewhat gloomy."* While resting at Bamako, Park used what medicines he had to treat the men suffering from dysentery and fever, but with little effect. He also decided to try to purge himself of dysentery with a heroic dose of calomel, which rendered him speechless and sleepless for six days. It also *'cured'* his dysentery, and he was ready to press on.

Nothing would stop Mungo Park except his own death. Every other man in his company might collapse and die, but he would pursue inexorably the single, all-consuming purpose of his life. Retreat was not an option, even though he must have known that the rest of his men were clearly less motivated: they were simply expendable. Of the 45 Europeans who set off from the Gambia, only 12 lived to see the Niger. They included Park himself, Martyn, and Anderson. Anderson had been carried much of the way and died a few weeks later. Even the loss of his brother-in-law was more of a blow to his mission than a cause for sorrow. For a man who had just led 33 men to their deaths Park was unforgivably remorseless:

*"I shall only observe that no event which took place during the journey ever threw the smallest gloom over my mind till I laid Anderson in the grave. I then felt myself, as if left a second time lonely and friendless amidst the wilds of Africa."*

Clearly, Park felt that such a loss of life was more than balanced by the ultimate prize of solving the mystery of where the Niger flowed to. He had not thought of turning back or of repeating the failure of his first journey. He had worked tirelessly night and day to reach this far. He had gone without food and sleep and survived both dysentery and malaria. He would sacrifice anything and anyone to fulfil his destiny.

The much reduced party embarked on a single boat converted from two canoes, and which was christened 'HMS Joliba' (or 'The Great Water'). Once on board and headed downstream, Park was determined that nothing should stop him reaching the sea and was ready to shoot his way through any real or fancied opposition. His decision to voyage down the Niger with the remaining seven men was both arrogant and reckless. He did not pay the necessary tribute or customs to local rulers, nor did he travel with any letter of safe conduct. Consequently, his descent of the Niger became a running battle with the local peoples, who insisted on their rights and were inflamed by his high-handed behaviour. When he was still over 1,000 kilometres from the sea, his boat foundered on the rapids at a place called Bussa. Under attack from the bank, Park and all the crew were drowned, except for Isaaco who lived to tell the tale. Ironically, after all the sacrifice of human life on the back of his ruthless ambition, the extent of Park's achievement was underestimated. He had reached the Bussa rapids on the Niger, over 1,200 kilometres from Timbuktu. But geographers at home had not the slightest idea how far Bussa was from Timbuktu and judged it to be only 80 miles.

Mungo Park was deeply religious and a convinced Calvinist. His faith carried him through pain and sickness, since he believed that all suffering was predestined. He was fully aware of the risks to his life. His contract for the second expedition included a payment of £3,000 for the support of his wife and family, in the event of his death. If nothing was heard from him for two and a half years from the date of departure, he would be assumed dead and the payment made. However, clearly Park was indifferent not just to his own fate, but also to that of others. The spirit with which he began his final stage of his enterprise is well illustrated by his letter to the head of the Colonial Office:

*"I shall set sail for the east with the fixed resolution to discover the termination of the Niger or perish in the attempt though all the Europeans who are with me should die, and though I were myself half dead, I would still persevere, and if I could not succeed in my journey, I would at least die on the Niger."*

Park was convinced that he was in some sense a chosen man, one whose destiny was to solve the riddle of the Niger. He also knew on his second expedition, as an officer with a column of soldiers behind him, that he had taken on a public role and a national responsibility. He saw himself with pride as the out-rider of commercial expansion, and as the spokesman for the distant interests of the king and the British government. In addition, he saw himself as God's interpreter, and doled out an Arabic New Testament to any potential convert he met on route.

There was above all a strong element of ambition in what Park accomplished, and a burning desire for fame and glory. The new passions of the nineteenth century were Commerce, Industry and Science. These offered new aspirational opportunities that had been denied to previous generations trapped in the more stratified society of the past. Ambitious young men like Stephenson, Watt, Cook and Park could recognise and seize their chances not only to better themselves, but also to achieve a national reputation. The journals of his second and final expedition to the Niger were published in 1805, a year before his death in 1806. As a child Mungo Park had wanted to be famous, to write and to see his name perpetuated. Exploration had made his dream a reality.

# 6  PALM OIL RUFFIANS

*"Every bar of yellow soap costs a drop of English blood."*

In the nineteenth century, after South Africa the most important part of the continent from a British merchant trader's point of view was the West Coast, and in particular the tropical forest region. By the end of the century cocoa had become the dominant export commodity, especially in the Gold Coast. Demand for the crop increased steadily as the drink became more and more popular in Europe. It was also an essential ingredient in the manufacture of chocolate, which was introduced in Switzerland in 1876. In areas to the north outside the tropical zone, groundnuts were also cultivated as a food source as well as an important ingredient in soap. Both crops were produced by African peasant farmers and required little in the way of capital investment. The smallholders who produced them also provided importers with a ready market for a variety of merchandise, mainly alcohol but also textiles, tools, and a wide assortment of knick-knacks.

Initially, however, the prime focus of British trade was further to the east along the Niger Delta, where palm oil was produced by Africans using little capital and rudimentary farming methods. The area became a magnet for British merchants, and for most of the century  palm oil was the single most important export from the coast of West Africa.

## Palm Oil

The oil palm grows along a wide belt just behind the coast of West Africa, and the oil from its fruit was already widely consumed and traded locally. In the 1840s British entrepreneurs in the area began buying it up for industrial purposes, to be used to oil factory machinery, and to make candles, margarine, and soap. The increased interest in palm oil was also partly the result of political pressure exerted by humanitarian movements throughout Europe on their governments, especially the British, to end the slave trade.

The growing traffic in palm oil did not put an end to slavery overnight. Even though slave exports from the coast declined, inland slave dealing remained important throughout the century. In fact, the trade in palm oil encouraged slavery, since the transport of the bulky oil required slave labour to paddle canoes down river, or to carry the loads on their heads overland to the coast. Slaves were also often employed to produce food for any trader employing a large work force to transport the oil. But steadily the new flow of trade shifted income from those who captured slaves to those who had palm oil for sale. It also benefited those communities which were well placed to profit as middlemen, first to ports directly on the coast and then to states inland.

The bulk of this trade was initially with the peoples living in the Niger Delta area, where the inhabitants were much quicker and more successful in developing an export trade in palm oil than the peoples in other coastal regions. One major consideration was that the palm oil was not easy to transport in quantity, and therefore its value was relatively low in proportion to its bulk. Canoe transport was the most efficient and economical way to transport the oil, compared with the alternative methods of head loading or cask rolling. The Niger Delta offered a ready-made system of waterways, and the surrounding region had an unusually dense population living in a relatively poor agricultural environment. There was therefore a surplus pool of labour to harvest the palm trees, as well as to manufacture and transport the oil.

These factors combined to create a boom in what became

known as the *'legitimate trade'*. By the 1870s, palm oil had become the primary cash crop of a number of territories along the West African coast, although in the final years of the century it was overtaken by cocoa as the dominant export commodity following the introduction of colonial European cocoa plantations in the Gold Coast and elsewhere.

## The Legitimate Trade

As part of their effort to stamp out slavery, and to encourage the development of a more repectable trade in other commodities, the British government based anti-slavery patrols on the offshore island of Fernando Po. From there they were able to intervene militarily anywhere in the Niger Delta that lay within the reach of their ships' guns. Under this protection, European traders came to live on the rivers, to buy palm oil and to prepare it for shipment.

The usual practice was for a group of businessmen to form a trading company or syndicate, from which each partner would benefit according to the capital he invested in it. A sailing vessel would be purchased or chartered, and a crew would be selected, with particular care being taken in the choice of captain, or *'supercargo'* as he was often known. The ship would then be stocked with merchandise that could be used for barter, as well as with items essential for carrying out the trade, such as pre-fabricated barrels for assembly on arrival by the coopers among the crew.

Many customs and practices of the new legitimate trade differed little from the slave trade, apart from the cargo to be loaded. A sailing ship entering the delta to load palm oil had to remain at anchor for several months. The captain would negotiate the customary formalities for his stay, including the payment of any necessary local taxes. When these were complete, the ship's masts would be removed, and a roof of palm thatch or bamboo mats erected over the upper deck, to give protection against the sun and heavy rain. This awning also served to convert the ship into a floating hulk or depot, on which the bartering of merchandise for produce would continue until the cargo was complete. At this point, the temporary roof would be dismantled, the masts re-erected, and the ship would unfurl her sails and head for home, fully laden with produce.

In the early days, no palm oil trading companies dared to set up a base on the shoreline, as they continued to live in fear of both the local climate and the hostility of the local inhabitants. Crews on board ship were always armed, and 'swivel guns' (small cannons on a rotating stand) were mounted on deck to repel boarders. The trading also continued to be conducted at arm's length via the local African rulers, their agents, and middlemen. They could make life extremely uncomfortable for the traders if any attempted to operate directly with the markets in the interior, as this would undermine their local price monopoly.

The traders in any case were conservative in their methods, and were quite content to stay in the creeks near the sea where life appeared healthier. There was also safety in numbers, and at least some form of mutual protection through their proximity to each other. The traders' reluctance to travel inland became so notorious that the Emir of Kontagora (in the north of present-day Nigeria) was once heard to remark that the Europeans must be some sort of fish, because they seemed unable to exist for long away from water.

The length of time taken on such enterprises varied considerably because the success of the ventures depended on a host of factors. These included the ability and the integrity of the supercargo, the state of the local trade at the time, the political activities of the local inhabitants, the weather encountered on sea voyages, and above all on the survival of those taking part. A voyage might last for a year or more, until the company had secured a sufficient return on its investment. During that period many would succumb to local diseases, and sadly some would not make the voyage home.

Sometimes in the early days, when a ship was ready to sail home with a full load, so many of the starting crew had perished that a fresh crew had to be sent from England to bring it home. And so, eventually companies decided to anchor their ships on a more permanent basis, and to turn them into what became known as *'floating hulks'*. These acted as local warehouses and received regular visits from supply ships, which not only took away the local produce, but also delivered the foreign merchandise to trade and barter with.

## Floating Hulks

The use of sailing vessels as floating depots was wasteful, but there were several advantages. Living on a ship instead of on land seemed to reduce, for reasons not then understood, the incidence of malaria. There was also no better place to be than on a ship anchored in mid-stream when fighting broke out periodically between local factions. In the 1850s the larger trading companies started to commission all manner of obsolete craft and moor them in the Niger River. Bonny and other ports resembled nautical museums with full size specimens. There were veteran *'Men-Of-War'* with double roofs and triple masts, retired Dutch and English *'East Indiamen'*, and at least one ocean-going liner called the *'Adriatic'.* Perhaps the most bizarre sight would have been the retired Isle of Man packet ship, named the *'Ben-ma-Chree'*, which had a wooden terrace with verandas and offices built over the hull. The interiors of the ships were often comfortably furnished, and some of the East Indiamen still had the original cabins with solid mahogany doors, panelled sideboards, and gilt mirrors. On deck there would be wicker chairs, sofas, and hammocks.

The European traders who lived on these hulks had a remarkably short shelf life. But their companies calculated that it was more economical to replace a few traders than an entire merchant ship's crew. Despite the obvious risks to their health, the traders were lured by the chance of acquiring a small fortune in the three years that were the usual term of service. There were many ways to supplement basic salaries, and the appalling death rate clearly offered excellent promotion prospects. Sadly, only a lucky few managed to reach the end of their term. Any who did survive were likely to return home only modestly rich, but completely broken in health. Not surprisingly, advertisements for new recruits were somewhat economical with the truth.

A typical advert in a London newspaper of the time shows how vacancies were filled:

> *Wanted young man, eighteen to twenty-five, as*
> *bookkeeper in West African factory.*
> *Unlimited shooting and fishing and fine tropical*
> *scenery, with a boat and crew at his disposal.*
> *Free quarters, salary £70 a year to start,*
> *with chance of rapid promotion.*

Not all of these incentives were entirely dishonest, given the circumstances, especially the promise of easy promotion. As if to confirm this prospect, on arrival many new recruits were shown around the graveyard of their predecessors. At Bonny in the Niger Delta, after an entire ship's crew had succumbed to disease and died, a second and then a third crew were despatched to the West African coast by the ship's owners, only to suffer the same fate. It was then decided that the ship should be scuttled and left to sink at anchor. There was only one survivor, an able seaman called Jack Twist, who was left behind to bury all his companions. Afterwards, he tried to console himself with the grim thought that *"the yarn can be told by none but me."*

Towards the end of the nineteenth century, Mary Kingsley,

one of the Victorian age's greatest explorers, was on one of her marathon journeys across West Africa. In Bonny she encountered Captain Boler one of the local factors trading there. He entertained her with the story of an incident that had taken place during a recent outbreak of disease, and which had killed nine out of the eleven European local residents. Apparently, during the fourth of the funerals, two junior clerks, who had been drinking heavily in fear and trepidation for their own safety, accidentally tumbled headlong into the grave. The coffin duly got lowered on top of them, and all three had to be hauled back out unceremoniously. A member of the funeral party was later overheard to remark with grim humour to the other survivors of the outbreak:

*"Barely necessary, though, was it? For those two had to have a grave of their own before next sundown."*

## Palm Oil Ruffians

The disreputable behaviour of the beleaguered traders marooned on these hulks soon earned them the label of *'palm oil ruffians'*. Many were bullies and were loathed by their assistants. If any man refused a duty, the palm oil ruffian would simply cut off his food rations. Many of these men had previously been operating in the slave trade. They may have changed the basis of their trading, but some continued to employ the same barbaric methods and treat the local inhabitants with deliberate and unprovoked cruelty. Other were more concerned to safeguard their own security, and hastily arranged marriages of convenience with the daughters of local chiefs. As a result, many mixed race children grew up on the hulks.

Life on board the hulks, especially in the absence of female company, was monotonous in the extreme. It is perhaps not surprising, with so much death and sickness around, that normal human standards would gradually erode. During the long hot days, European traders would gaze anxiously at the shore, waiting for a canoe laden with palm oil to approach, and speculate on whether it was heading for their hulk or a rival vessel. Their only excitement was to watch crocodiles floating along the stream. Otherwise, their work was a tedious routine of supervising the coopers who assembled the barrels and the local workers who rendered the palm oil to remove any impurities and fill the barrels ready for shipment.

The palm oil ruffians often relied on alcohol to lubricate the trading porocess. Local chiefs would often be given a liquid breakfast on board the hulks, as a preliminary to bartering the palm oil for cloth, gin, salt, beads, and gunpowder. The arrival of a mail boat at the coast could also be a cause for drunken celebration. Sometimes at night European traders who had consumed too much alcohol would even raid rival hulks and demand whisky with menaces. After decades of heavy drinking, the sea floor under the hulks became littered with bottles. When one ship's captain was approaching the port of Opobo for the first time, he enquired what sort of bottom he might expect when he dropped anchor. The local African pilot was said to have replied:

*"All the same bottom here, sir. Soda water, whisky bottle, gin bottle bottom, sir."*

Even the burial of a dead comrade was an excuse for a boisterous party. The coffins often used were empty wooden cases that had contained the lengthy Dane guns popularly used for barter. If the deceased had been a tall man, then the end of the case might have to be removed, so that the head could stick out. The head would then be covered with a top hat, the rim of which would be nailed to the case. This led to the ceremonies being called *'gun case and top hat funerals'*. A drunken funeral party would then weave its way to the grave that had been dug, usually to find that it was already full of water that had seeped in from the surrounding swamps. A small service would be held, and then the makeshift coffin would be lowered into the watery grave.

The debauched lifestyle, however, did in the end take its toll on the palm oil ruffians. In 1887, one of the traders called John Whitford published a book on his experiences. In it he described the haggard looks of traders ravaged by the deadly combination of a hostile climate and too much drinking:

*"If a stranger to the rivers, as you ascend the outer staircase you are astonished by the ghost-like appearance of an over-grown white boy meeting you, ornamented with a bald head; his once plump and ruddy features are shrunken and bleached yellowish-white. You feel very sorry for him as he states that he has just got up from an attack of fever, during the delirium attendant upon which his hair was suddenly removed; but with brightening eyes he adds cheerfully that his three years' term of servitude will soon terminate, and then he will gladly go home to his parents and friends."*

Perhaps to compensate for their rough existence, the palm oil ruffians developed an almost surreal lifestyle. Pyjamas and sun helmet became regulation dress. Africans employed on the canoes attached to each company would be dressed outlandishly in highland tartan, or in red jackets and blue trousers. There was also some eccentric behaviour, such as one trader who prayed aloud on deck, berating his various assistants for their various sins, and then begging God for forgiveness on their behalf.

John Whitford also described his own daily morning routine:

*"The model palm-oil trader's voice is heard long before daybreak resounding beneath the dark, dismal roof of the hulk, summoning coopers, carpenters, white men, Accra men, and Krooboys from slumber to labour. After giving coffee and biscuits to the white men, he goes in a boat to the beach, tumbles out the sleepers there, and sets each gang to their particular work. He then returns on board, presides at the barter business half an hour before breakfast, when he enjoys another bath, and whilst having his toilet*

*prays aloud in his thinly partitioned cabin and is heard all over the quarter-deck. It is rather uncomfortable for his clerks to hear their names mixed up in soliloquy; but thus he warns them of shortcomings, not only in earthly, but hulkly and other affairs."*

However, the majority of traders had a less robust constitution and were gradually worn down by the endless tedium of coastal life. Some even became unhinged by the whole experience, including one clerk who became so angry after a quarrel with his boss on shore that he rushed back to the ship and plunged his cigar into a barrel of gunpowder. The resultant explosion destroyed the hulk, leaving only one survivor, who was fortunate to have been blown out of the stern porthole.

## The Trust System

The most insidious custom and practice of trading life in the Niger Delta during the time of the palm oil ruffians was the Trust System. The European traders extended goods on *'trust'*, whxch had to be repaid in palm oil at a later date. In the past, Africans had in effect supplied their own human capital for the slave trade, but now they needed to borrow capital from the Europeans to trade in oil. The Trust System was at the core of all trade in the delta. It was also the cause of much trading strife between rival African trading units or *'houses'*, which in turn prevented trading companies from settling their own disputes.

The usual arrangement was for a young man to become apprenticed to a head of one of the local houses, and to work his way up the ladder to the responsible position of being trusted to handle transactions on his boss's behalf. His boss would then arrange for the supercargo as the shipowner's representative on board to advance the youth an agreed value of goods on trust. When the youth reached his trading post, he would in turn advance some of the goods to the workers who had agreed to gather the palm fruits for him and to process the oil.

When the processed oil was ready, he would settle whatever balances remained, and then advance more goods as incentives for his next visit. As his source of supply might be fifty or sixty kilometres upstream, it could take many days before he was able to return to the supercargo who had given him credit. But when he did arrive back, he would redeem the goods advanced to him by delivering his oil, after which he would expect the European trader to give him another advance of goods on trust for his next trip.

Although the Trust System satisfied a local trader's continual need for financial backing, it was also a convenient method by which a supercargo was able to boost his purchases of oil. It also enabled him to bind a man and his trade to him, because the African trader would be unable to switch his loyalties to another European trader without first clearing his debt. If any man attempted to do so, seduced by better terms offered by another supercargo, then the first supercargo would simply hijack the African trader's returning canoes, or sometimes the canoes of his relatives or partners, and seize the oil in them as payment for the outstanding debt. This practice, known as *'chopping oil'*, was also sometimes used by unscrupulous supercargoes when they were going through a bad patch of trade, and by newcomers trying to break a local monopoly to gain a foothold in a particular area.

When the wealthier local African rulers also began to give out *'trust'* the practice of *'chopping oil'* got completely out of hand. In some cases, serious fighting took place, resulting in deaths and injuries as well as damage to property. The supercargoes struggled to get control of the situation as it rapidly deteriorated. However, it did not help matters that they were constantly ignoring laws, rules, or conventional ways of doing things. Some of the supercargoes were virtually a law unto themselves. Consequently, the only remedy that seemed left to the local African leaders was to ban their people from having any dealings at all with the European traders. Events might have spiralled completely out of control on the Delta, if it were not for the sudden and unexpected arrival off the coast of a large fleet of buccaneer ships. This common threat forced the supercargoes to pool their resources and chase the pirates from the mouth of the river.

This emergency brought all the European traders to their senses. They realised that their commercial future would be in jeopardy if they allowed the vicious rivalry between them to continue. And so, in 1853, they agreed to put aside their differences and to work together. In addition, a mutual settlement was made to establish the first courts in the Delta for the arbitration of any future commercial disagreements. These courts were to be composed of both African and European traders, and their decisions would be enforced by commercial sanctions. They were also validated in British law by the authority of the British Consul who had recently been appointed to administer the Bights of Benin and Biafra.

## The Rise Of The Trading Companies

The wild and lawless world of the palm oil ruffians was soon to be curtailed further. In the 1870s the stronger companies overtook the weak, and those left in the business started to build permanent establishments ashore. These were called *'factories'*, *'beaches'* or *'ventures'*, and were often quaintly named after the hulks that had preceded them, such as *'Matilda'* in Calabar. The typical factory was situated at the edge of a river, and usually consisted of a pier, a wharf, and a large house with a veranda, containing the quarters for the agent and clerks on the first floor and a store on the ground floor. Nearby were the sheds for produce and sleeping places for the African employees. The sites were rarely freehold, but usually owned by the local rulers. Tenure was either leasehold as in the port of Calabar, or based on paying the *'comey'* trading as in the towns at the mouth of the River Brass.

Most of the semi-skilled and unskilled labour at the factories and on the river vessels was carried out by men from the Liberian Kru coast. These Kru men would beg lifts from southbound ocean ships that sailed past their villages, and travel with them to whichever port they desired along the west coast. On reaching their destinations, they would then contract out their labour for fixed periods, at the end of which they would return home by the same means as they had arrived. All skilled labour, however, was provided by men from the Christian mission stations in the Gold Coast and Sierra Leone, where they had received some basic technical education.

Later, even larger enterprises entered the trade with greater capital investment, and in some cases with government subsidy and backing. It was the arrival of the steamship in particular that revolutionised the trade on the river. Steamships made river navigation possible, whereas sailing boats had a hopeless task against wind and current. One of the pioneers of steamboat navigation was a Liverpool merchant named Macgregor Laird. The city had lost the slave trade but not its interest in West Africa. Already there was a growing trade in palm oil, and the Liverpool merchants were eager to expand their business. So, with the now celebrated explorer Richard Lander in his party, Macgregor Laird set sail in 1832 on the first of what were many attempts to penetrate the interior by river. Despite taking various precautions, his voyages paid a heavy toll in human life and were only partly successful in navigating the river upstream.

Nevertheless, in 1841 the British government decided to launch an even more ambitious attempt to navigate the Niger. The expedition would bring with it steamboats to open the way for river trade, and the plan was to set up a cotton plantation colony in the open savanna land near the confluence of the Benue and Niger rivers. There the leaders of the humanitarian movement in Britain hoped to set up a settlement for freed slaves modelled on the one already established in Sierra Leone. The idea was that this new community would introduce new farming techniques and promote trade with the local inhabitants, while at the same time increase the spread of Christianity into the dark interior of the continent. A grand expeditionary force was therefore assembled. Three ships, specially equipped with the latest ventilating devices, were despatched, under the command of Captain Trotter and a volunteer crew from the Royal Navy. A model farm, complete with the latest equipment, was loaded on board. The Reverend Samuel Crowther, later to become the first black Bishop of the Niger, accompanied the expedition to spread the light.

The town of Lokoja, where the Niger meets the Benue, was reached safely and without major incident. The model farm was duly disembarked and established on a strip of ground purchased from local chiefs. But within two months 48 of the 145 Europeans were dead, struck down with fever. With great difficulty the ships were worked back down the river to the delta, where some of the Caribbean labourers attached to the expedition were butchered. The model farm itself was stranded and was later evacuated. The British government, never terribly enthusiastic, abandoned the expedition. This disaster for some years dampened whatever eagerness there had been to open up the Niger for trade.

And so, the situation on the Niger did not change, until news reached Britain in 1852 that Dr Barth, a member of a government sponsored overland expedition that had set out from Tripoli in 1850, had crossed the River Benue at Yola in June 1851. This new development reawakened interest sufficiently for the British government to consider arranging the rescue of Dr Barth, on the basis that his experiences could lead to a more thorough exploration of the River Benue. And so, Macgregor Laird was asked to organise yet another expedition.

This time no expense was to be spared, and a 100 foot iron-clad, screw-propelled steamship '*The Pleiad*' was specially commissioned for the journey. Internally, the ship was handsomely equipped, including five state rooms for the officers, a library, a steward's pantry, and a bath. The rear cabin was equally elegantly fitted with mahogany tables, a green leather sofa, a bronze chandelier, marble sideboards, and mirrors on either side of the entrance. A system  of moveable shutters was installed to provide healthy ventilation throughout, and the ship was also armed to the hilt with all the latest military equipment. The mission's sole and apparently straightforward objective was to explore the River Niger and its eastern tributary the River Benue as far as it was possible to go and to assess the chances of trade with the local people.

The expedition set off for the West African Coast in 1854 with William Baikie on board, a young Scot who had served in the Royal Navy on ships in the Mediterranean but had no previous African experience. He had been recruited for his medical qualifications as the Medical Officer and Naturalist on board. But when '*The Pleiad*' reached the West African Coast, the crew received the news that the leader of the expedition, John Beecroft, who was to join the mission in Calabar, had died. As Blaikie was second in command of the ship, he was the automatic choice to take charge. Under his leadership, it was to become a ground-breaking expedition that opened the way for future expansion of commercial activity on the river. For, after a month on the river, Baikie and his team had managed to travel further up the Niger and Benue rivers than any previous European expedition, and they had returned to the coast without any loss of life.

He later attributed this success to a number of factors, which were to set new guidelines for future European trading business ventures in West Africa. Firstly, the use of a steamship to navigate the interior had been vindicated. Secondly, he had employed fewer Europeans and hired local people in their place, because they showed greater resistance to the diseases that had decimated previous expeditionary forces. And lastly, he had used the opportunity to test his theory that regular doses of quinine could reduce the high percentage of European officers and crew who had lost their lives to malaria and other tropical diseases on previous explorations.

In Baikie's view, the prospects for future trade were now more positive, and he and his team had identified during the voyage a number of potential locations for future more permanent trading posts on the riverbanks. At the same time, as a committed Abolitionist he was able to argue persuasively the case for *'legitimate trade'* as a more humane and rational alternative to the slave trade. In his analysis, commercial trading provided a long term practical solution, since it would be attractive to local leaders who were concerned at the impact of the Atlantic Slave Trade on their communities. In order to give traders greater security, he also recommended that the naval squadron that patrolled the Atlantic coastline should be made permanent. It should also be given greater powers to blockade slaving ports, as well as to punish the officers and crew of any ship that attempted to continue the slave trade. He thought that these tactics would allow *'legitimate trade'* to flourish, and that fresh expeditionary forces would be able to open up a lucrative new market for British business.

In 1857, Baikie was asked to lead a second expedition to the West African coast. The objective was to renew negotiations on the Niger River with the local Igbo population and to get their leaders to consent to the establishment of a string of British trading stations on the riverside at strategic locations. But, when his small steamer was shipwrecked near the confluence of the Niger and Benue Rivers, Baikie and his team were stranded and had to be rescued. The expedition was aborted, but Baikie and a few others stayed on to complete the mission and established a successful trading station.

In less than five years he succeeded in opening up the navigation of the Niger for commercial traffic and in establishing a thriving market town at Lokoja. There he became a popular figure who was respected as the local doctor, minister, schoolteacher, and magistrate. At the same time, he was an effective ambassador for British interests in the area, giving them a head start over their rival European competitors. A fuller account of Baikie's exploits is given in the next chapter.

In 1862, the British Government acknowledged Baikie's efforts, and began to support his local enterprise with supplies and trading goods. Three years later, however, he was forced through ill-health to leave his post, and died in Sierra Leone on the journey back to England. However, in a few short years he had set an example for all European traders to emulate, and he had signposted the way to a lucrative commercial opportunity for them to exploit. His settlement at Lojoka later became the military headquarters for the Royal Niger Company, the British mercantile company that was to become the dominant trading operation on the river.

## The Royal Niger Company

Through the use of quinine and the steamship, Baikie had succeeded in solving the technical problems of navigating the lower Niger River. Very soon steamboats became a regular feature of the local scene, sailing up to the junction with the Benue River and on up both rivers. This carried the riverside trade well into the savanna region, as well as opening up new points of trade on the lower river. Crucially, the steamers gave the European traders access to the palm producing regions that had previously only navigable by using much narrower canoe routes. The local African states of the delta thus found their trade restricted, and their future expansion limited. To make matters worse, substitutes for palm oil, such as peanut oil and petroleum, began to come on to European markets at lower prices.

The price of palm oil remained on an upward curve through the 1850s, but in 1862 it began to drop. In fact, it began to decline so rapidly that the Niger Delta states were unable to maintain their exports at anything like previous levels, even by increasing output and shipping larger quantities. Social unrest also began to spread, as ex-slaves who had begun as canoe-paddlers managed to work their way into the ranks of traders. They then became unhappy at being denied the power and prestige to match their new-found wealth. Revolts broke out all the over the Niger Delta area, and the British navy had to be called in on several occasions to help shore up the faltering regime of the old local trading houses. In 1869, part of the population of Bonny even broke away under an ex-slave named Jaja to set up its own independent state called 'Opobo', and quickly assumed control of all the markets Bonny had once dominated. Again, the British had to intervene, and Jaja was deported and died in exile in the Caribbean.

During this turbulent period, the world of the palm oil ruffians also came to an end. Factories were transferred to the shore in the 1870s, and the worm-eaten hulks were either beached or sunk at their moorings. By the time that the Royal Niger Company was set up in 1886, it could claim to have as many as 100 local factories. Many admittedly were little more than re-fuelling stations, where wood was cut and stacked for the river steamers. These were usually managed by a Kru man, who lived there with his family in a small thatch-roofed mud hut provided on a plot of land. From there a paved causeway would lead down to another hut at the waterside known as the 'canteen', which was used as a retail store.

By contrast, the company's headquarters at Akassa developed into a small town of 14 hectares, with its own post office, canteen, staff quarters for all European employees, and extensive stores made of corrugated iron sheets or brick. There was also a workshop to deal with ship repairs, a substantial jetty that could serve ocean going ships, and a light railway for moving cargo between the jetty and the main buildings. The military resources of the company consisted of 424 armed African constabulary commanded by British officers, river steamers with light guns, and a battery of five seven-pounder guns. The administration controlled over 1,500 kilometres from Garua on the Benue River and 800 kilometres from Rabbah on the Niger River to the sea. The company had little jurisdiction over the land, but complete control of the waterways. The rivers as a result became safe highways for European trading companies, and a secure platform for large scale exploitation of trade with the interior.

It was a far cry from Baikie's modest trading post at Lokoja, but he had prepared the ground for the Royal Niger Company to expand commercial activity on the Niger. The company existed for a comparatively short time (1879–1900), but it was instrumental in the formation of Colonial Nigeria, as it enabled the British Empire to establish control over the lower Niger against the German competition led by Bismarck during the 1890s. In 1900, the company-controlled territories became the Southern Nigeria Protectorate, which was in turn united with the Northern Nigeria Protectorate to form the Colony and Protectorate of Nigeria in 1914, which eventually gained Independence within the same borders as the Federal Republic of Nigeria in 1960.

# 7 WILLIAM BAIKIE

*(1825-1864)*

William Baikie was born in 1825 in Kirkwall in the Orkney Islands. After taking a degree in medicine at Edinburgh University, at the age of 23 he entered the Royal Navy as an Assistant Surgeon. He served in this capacity on several ships in the Mediterranean fleet, before being transferred to work at the naval hospital in Portsmouth for three years. In his final year Baikie heard about a British expedition leaving for Africa, which was being sponsored by a Liverpool merchant Macgregor Laird. He was appointed as Medical Officer and Naturalist, two positions which were often combined in Victorian times. And in June 1854 he joined the expedition's steamship the *'The Pleiad'* on the coast at Sierra Leone to prepare for the trip inland.

The expedition's primary objectives were to navigate the Niger River and its eastern tributary the Benue River as far as it was possible to reach, and on the way to assess the prospects of developing a viable business with the local population that lived along the riverbanks. The expedition was also asked if it could rescue Heinrich Barth, a German explorer who had in 1851 crossed the upper reaches of the Benue but had since gone missing. In the end they could find no trace of him, as he had already left for Timbuktu on another leg of his own five year West African exploration.

The leader of the British expeditionary force was intended to be John Beecroft, Her Majesty's Consul for the Bight of Biafra. He was an experienced navigator who had already embarked on a number of missions into the interior, using steam ships to penetrate further up the Niger River, the Cross River and the Benin River than previous official British expeditions had succeeded in doing. But when *'The Pleiad'* arrived on the coast, they were given the sad news that Beecroft had died. Baikie was the next most senior officer, so he immediately assumed command of the expeditionary force. In his own words:

*"I resolved to continue the expedition, as I considered that, the preparations being so far advanced, and results of no little importance being expected, it would be wrong not to make the attempt."*

His crew was made up of 12 Europeans and 53 Africans. The plan was to enter the river in the rainy season when the waters were rising, and navigation upstream would be easier.

Baikie as a trained doctor would have been aware of the risks and dangers of leaving the coast to explore the inland river network. Moreover, the official letter commissioning had warned Beecroft of the dangers:

*"Finally, you are strictly enjoined to be careful of the health of the party entrusted to your charge, and to afford them the benefit of your experience as to the best mode of maintaining health in African rivers; and should, unfortunately, fever break out and assume a threatening appearance, you are to remember that you are not called upon to persevere in the ascent of the river, but that your first care is the safety of your people."*

As a medical practitioner, Baikie was also keen to investigate the effect of regular doses of quinine on his men. In his diary of the voyage, he wrote:

*"Being now fairly in the river, we commenced giving, morning and evening, to all the Europeans on board, two-thirds of a glass of quinine wine, which contained about five grains of quinine, believing this would act as a prophylactic or preventive, while exposed – as everyone must be while in the Delta – to the influence of malaria."*

The early signs were promising:

*"We had now been a month in the river, and the health of all on board was perfect, and being quite clear of the swamps of the Delta, we were in great hopes that this unlooked-for exemption*

*from disease might continue."*

Even when one of his senior officers went down with fever, Baikie was delighted to observe his rapid recovery:

*"Mr May was now taken ill, showing decided symptoms of remittent fever, so I had to take him in hand.... Mr May was now so much better, that he was able to resume his usual duties, so speedy was his recovery from the attack under the modern rational treatment."*

The 1854 expedition surpassed all expectations. Baikie himself wrote:

*"We have discovered a navigable river, an available highway, conducting us into the very heart of a large continent. We have found these regions to be highly favoured by nature, teeming with animal life, and with fertile soils abounding in valuable vegetable products. We have met on friendly terms with numerous tribes, all endowed by nature with what I might term the 'commercial faculty,' ready and anxious to trade with us."*

His team had managed to navigate and record scientific data along over 800 kilometres of river, including constant latitude and longitude readings. Indeed, *'The Pleiad'* had sailed 400 kilometres further along the Benue than other expeditions had dared to venture before. The ship arrived back at the mouth of the Niger exactly sixteen weeks after they had set out. In an era when similar voyages would have lost three quarters of the crew to disease, Baikie accomplished the journey without the loss of a single life.

Baikie later attributed this success to the employment of as few Europeans as possible, and to the recruitment of Africans as crew. Indigenous to the region, as might be expected, they had greater resistance to the local diseases that had claimed so many European lives. The survival of all the European members of the crew he attributed to the use of quinine as a prophylactic. He later wrote with some satisfaction:

*"Of the measures employed as hygienic most were of a general nature, the only more specific one being the free use of quinine… Under proper precautions, Europeans may not only live quietly, but even commit with impunity what, some years ago, would have been considered as terrible indiscretions."*

He congratulated himself that throughout the whole journey he had slept on the deck of *'The Pleiad'*, and that he had been awoken at regular intervals each night to make meteorological observations. Nevertheless, although he had proved that the use of quinine was an effective prophylactic, the cause of the endemic fever in Europeans stationed on the West African coast was still a mystery.

Baikie himself realised that quinine had its limitations, and that other precautions were necessary. He rounded on the usual suspects:

*"The other means of avoiding disease are such as reason and common sense would suggest – namely, avoiding night exposure, sleeping in the open air, or delay in sickly spots, &c., and for the Europeans a rather generous diet, with the frequent use of the shower-bath."*

He mocked other theories as to how the disease was caught:

*"At one time sulphuretted hydrogen was pronounced to be the origo mali, the theorists forgetting that if so, Harrowgate and Strathpeffer would be highly dangerous spots."*

Blaikie's own pet theory was that it was caused by a:

*"poison, the nature of which we are as yet ignorant may arise from a dry soil. It is certainly more abundant where there is moisture, and generally more intense; but all that is required for its production are a certain amount of heat and previous moisture."*

The truth is that, like all his contemporaries, he did not really have a clue.

When Baikie returned to Britain, he spent the next year writing up the notes from his Niger expedition and in 1856 published an account of his travels under the title *"Narrative of an Exploring Voyage up the Rivers Kwo'ra and Bi'nue, Commonly Known as the Niger and Tsadda, in 1854"*. His memoirs would have been excellent propaganda for those in Britain who were promoting the *'legitimate trade'*. And so, it would have been no surprise that in 1857 Baikie returned to the West African coast to command his second expedition of exploration up the Niger. The strategic objectives of the mission were to build good relations with the local population living along the banks of the river, and to find opportunities to set up trading posts at strategic locations along the way.

Building on the connections he had made three years earlier, Baikie received a good initial reception from the local Igbo leaders. On this journey the expedition was travelling in a small fleet, the steamship the *'Dayspring'* accompanied by its support ship the *'George'*. And, when the boats reached the junction of the Niger and Benue Rivers, the crew of the *'George'* stayed behind to set up a trading post. As the *'Dayspring'* proceeded further up the Niger, it came to grief when it struck hidden rocks near the town of Jebba. Baikie successfully offloaded all the crew and cargo, and he then set up camp to wait patiently for a rescue party. Baikie continued with his trial of quinine to ward off disease and was able to keep the crew together and alive for over a year until they could be rescued. Eventually, one of the officers, Lieutenant Glover, managed to trek overland to Lagos on the coast and then on to Sierra Leone to raise the alarm. When the rescue party finally did arrive, most of the other explorers returned to England and left Baikie and a few others to carry on the exploration.

Baikie was determined to fulfil his mission and immediately began negotiations to establish a British Consulate in the area. But he faced stern opposition to the idea from the local leaders, possibly because Baikie was opposed to the slave trade that still provided a generous income for them. So, he moved his base camp further up the river to the town of Lokoja, where he bought a piece of land and was able to set up a more permanent settlement. He was not deterred by the previous ill-fated attempt in 1841 to set up a model farm in the same location at a huge loss of life. He managed to survive there for five years, becoming fully integrated into the local community. After purchasing the site and concluding a treaty with the local emir, he proceeded to clear the ground, build houses, form enclosures, and pave the way for a future town.

Construction work began in 1860, with Baikie, Dalton the *'Dayspring'* zoologist, and a dozen African labourers clearing the first 100 acres themselves. By the end of the following year Baikie was the only European left in the area. But he chose to remain there doggedly for three more years studying the country and its peoples. As the founding father of the Lokoja settlement, Baikie became respected locally as a doctor, minister, schoolteacher, and magistrate. His influence on local events at the time was such that the local Igbo language still uses the word *'beke'*, a corruption of his surname, as the phrase for *'white man'*, and an extension of the same derivation *'ala Beke'* for Baikie's country, meaning Britain. He also made several journeys inland to explore the area that lay beyond the riverside. On his travels he collected the vocabularies of nearly fifty African languages and found time to translate some of the Bible, especially the Psalms, into Arabic and Hausa languages. On one particularly arduous trip he travelled on horseback for over three months to reach Kano, the principal market town of northern Nigeria.

In less than five years, Baikie opened the Niger River to safe navigation from the coast, constructed roads, and established a market to which the local produce could be brought for sale and barter. More than two thousand traders visited the market in its first three years of operation. Only once during his stay did he have to employ any armed force to protect the settlement, which also became a haven for anyone fleeing the slave trade. But by 1864 Baikie was becoming exhausted physically and mentally from the constant pressure of running the Lokoja trading settlement. He also began to question the point of staying any longer in his self-imposed exile.

And so he asked the British Government for someone to relieve him of his post, so that he could return to England. In August 1864, 'HMS Investigator', arrived to take him back to Sierra Leone. There he decided to spend some time sorting out his manuscripts and natural history collection before returning to Britain. But while he was recovering his strength for the return journey to England, he was suddenly struck down by a deadly fever. He took ill on December 10 and died two days later, aged just 39. He was buried with full military honours in the old cemetery in Sierra Leone.

In an age which called for daring and courage from its emissaries to Africa, Baikie was a match for any other British explorer, but he differed from many in that he was an educated, scientific observer of the African scene, an intellectual rather than a risk taker. He had done much to establish British influence on the Niger, and his settlement at Lojoka later became the military headquarters for George Goldie's Royal Niger Company, the British mercantile company that controlled trade on the river. Baikie himself wanted to be remembered for two things, as the pioneer who opened the interior of Nigeria to British trade, but also as an influential voice speaking out against the slave trade.

In his memoirs Baikie made an impassioned denouncement of the Atlantic Slave Trade and expressed his frustration that it was taking so long to stamp out. He continued to argue that the African Squadron should be made permanent and given greater powers to patrol the coastline, and that any ships caught pursuing the slave trade should be should be declared to be pirate vessels and punished accordingly. In his view, these two practical initiatives would encourage the local population to abandon the pernicious slave trade, and convince them that they would derive more benefit from commerce.

William Baikie believed that in his long career he had personally laid the foundation on the Niger and Benue Rivers for a more legitimate trade to flourish. This was the legacy he yearned for, and it is suitably reflected in his memorial inscription:

*William Balfour Baikie, MDRN, FRGS, FBS, FSA(Scot).*
*Born at Kirkwall 27th August 1825.*
*The explorer of the Niger and Tchadda, the translator of the Bible into the languages of Central Africa, and the pioneer of education, commerce, and progress, among its many nations. He devoted life, means, and talents, to make the heathen savage and slave, free and Christian man. For Africa, he opened new paths to light, wealth and liberty – for Europe, new fields of science, enterprize and beneficence. He won for Britain new honour and influence, and for himself the respect, affection, and confidence of the chiefs and people. He earned the love of those whom he commanded, and the thanks of those whom he served, and left to all a brave example of humanity, perseverance, and self-sacrifice to duty. But the climate, from which his care, skill, and kindness, shielded so many, was fatal to himself, and when, relieved at last though too late, he sought to restore his failing health by rest and home, he found them both only in the grave.*
*He died at Sierra Leone 12th December 1864.*

# 8 CHRISTIAN MISSIONARIES

*"They speak in an unknown tongue, but they show
their white teeth and look delighted."*

Early missionary attempts in West Africa ended in failure. In 1515, the Oba of Benin asked for Portuguese missionaries to visit his court, but when they arrived the Oba was away fighting a war. He invited the missionaries to join him in the fighting and said that his lessons in religion would have to wait, *"because he needed leisure for such mystery"*. When he returned from the war a year later, he asked for one of his sons to be baptised and taught to read. But the Oba himself was soon back on the warpath, and so the missionaries gave up their mission and returned home to Portugal. Three other missionaries arrived in 1538, but by then Portuguese trade with Benin had declined, and so had the Oba's interest in religion. The missionaries did not help their cause by refusing to supply the Oba with the guns he needed to pursue his military campaigns.

Thereafter, the Portuguese missionary effort in Benin was fitful and intermittent, and it failed to displace the traditional religion. In the middle of the seventeenth century Spanish and Italian Capuchin monks made a renewed effort at converting the Oba and his people. They were welcomed with generous hospitality and given rooms in the royal palace. But they were denied access to the Oba, whom they only saw twice in ten months, and were not given the services of an interpreter. Then, when they tried to disrupt a religious festival involving human sacrifice, they were run out of town by an angry mob and subsequently deported.

In neighbouring Warri in the 1570s the Portuguese seemed to

have more success in establishing a foothold for their Christian faith. There the ruling Olu was keen to maintain his independence from the neighbouring kingdom of Benin and decided to enlist Portuguese support. He welcomed the visit of missionaries from the Portuguese island of Sao Tome, and allowed his crown prince to be baptised with the name of Sebastian. This prince later sent one of his own sons to Portugal to be educated, who returned home with a Portuguese wife. The son of this marriage, when he became Olu, fostered even closer relations with the Portuguese missionaries. Indeed, for a century and a half the Warri rulers were well known abroad as Christian converts.

But Christianity did not spread beyond the court, and even its hold at court was shaky. Eventually the traditional religion reasserted itself, and in 1733 the ruling family began to turn against Christianity. During the rest of the eighteenth century, the missionary enthusiasm of countries in Europe declined, and few missionaries came to Warri. And so, by the beginning of the nineteenth century there was little to show for these earlier missionary efforts.

## The Evangelical Movement

The abolition of slave owning in 1807 and of slave trading in 1833 throughout the British Empire proved to be two important turning points. Outlawing the slave trade and converting freed slaves became a powerful motive for setting up European Christian missions. In addition, compassion in Europe for the plight of slaves meant that money could be raised to fund the considerable expense of setting up a mission. By the 1830s Sierra Leone and Liberia, both colonies set up by freed slaves, became important centres of Christian practice in West Africa. The freed slaves who arrived in these colonies from America were already converted Christians. And it was from there that the missionary movement began to take root and establish at last a more permanent foothold in West Africa, from which it could expand its operations and spread its religion.

The Niger Expedition in 1841, although it ended in failure, captured the public imagination, and marked the beginning of a new missionary drive in West Africa, with Britain now seeing itself as a powerful agent of civilisation. The driving force behind this new missionary movement was the evangelical revival in England led by John Wesley, which had close ties with the anti-slavery movement. British efforts to stop the slave trade through diplomacy in Europe and naval patrols in the Atlantic had not radically reduced the number of slaves taken out of Africa. The coastline was simply too great. Thomas Buxton, an evangelical preacher and one of the leading lights in the anti-slavery movement, believed that the problem could only be solved at source on the mainland of West Africa. And he campaigned that the Christian church should be in the vanguard of a renewed effort to stamp out the slave trade.

Buxton urged his fellow Christians to join his noble crusade:

*"We must elevate the minds of her people and call forth the resources of her soil...let missionaries and schoolmasters, the plough and the spade, go together and agriculture will flourish; the avenues to legitimate commerce will be spread; confidence between man and man will be inspired; whilst civilisation will advance as the natural effect, and Christianity operate as the proximate cause of this happy change."*

His plan for achieving this programme was that the British government should reinforce the naval patrol, which was endeavouring to blockade the coast, with action on land. He urged the government to finance expeditions up the great rivers of the West African coast into the interior, in order to make treaties with local rulers. His theory was that very soon private individuals and companies would follow the lead of government and invest their own capital, and that ultimately these new enterprises would displace the slave trade. In his vision of the future, the new trade would be less restrictive and dominated by local rulers and would lead to the emergence of both a free peasantry and a new commercial and industrial class.

For this reason, and because of the hostile climate, the government and trading companies began to rely on Africans from Sierra Leone and the Americas as their intermediaries. Wide publicity, particularly in Sierra Leone, encouraged the voluntary migration of the liberated Africans there who wanted to return to their homelands along the coast. This led in turn to a rapid extension of the work of Wesleyan Methodists and the Catholic Missionary Society, from Sierra Leone in the west as far as Badagry in the coastal area of what is present-day Nigeria. Scottish missionaries in Jamaica, anxious to encourage a similar migration from the Caribbean, also established a mission sponsored by the United Presbyterian Church further to the east at Calabar in 1846.

The key to this expansion was that, unlike the palm oil ruffians who conducted their business at arm's length from their hulks moored along the shoreline, the new African agents were prepared to venture inland. They would travel under the benign protection of the British government and with the inspired guidance of the European missionaries on the coast. Deep into the interior, it was hoped that they would be able to set up trading posts at strategic locations, where they would live together in little colonies. Initially, these were sited on the banks of the major rivers such as the Niger, Benue, and Cross. The underlying objective was that these Christian communities could act as beacons of civilisation, from which the light would radiate to the surrounding regions.

## The Bible And The Plough

The missionaries wanted not only to abolish the Atlantic Slave Trade but all forms of slavery. They were committed to putting an end to all practices which were alien to their Christian code, such as human sacrifice, the murder of twins and cannibalism. In every possible way they wanted to bring down the old society on which the slave trade was based, and to set up in its place a new social order. But above all they wanted to persuade Africans to abandon their own gods for the Christian God and to live a Christian way of life. Alongside religious instruction, the missionaries also taught basic technical and craft skills to equip the new converts for their new careers.

Indeed, the role of these missionary pioneers was a truly multi-tasking one. As catechists and teachers, they preached the new faith and taught new skills. As carpenters and masons, they upgraded the standard of housing and built the roads and bridges to make a highway for legitimate trade. And as commercial agents, they encouraged the cultivation of crops like cotton and indigo, which they bought for the European market in return for European manufactured goods. Commerce and Christianity in future would march hand in hand. In the words of Buxton, that would become the battle-cry of missionaries for years to come:

*"It is the Bible and the Plough that must regenerate Africa".*

In the minds of the nineteenth century humanitarian movement, commerce and religion were inseparable. The promotion of trade would lead to conversion, and vice versa. There was a widespread belief among missionary strategists that the spread of trade and the development of agriculture and industry were essential conditions for the success of Christian evangelism. Some leading figures of missionary societies were even directors of the trading companies that were operating in their region of West Africa, and occasionally missions went directly into trading in their own right. Perhaps the most successful venture was the Basel Mission on the Gold Coast, which set up a trading company to develop cotton production.

The missions aimed to introduce Christian trading standards

to the area, which in practice largely meant a commitment not to deal in guns or alcohol. The objective was that missionaries would create hubs of local industry and self-sufficient communities, where converts could live godly lives and provide for all their worldly needs. The farmers and artisans, teachers and doctors in these communities were thought to have as critical a role in the missionary effort as the ordained preachers. Indeed, many of them were also competent craftsmen, and able to practice a trade should the need arise. In addition, while the missions continued to be supported by funds from the home base, missionaries had to give a strict account of their expenditure of funds. And so, in a desire to make their missions more self-sufficient and less reliant on their parent organisation, many missionaries began to operate as small businessmen in their local area.

Although missionaries liked to distance themselves from their profit seeking fellow countrymen, the truth is that traders and missionaries were closely inter-dependent. Firstly, it was in the interests of both groups to persuade African rulers to abandon the slave trade. Secondly, industrialists in Britain were anxious to find new markets for their goods, and to ensure regular supplies of palm oil and other West African products for their factories. By evangelising the interior, manpower could be redirected to the production of palm oil, the felling of timber or the harvesting of cotton. Moreover, by moving into often uncharted territory for Europeans, Christian missions could open up new commercial avenues for the trading companies to exploit. At the same time, the expansion of European trade and political influence would greatly facilitate the work of the missionaries. Consequently, the early expeditions up the Niger in the nineteenth century were jointly sponsored by the missionary movement and by business interests.

Traders and missionaries often quarrelled, but they had to co-operate most of the time. Mission funds came largely from the church offerings of faithful worshippers in Europe, but often missions ran short of funds on the ground. Therefore, the occasional contribution of £50 or £100 from a Liverpool, Glasgow or London merchant made a considerable difference to the missionary budget. And, when in 1853 a regular mail-boat service was established, many missionaries depended upon these trading vessels for their outward and return passage, as well as for the delivery of freight and correspondence. Even the richest missionary society could not afford the expense of owning and maintaining its own ship. Traders took on passengers and freight from the missions as a favour, and they quite often travelled free of charge.

Missions also could not afford to set up the sort of establishment that a trader maintained in his hulk at Calabar or his factory at Badagry. It was more economical and convenient for a mission to hire a local trader's canoe than to try to pay for its own canoe and canoe men. Usually, missionaries received from their local trading post any provisions or other goods they required on bills of credit. The merchant would present then this for payment at the mission headquarters in Europe. The traders acted also as bankers to the missionaries.

In return, the missionaries created some social life to the traders. They brought European wives and occasionally families, and so provided a settled family life that a lonely trader greatly appreciated. The traders themselves generally kept local women, and the reputation of the palm oil ruffians was well known to the missionaries. They wrote a good deal about their degenerate behaviour, which was at odds with the moral code they were preaching. But it was not the personal morality of the traders that separated them from the missionaries so much as their way of trading. A major bone of contention was the iniquitous Trust System, which locked Africans into long term debts that they were unable to pay off.

# The Political Agenda

From the beginning, missionary propaganda was inextricably linked into the political narrative of the time. They were the standard bearers of British influence, since unlike the traders and colonial administrators they were prepared to move inland and to settle in local communities, to speak their languages and to profess an interest in their welfare. The missionaries had no physical force with which to implement their social reforms, but instead sought to do so under the patronage of the local rulers. They in turn realised that the missionaries could be a considerable political asset, and act as a communications channel between their people and the British government officials on the coast.

However, while the political status of the missionaries grew, the influence of the rulers began to decline among their subjects, as Christian converts transferred their allegiance to the missions. The missionaries were also extremely patriotic and committed to promoting British interests. As a schoolboy joke in England had it at the time:

*"Africa is a British Colony. For this England is much indebted to her missionaries. When the missionary arrives in a hitherto unknown part, he calls the natives to him. When they have gathered around him, he makes them kneel down and close their eyes. This done, he hoists the British flag and proclaims the country British territory."*

As a result, the missionaries sometimes found themselves caught in a vice between their twin loyalties to the local elites and to the British authorities. They had to cultivate the rulers, in order to get permission to establish their mission stations, and to be able to move about freely to evangelise. They had to bribe them with European gifts, to give political advice when asked, and to act as secretaries when the rulers needed to communicate with the authorities. In general, they preferred to operate in compliance with local politics, as they feared that the imposition of a European administration would mean that their prestige and influence as local advisers would diminish.

But at the same time, Christian Missions in West Africa had to balance their relationship with colonial officials, who guaranteed their security and personal safety. Their concern over their safety is illustrated by the fact that Hope Waddell, one of the leading missionaries of the day, refused to leave Britain for Calabar in 1845 until he had received assurances from the Admiralty that the navy in West Africa would offer him *"every protection"*. In return, missionaries on occasion provided the British government with geographical and strategic data that could be used for military intelligence.

The administrators themselves remained largely ignorant of the indigenous customs and behaviour. They therefore relied on the missionaries with their local know-how to step in to restore calm whenever their actions had in some way violated local customs. Missionaries were also appreciated by the authorities for their role in acclimatising local peoples to the machinery of British rule, by patiently explaining to the local rulers what was required of them. Their presence on the ground promoted some measure of understanding, encouraged mutual confidence, and engendered a peaceful atmosphere. Unwittingly or wittingly, the missionaries prepared the way for British occupation and commercial exploitation, without the need for machine guns.

Some missionaries, such as Reverend J. B. Wood, a missionary of the Church Mission Society to Abeokuta in western Nigeria, became deeply immersed in local politics. So great was his interest in Yoruba politics that he refused to be transferred to Sierra Leone, where he was offered the well paid post of Colonial Chaplain. Nor, despite repeated pleas from the CMS hierarchy, could he be persuaded to take up the newly created position of Bishop of Yorubaland, as this would have turned him into a full time church administrator. Appointed Superintendent of the CMS interior mission in 1883, Wood identified himself with local politics until his death in 1897, and he endeavoured to act as conciliator during a suicidal civil war between the Egba and Ibadan factions which lasted for sixteen years. He repeatedly appealed to the British government to intervene and put a stop to the fighting. But at the same time, he used his own influence over the local rulers to end the war, by persuading each of them that he would be able to help them resolve their political differences. Wood himself was convinced that, if he had been given what he called the *"material force"* of just 100 soldiers, the war would have come to an end much sooner.

Further to the east in the Niger Delta area, the influence of the missionaries on local society was just as profound. Two rival kings, Eyo Honesty of Creek Town and Eyamba of Duke Town, competed for their patronage. Eyo in particular was receptive to the missionaries' powers of persuasion and evangelical fervour. In 1850, just after he had declared sovereignty over the whole of Old Calabar, Eyo took the radical step of outlawing the common practice of sacrificing slaves on the death of their master, so that in future only criminals would be executed.

This concession opened the door to further interference by the British in Efik society, and to a raft of new reforms soon demanded by the local consular authority. The missionaries and traders joined forces to form the *"Society for the Abolition of Inhuman and Superstitious Customs and for Promoting Civilisation in Old Calabar"*, which dedicated itself to the eradication of what they considered un-Christian local practices such as infanticide and the murder of twins. Missionary activity then began to erode Eyo's authority, as slaves took the opportunity to convert to Christianity against his wishes. Moreover, news of events in his territory was regularly leaked to the authorities by the missionaries. Although Eyo protested, he realised that he had little power to resist as the missionaries had the backing of a large British naval presence in the area.

When Eyamba, the ruler of neighbouring Duke Town, attempted to expel the local missionaries, he soon backed down for fear that *"the Queen of England be vexed too much"*. And the imperial show of force culminated in 1855 when the Old Calabar was destroyed by the guns of the Royal Navy, as a punishment for its active resistance to the missionaries. In exchange for rebuilding their town, the chiefs were forced to accept the missionaries, as well as their radical programme of reform. They agreed to abolish human sacrifice and to hand over twins and orphans to missionaries, instead of killing them. The local British Consul, in concluding the arrangements, declared that:

*"Queen Victoria and her gentlemen wish commerce and Christianity to flourish wherever the English flag was."*

Then, after a final show of defiance in Duke Town, the local Efik chiefs received the stark warning that, if they continued to *"molest"* the missionaries, they would incur the *"displeasure"* of the Queen of England. They soon came to heel, no doubt chastened by the arrival of a gunboat on the scene, which was aptly named *'HMS Scourge'*. Thereafter the interference of the missionaries in Efik society became all too pervasive. Among the alien and inappropriate measures they introduced into local Efik society were the European form of marriage and inscribed graves. The extent of their influence is perhaps best summed up by the text of a law passed by Creek Town in 1873:

*"Henceforth on God's day no market to be held in any part of Creek Town territory; no sale of strong drink, either native or imported in doorways or verandahs; no work; no play; no devil firing of guns; no Egbo processions; no palaver."*

## Missionary Preparations

Not all missionaries, however, were quite so domineering and insensitive to local traditions. Most new recruits set sail with more worthy ambitions, inspired only by their faith, and impeccable in their charitable intentions towards their fellow men. They were in many cases blissfully ignorant of the trials and tribulations that awaited them. The missionary societies, however, were only too aware of the sinister reputation of the West African coast, of its unhealthy climate and all too prevalent disease. They therefore made sure that their missionaries were as meticulously and comprehensively equipped for their overseas assignments as possible. Nothing was left to chance and detailed instructions and guidance were handed out to all new recruits.

Standard equipment for the British male missionary comprised of:

*1 pith helmet from the Army and Navy Stores*
*1 Willesden canvas tent by Edgington*
*1 White African tin box by Farwig*
*1 billhook*
*1 hatchet*
*1 fishmonger's knife*
*1 snider rifle, plus 50 cartridges*

In addition, it was recommended that he would need:

*1 travelling tin bath*
*1 umbrella with three white covers*
*4 pairs of sleeping trousers*
*1 small meat mincer*
*2 white tablecloths*
*7 yards of mosquito netting*

There was also a standard list of 66 food items that any self-respecting Christian missionary would need to keep in stock, and which were calculated to be sufficient to last a couple of years. The regulation supply order was also quite precise in its selection of some of the items such as:

*24 tins of Mason's Concentrated Beef Tea*
*12 tins of Edwards' Dried Soup*
*12 pounds of Johnson's Cornflour*
*4 pounds of Madras Curry Powder*
*10 tins of Bartlett's Pears*

In addition, there was a prescribed list of the essential medicines and medical equipments to take such as:

*Forceps*
*Hypodermic needles*
*12 bottles of Opium tablets*
*Half a pound of Sulphur to combat itching*
*5 bottles of Eno's Fruit Salts*
*1 Bedpan*
*1 packet of Livingstone's Rousers to be taken as laxatives.*

In the early years of the nineteenth century the expected role of European women who travelled to West Africa was predominantly to support their husbands or brothers in their mission. But in the boom years for Christian Missions at the end of the nineteenth century and beginning of the twentieth century, there was a growing demand in all missionary societies for unmarried women to volunteer to work as missionaries in their own right. One recruitment advertisement from 1887 has to modern eyes a somewhat ambiguous message in the final line, which would doubtless have been lost on a prim Victorian audience:

<u>*Wanted immediately - Three ladies for Africa*</u>
*Must be wholehearted missionaries, physically strong,*
*and thoroughly understanding the principle:*
*'In honour preferring one another'.*

Useful but different advice was given to female missionaries on how to equip and conduct themselves in foreign parts. It is not known how many followed the advice, but the regular recommended outfit included the following more feminine items:

<u>Underclothing</u>
*2 or 3 thin petticoats; 2 or 3 pairs of woollen knickerbockers if liked; 6 high-necked and short-sleeved woollen combinations; 6 pairs of thin Cashmere stockings; 4 pairs of canvas corsets; 4 or 6 cotton bodices; 2 cholera belts; 2 dozen pocket handkerchiefs; 1 flannel dressing gown; and 4 woollen nightdresses.*

<u>Dresses and Blouses</u>
*12 cotton blouses; plus 2 or 3 thin flannel blouses for walking; 3 or 4 skirts,*

*including a cycling skirt; 1 plain evening dress or silk blouse for evening wear; 1 better dress; and a Sunday frock if liked.*

She was also expected to supply herself with plenty of toilet soap.

A lady missionary was also advised to solicit useful gifts before departure from friends and well-wishers, such as:

*"bicycle; sewing machine; clock; afternoon tea-set, picture frames; a small wringing machine for her laundry; a cushion for an easy chair; an eiderdown quilt; and eau-de-cologne."*

She was also recommended a list of small gifts and trinkets that she could give away:

*"coloured handkerchiefs; small looking-glasses; coloured pencils (much prized); knives and scissors; paper and pencils; and small cakes of scented soap".*

Finally, there was a list of foodstuffs for consumption on the trek to the lady missionary's destination:

*"plenty of biscuits are needed for lunching by the roadside, and Huntly and Palmer's are particularly recommended; tinned meat from the Army and Navy Stores is to be avoided at all costs".*

Experienced missionaries were also only too willing to offer their advice to new recruits, and head offices of the missions were bombarded with handy tips. Top of most lists was the advice that a pith helmet and umbrella should always be used when out in the open, as the sun was considered the greatest enemy in Africa. A host of other health precautions were recommended, including:

*"taking 10 grains of quinine each morning; wearing tweed after sunset; and wrapping up in an overcoat after being soaked in a downpour."*

There were suggestions on how to barter and to run a store, including the warning not to sell any toy dolls or animals, for fear that they might be adopted as fetishes by the locals:

*"We should jealously guard our mission barter store from containing any article that will minister to the superstition, vanity and bad customs of our parishioners."*

One general rule was to avoid any form of hardship:

*"To begin in good time to make a comfortable bed for the night; never to walk in*

*the rain and to avoid getting the feet wet."*

Armed with such sage counsels, the new missionaries set sail to Africa to set up their mission stations. A key first task on arrival at the coast was to hire porters. Transportation in the tropical rain forest belt of West Africa could be extremely arduous. Except for a few stretches of navigable river, the major communication routes consisted of narrow and winding forest paths. Moreover, the warm and humid climate was unhealthy for bullocks or horses, let alone camels. And so, missionaries for most of the nineteenth century travelled on foot or were carried in hammocks. There was an unwritten rule that you replaced your hammock bearers every ten miles or so. However, German missionaries economised on this expenditure by only paying the bearers for the time they were actually carrying the hammock. Towards the end of the century, some missionaries were able to advance to the luxury of moving around by bicycle, which was seen as a major breakthrough at the time.

## The Mission House

Another early duty of the missionaries was to recruit labour for their building operations. There was no thought of adapting local products and materials to European use. Instead, complete European houses were imported in prefabricated units. But the greatest problem that missions faced was finding a roofing material suitable for the climate and which met European standards. Africans roofed their houses with grass laid on top of broad leaves. If kept in good repair, this made excellent roofing and its greatest merit was that it kept the houses cool. But practically every dry season there were outbreaks of fire, which might consume as much as a third of the houses in a town. As a result, valuable possessions were stored in a small windowless room with a mud ceiling, which was likely to escape damage if the roof burnt. It was also necessary to smoke the roofs to keep them resistant to decay and free of vermin.

British missionaries, who considered windowless rooms and grass roofs to be unhygienic, embarked on a series of experiments to devise alternative and more acceptable roofing that would be equally durable, cool, and resistant to rain. They found that they were unable to make tiles that would stand up to the local weather, and so they experimented with rolls of felt covered with several coats of tar. The Basel mission in Ghana was famous for its teaching of building crafts, and their founder, Andreas Riis, became known as *'Osiadan'*, the house builder. In place of the traditional round mud houses roofed with grass and without windows, the Basel mission built rectangular houses with windows and doors, roofed with shingles. However, despite all this ingenuity, the problem of roofing was not settled until the invention of corrugated iron sheeting towards the end of the nineteenth century.

The first mission houses and churches were patterned after West African architectural styles, while missionaries waited for materials from abroad to build more permanent structures. In the larger towns the structure of the mission house was intended to impress, and to provide a model to raise the overall standard of housing in the community. A church and a school were usually located nearby. There were also houses for teachers, school boarders, interpreters, returned slaves and other refugees, as well as carpenters' workshops and other industrial buildings.

With the growing number of converts, the peaceful co-existence of the Christian community with the rest of the local population proved to be increasingly difficult to maintain. Christian converts were regarded by the rest of their people as social outcasts and were subjected to varying degrees of discrimination and intimidation. Often, they were shunned and excluded from ordinary society, and occasionally families of the converts even expelled them from their homes. As a result, it became the norm for missionaries to set up separate living quarters for converts, usually on the lands acquired for the mission stations, and these compounds became known as 'salems'.

The mission stations operated under the auspices of the local rulers, and this placed the missionaries in an awkward dilemma, since they were obliged to obey a civil authority which they considered to be ungodly. Many missionaries believed themselves to be above the law and vowed to defend the independence of the mission house with force if necessary. Some in their religious zeal showed a blatant disrespect for local customs and practices in general. In 1849, Samuel Egerton in Calabar famously broke the sacred Ekpe drum in a fit of temper outside the town hall. He later had to apologise publicly at the end of one of the local festivals. In 1856, another missionary in Awaye in Yorubaland interrupted the local Sango festival to hurl abuse at the local rulers and priests. He then caused further offence by playing his mouth organ very loudly, and asking his schoolboys to sing at the top of their voices. As a result, he was one of the few white missionaries in West Africa to suffer personal violence.

## Christian Converts

The application of Christian doctrine in the nineteenth century was much stricter than it had been in previous centuries. Missionaries had previously been relaxed about African religious practices merging with Christianity. So, for example, polygamy was not considered as adultery, but rather as the lesser sin of concubinage. But Christian missionaries who came from Europe in the early nineteenth century utterly disapproved of how Africans worshipped. They did not tolerate polygamous households, strenuously rejected any form of ancestor worship, and were particularly severe on such practices as personal bondage or slavery. Any objects or animals which people worshipped were to be destroyed, and any cruelty in rituals or punishment was unacceptable. Many missionaries even disapproved of traditional African costume and dance. Occasionally the missionary code of behaviour could take extreme forms, such as a fine of one shilling on the Gold Coast for firing a gun, and an outright ban on drumming in the model town of Abokobi in Yorubaland.

This was the age when Christianity, enlightenment and progress were devoutly believed to be a holy trinity. Local traditional religion was therefore viewed with contempt, as being both irrational and unscientific. Missionaries were aghast at the superstition, idolatry and devil worship encountered, and wanted to see these evil practices destroyed at any cost. The historical pattern in Europe, of a gradual progress from pagan religions and witchcraft to a general acceptance of Christian ideals, was fondly expected to be repeated in Africa. The missionaries' duty was to hasten this inexorable process. They were, therefore, often unable to distinguish between the harmful and harmless in African culture. Because some performers in traditional masquerades were strongly suspected of rape and other abuses of women, the white European missionaries were unable to countenance any of the dramatic performances and dances that were the local African peoples' cultural outlet.

There were also tensions between missionaries and local communities over their methods of conversion, especially if the African converts were encouraged to show contempt for their African traditions. In some cases, little or no conflict followed conversions, as the converts were either strangers to the area or were already social outcasts. Other converts were designated by heads of household to serve the Christian God as a token of friendship to the missionary, just as other members of the family were customarily assigned to local gods. Family heads were essentially hedging their bets and ensuring they would receive the goodwill of a variety of gods to cover any eventuality.

Another source of friction was the number of lawsuits involving mission staff or converts who sought the protection of the mission. Impatient with the pace or conduct of local justice, missionaries would often repudiate the local legal framework or criticise court procedure. Some even went as far as to claim jurisdiction not only over legal disputes between members of the mission community, but also over any case that involved a single member of the mission community.

It was not long before African Christians wanted to worship without any European intermediaries and in their own style. Enlightened Christian missionaries also knew that if Christianity was to flourish, Africans would have to be ordained. Some Africans, such as Samuel Ajayi Crowther, who eventually became the first African Bishop in the Anglican Church, were sent to Britain for training. He had been captured as a slave in 1822, but the slave ship in which he was held was intercepted and he was taken to Freetown in Sierra Leone. There he was educated, baptised, and sent to London for further instruction. Subsequently he was commissioned by the Church Missionary Society to set up the Niger Mission. He later met Queen Victoria and read the Lord's Prayer to her in his own language of Yoruba, which she described as *"soft and melodious"*.

Other African missionaries were trained in local institutions, the most famous of which was Fourah Bay College in Sierra Leone, which was founded in 1827 and achieved university college status in 1876. Many of those educated there were eager to return to their countries of origin, where their education qualified them for employment as interpreters and clerks for European commercial companies, or for a junior position in one of the government departments. However, this was always regarded by the the colonial authorities as a secondary and almost accidental outcome of their education. The primary objective for the administration was that the students after graduation should support the local missions in their efforts to spread the Christian faith further along the coast to the inhabitants of the Gold Coast and Nigeria. There they became known as *'Saros'* - a contraction of Sierra Leones.

## Missions And Education

In general, however, adult education was limited in both aim and achievement. The driving force behind the work was a desire to teach converts and would-be converts to read the Bible. Indeed, nothing shows the zeal of the pioneering missionaries better than the time and effort devoted to the study of local languages, often converting the spoken language into written texts for the first time. However, few of the adult converts were taught to write in their own vernacular, and most never learned to read handwritten script. They were also not taught to read and write in English, which was the most important difference between the education programmes for adults and children.

For, in the teaching of children the missionaries were obliged to respond to the pent-up demand of many African parents for their children to be trained in the English language, so that they could acquire the knowledge and skills of measurement and basic accounting for the purposes of trade with Europeans. As one spokesman for the Efik people in the Niger Delta area put it:

*"They all get learning when young, but our children grow up like goats…A school to teach our children to saby book like white people will be very good thing."*

For more than a century children's education in West Africa remained almost entirely in the hands of the Christian Missions. Elementary schooling was free, but various inducements were necessary to ensure regular attendance. Pupils were accustomed to receiving little gifts from Europe, such as clothes, copy books, slates, and pencils. At the annual public examinations, when the school was dressed up and shown off to the public, prizes were liberally awarded. Every Christmas, schools had feasts to attract the local population, and on other occasions there would be a parade through town to show other children and their parents what they were missing. Despite these incentives, the initial response in a community would generally be disappointing. Some parents objected to losing the services of their children on the farm in the key seasons, while others complained that the school taught children to show disrespect to their parents and to tradition. The children themselves, used to outdoor life, found it difficult to be confined between benches all day long.

Ambitiously, the first schools covered all subjects in the curriculum, except physical exercise. When Samuel Crowther opened the first school in Onitsha in 1858, 14 children came regularly at first and all were girls between six and ten years of age. He observed that:

*"The boys...like to rove about in the plantations with their bows and bamboo pointed arrows in their hands to hunt for birds, rats and lizards all day long without success: but now and then, half a dozen or more of them would rush into the school house and proudly gaze at the alphabet board and with an air of disdain mimick the names of the letters as pronounce by the schoolmaster and repeated by the girls, as if they were a thing only fit for females and too much confining to them as free rovers of the fields."*

Farm work, particularly in the dry season, made boys' attendance particularly irregular, and this was a difficulty schools had to live with. The only effective counter-measure was to persuade parents to allow them to be brought up by the missionary in his own household.

For this reason, the boarding school became a regular feature of the mission station. It was also fondly expected that from among the boarders would be found the future leaders and priests of the church. The lifestyle and routine of boarders could vary from the warmth of a genial and supportive household to the harsh and unforgiving regime of an approved school. In general, discipline and hard work were the cornerstones. The records are full of the strenuous efforts of missionaries to keep the morality of their boarders up to scratch, and to prevent them being corrupted by the local community. One mission, for example, introduced the regulation that:

*"Girls were not allowed to go wash clothes at the brook, as the company at these washing streams is so bad."*

The main object of all education was religious instruction, especially for younger children, who could be easily weaned from their pagan ways and the prejudices of their unwilling parents. The elementary schools were the principal agent of evangelisation. The schools openly propagated the ideas of Christianity, as well as the basic doctrines of their particular denomination, while teaching literacy and a little arithmetic to the children. The common curriculum consisted of the '4 Rs'- Religion, Reading, Writing and Arithmetic, with Sewing for girls where there was a lady teacher on the staff. Particular emphasis was placed on the Bible and on translations of religious tracts in the local vernacular. The focus was on character training and spiritual development, and little effort was given to raising the status or material standing of the pupils and converts in society. To this end the children were overdosed on religion, and their behaviour was closely monitored. They were expected to grow up in a strict moral code and lapses such as traditional singing or dancing were not tolerated, and sometimes severely punished.

In many areas the missions were reluctant to offer higher education to their converts, and few missions had formal training institutions for their employees. Many even believed that adult education was counter-productive. In the Niger Mission even the African Bishop Crowther considered that the best people to disseminate Christianity were those without formal education, such as itinerant shoemakers, government messengers or stewards aboard ships. In his view, because they were unsophisticated, they had no pretensions and worshipped with a greater sense of reverence. If they needed any training at all, they were given periodic courses in Bible study.

From the mission standpoint, therefore, higher education was not conducive to the spread of Christianity. Many of the mission converts used any advantage to win themselves employment in government service or in a commercial enterprise. In Bishop Crowther's experience, they often transferred their allegiance to the Royal Niger Company or became traders in their own right. The missions considered that advanced education was the government's responsibility and so withdrew from grammar school education. They concentrated their energies on elementary education, and these schools became their most effective recruiting ground.

## Medical Missions

Missionaries were among the first Europeans to introduce western medicine to Africa on any permanent basis. Previously European barbers who were stationed at the Europeans forts and castles along the coast of West Africa doubled up as surgeons. They occasionally offered medical services to Africans, but their medical knowledge was often inadequate. In the nineteenth century, missions were quick to see the benefit of including medical practitioners among their staff. Local African therapies did provide a basic standard of health care, but they were severely limited when it came to surgery and internal medicine. The impact of western medicine could be dramatic, and contemporary mission medical records are full of enthusiastic notes on the awesome effect that cataract surgery could have on African patients.

The minimum recommended staffing for a mission station was a doctor and a nurse. The nurse acted as anaesthetist, house surgeon and trainer of local staff. Conditions at first were primitive, with a bed sometimes being used as an operating table, enamel vegetable bowls as instrument trays, and a saucepan as a steriliser. In due course, a second qualified medical colleague might be added to the staff. The initial thatched buildings would also be replaced by wattle and daub, and the first primitive bedsteads would be replaced by wooden frames with cowhide mattresses. Branch dispensaries would later be opened at convenient locations around the main hospital. Eventually, as the number of beds needed in clinics and hospitals increased, missions began to develop training programmes, generally for local girls as nurses and for local boys as clinical assistants.

For medical missionaries healing and conversion went hand-in-hand. But evangelical work was their prime concern, and a thorough knowledge of the Bible was a pre-requisite for any appointment. Indeed, in the early days of the Church Missionary Society a well-known London surgeon was rejected on the basis that he could not recite the full list of the kings of Israel and Judah. The missions also laid great store in their medical workers learning the local vernacular language of the area where they were posted. In order to spread the word, home visits in the local community were seen as an essential feature of the early stages of a medical mission. Through them the medical missionaries were able to advertise their services and to proclaim their Christian religion to the local inhabitants.

At a later stage, when facilities improved, anyone with a serious illness in the districts which the medical missionaries visited would be routinely brought into the central hospital for treatment. Even at the hospital, medical staff were expected to take every opportunity to convert the patients in their care to the Christian faith. Medical missionary work had the advantage that the doctors did not need to go out looking for a congregation because it came to them. Patients who had been relieved of their pain or cured of illness were fertile ground for conversion, as well as being a captive audience. The mission would therefore organise regular church services for both in-patients and outpatients to attend, together with any friends or family who were accompanying them. Lantern-slide lectures also were given on the wards, and more intimate personal conversations obviously took place at the bedside. Medical missionaries in effect assumed the role of hospital chaplains, and their clerical colleagues back at the mission house were only required to visit to give Holy Communion or the occasional baptism.

## The Anti-Liquor Campaign

As part of their programme of moral and social regeneration, missionaries were in the vanguard of the campaign against the damage being caused to the fabric of local society by alcohol, the white man's *'firewater'*. Trade in spirits had been one of the most important commodities since the beginning of the slave trade. Until the 1860s, almost the entire spirit trade on the West African coast had been in the hands of English distillers who exported Caribbean rum. But the absence of any custom duties or other regulations allowed the French and Germans to supplant rum with inferior and cheaper spirits, mainly gin made from potatoes. By the end of the century much of this gin was distilled in Germany and Holland, but most of it was carried on British ships and made to the order of British merchants. In 1897, European companies exported almost 3 million gallons of liquor to West Africa. This compares with a mere 180,000 gallons of British exports to the whole of the Empire. The Europeans on the coast were themselves inveterate drinkers, but they steadfastly refused to have anything to do with these imported spirits, preferring more select brands from British distilleries.

The coastal areas of West Africa were the ones mainly affected by this trade, especially the Niger Delta. European liquor became an essential part of marriage, funeral, and other religious ceremonies. It was also the chief incentive used to encourage oil production in the interior. Many workers spent the greater part of their earnings on drink, rather than on goods that would have improved their standard of living. In the opinion of British administrators, the traffic was doing incalculable harm. Yet they did nothing to control its flow, or to regulate the quality and strength of the spirits imported.

Agitation from the Temperance Movement lobby back home, however, led to an agreement at a conference of European powers at Brussels in 1890, which imposed a ban on the distribution and consumption of alcohol in areas where its use had not yet been established, such as Muslim Northern Nigeria. However, the French and German governments vetoed a second British proposal to impose a punitive export tariff. As a result, the Brussels Agreement was doomed to dismal failure. But, as the Anti-Liquor Campaign gained momentum, the entrepreneur George Goldie saw an opportunity in the Niger Delta to gain a competitive edge for the Royal Niger Company over the Liverpool shipowners who were his main rivals.

When one of his factories was ransacked by a drunken mob, he used the incident to parade his company's credentials as Anti-Liquor Campaigners. The story caused a sensation in Britain when it was reported that the gang, after consuming large quantities of gin in the storerooms, had cannibalised a number of the company's employees. With the news still fresh, in 1895 Goldie made a speech to the Native Races and Liquor Traffic Commission and confounded his audience by advocating a complete ban on alcohol. His remarks fuelled a frenzy of Anti-Liquor emotion among the missionary societies, and the hysteria became infectious. In Abeokuta in Western Nigeria over 8,000 signatures were collected and sent to Britain on a sheet of paper said to have been 250 feet long.

The cause was taken up by Bishop Herbert Tugwell, one of the most devout Christians ever to leave Britain for West Africa. Tugwell was a zealot who was relentless in the pursuit of his goals and brooked no dissent from black African or white European. Horrified by an epidemic of venereal disease among Europeans in Lagos, he compelled them to agree to terminate the employment of all African women in their employment. The Anti-Liquor Campaign was another moral crusade into which he threw himself with great enthusiasm. He railed at the British colonial administration for its dependence on revenues from its tax on liquor, which he regarded as *"a scandal and disgrace, a dark blot on an otherwise splendid system of administration"*. He mobilised public opinion by embarking on an ambitious and gruelling 1,000 mile tour of his episcopate on foot.

On his return to Lagos, he was dramatically arrested on a trumped-up charge of libel made by traders in Lagos. They were particularly incensed by the bishop's claim that three quarters of deaths among Europeans in West Africa could be ascribed to the effects of alcohol. Tugwell was prepared to face trial and to make himself a martyr for his cause, but the administration backed down to save face. Under constant pressure from public opinion, it was persuaded to increase the liquor tax progressively, much to the traders' annoyance. Then in 1905 the administration put its own house in order, by regulating the quality and strength of liquor. Tugwell was not fully satisfied and continued to pursue his dogged campaign for an outright ban on alcohol. But when he advocated direct taxation as the rational solution to the liquor problem, he alienated the educated African elite in Lagos for whom this concept was anathema.

Differences of opinion on the issue also broke out between the Christian missions. The Anti-Liquor movement dissolved into a one mission campaign by the Church Missionary Society. Only under duress did the heads of the Catholic missions in Nigeria agree to attend the Royal Commission of Inquiry established in 1908 to investigate the whole affair. They argued that Nigerians were by and large a sober people, and therefore that an alcohol ban would serve no purpose. The delegation from the Wesleyan Mission even suggested that the evils of alcohol had been wildly exaggerated. Of the four remaining European missionaries present at the inquiry, three refused to give evidence. The fourth delegate was a well-known alcoholic, whose outrageous conduct led to his recall to England for drunkenness in the following year. And so, the high hopes of the Anti-Liquor campaigners were dashed, and their cause came to an ignominious and inglorious end.

## Mission Life

Whatever the individual or corporate goals missionaries aspired to, they readily appreciated the need for a good press back home, in order to secure funds to support their enterprise. They therefore became inveterate diarists and letter writers, and a large number of them also wrote books about their experiences. These were consumed eagerly by their supporters at home, who were voracious in their appetite for news from the mission stations, and for confirmation that the cause they were supporting was a just and godly one. Mission journals had a wide readership, and once a year there was a great gathering at Exeter Hall in London of missionary and humanitarian societies. At these meetings, missionaries from foreign fields were a great attraction. Their letters were sometimes read out loud, if they could not appear in person.

One of the most meticulous and revealing diarists of the nineteenth century was Anna Hinderer, who in 1853 set up a mission with her husband David at Ibadan in western Nigeria. After her death, her memoirs were published in book form as

*"Seventeen Years In The Yoruba Country"*. Her enthusiasm for the challenges facing her was boundless in the early days:

*"When I see what is the need, I feel that if I had twenty lives I would gladly give them to be the means of a little good to these poor but affectionate and well-meaning people who, though black enough their skins may be, have never-dying souls, which need to be led to our Saviour, to be washed by the blood of the Lamb".*

Throughout her time on the mission station, she corresponded regularly with the Sunday School children she had left behind in Lowestoft, England. She encouraged them to collect items for her toy box. In return she sent them stories about everyday life at the mission station in Ibadan, especially about the habits and customs of the African children in the mission. One popular topic was her detailed description of how the hair of the African girls in her mission was plaited. Over time a bond developed between the two Christian communities in Ibadan and Lowestoft, and this was sealed when a child belonging to a couple of African converts was baptised with the name Francis Lowestoft Akielle.

As Sunday was the special day for Christian converts at her mission, Hinderer decided to send the children an account of the day for the church Sunday School magazine. The routine that she describes incidentally gives us an insight into how basic education was delivered:

*The day would begin at 8.30 am with the sounding of the first bell and a procession towards the mission station of local people, with their own grass bags or bright coloured ones from England on their heads containing their books.*

*Men and women were taught in separate classes at either side of the church, and classes were graded at different stages from the illiterate to the advanced. Some would have only a basic Primer, but the more adadvanced in the new art of reading would have printed sections from the Bible.*

*Morning lessons began with the reading of a Bible story, which the class had to repeat back to test their comprehension. Then they were taught a text or a verse of a hymn, and the last quarter was always dedicated to the rote learning of a catechism. A church service then took place followed by a midday meal, which most people had carried with them from home.*

*There was then a second school session in the afternoon, with the same routine as the first, except that the final quarter was devoted to questions on the sermon. This was followed by another church service, which closed around 5.30 to allow everyone to return home safely before dark.*

Afterwards, Anna would spend the evening with the children of the mission gathered around her, as they repeated passages learned off by heart and sang *"English and Yoruba hymns to sweet English tunes, with the harmonium".*

Hinderer and her husband would make frequent tours of their district to recruit new converts to the Christian faith and were assiduous in the attention that they gave to the converts in their care. But in due course, as with many other missionaries, the hard work and the hostile climate took their toll both mentally and physically. Her mission was caught up in a war zone, and a note of disillusion begins to creep into her journals. At the end of a particularly tiring day, she writes with an air of resignation:

*"These are the most troublesome people. You must either let them go on as they please or hold them with a strong hand."*

Hinderer was also plagued by frequent sickness from malaria and other diseases. Of the ten missionaries who travelled out with the Hinderers from England, only four were alive after a couple of years. Eventually Anna too succumbed to yet another bout of fever. After her death her journals were published as a tribute to:

*"one whose health had been utterly ruined by the pestilential climate of Africa; the dangers of which she had encountered for the love of Christ."*

European missionaries in West Africa and their families were constantly struck down by fevers and other debilitating illnesses. Their mortality rate was extremely high, with many dying in their very first year. The fate of Anna and her colleagues was not untypical, and the sad result of the many lives sacrificed in the service of their Christain faith was that mission cemeteries and isolated graves littered the coast and interior of West Africa. In Sierra Leone 22 missionaries of the Wesleyan Methodist Missionary Society died in only 25 years, eight in one year alone.

European missionaries therefore were prudently contracted for two years only, and a concerted effort was made to train up local African preachers to take over the work. Some preachers were even recruited from the Caribbean, as it was thought that they would be more able to withstand the climate. All missionaries had to be prepared for the worst from malaria, and until the mystery of its cause was unlocked by Robert Ross in 1897, various potions were taken to reduce its effects, including *'Warburg's Fever Tincture'*, according to one missionary *"the most vile drug that man ever invented"*.

## Missionary Critics

Not everyone, however, was entirely sympathetic towards the missionaries or applauded their sacrifice. Some refused to swallow their propaganda and challenged whether they were having a wholly beneficial effect on the local population. A particularly severe critic was Mary Kingsley, an emancipated woman with strong and often controversial views, who made two journeys to West Africa. Her interests were mainly biological and anthropological, but her travels necessarily brought her into contact with missionaries. She was unimpressed by the technical training in printing, bookbinding and tailoring offered by the Protestant missions to their Christian converts. Although in her view the Wesleyan missions could be congratulated for teaching the more relevant skills of bricklaying, carpentry and blacksmithing, only the Catholic missions taught what Kingsley considered the skills that Africans most needed: improved methods of agriculture and plantation farming.

Kingsley was particularly critical of the effect that missionary life was having on the Africans themselves. She condemned the notorious *'Hubbard'* garment that girls were always obliged to wear. The Hubbard was a shapeless kind of smock introduced to African missions in the interest of female modesty and produced in their thousand at sewing circles by pious ladies throughout Europe. It consisted of a yoke around the shoulders, fastened at the back by three buttons, two of which were usually missing. From the yoke protruded short sleeves, to which were attached flaps that reached down to the ankles. To make matters worse, Hubbards were made in an extra-large size only, to accommodate the ample figure which the European ladies imagined their African counterparts to have. Any woman leaning forward to tend a fire or stir a cooking pot inevitably ended up with her Hubbard dragging on the ground or falling into the pot. The result was that they were always grubby. Kingsley commented that *"it is not in nature for people to be made to fit these things."* She condemned the Hubbard as:

*"one of the factors producing the well-known torpidity of the mission-trained girl; and they should be suppressed in her interest, apart from their appearance, which is enough to constitute a hanging matter."*

Kingsley was equally forthright in her views of some of the missionary attitudes she encountered. Missionaries were prone to blame their failure to make conversions on the effects of alcohol or the sinful practice of polygamy. Many mission accounts coming out of Africa contained broadsides against the evils of drink or thinly veiled criticisms of the plurality of wives, which was not a subject to be mentioned too bluntly to a Victorian matron. Kingsley believed that the missions were guilty of using attacks on the liquor trade to whip up support at home, where the temperance movement was growing in popularity. As for polygamy, Kingsley thought that it was quite impossible for one African wife to do all the work expected by an African male: cooking, tending the house, fetching water, cultivating the land, and looking after the children. She also believed that the women themselves were more than happy with sharing their man, if they received as much cloth and beads as any of the other wives.

In her view, the fundamental reason for missionary failure in Africa was that the missionaries were unable to recognise that the difference between themselves and the Africans was not a difference of degree, but a difference of kind. The black man was not in her opinion an underdeveloped white man. The missionaries were therefore misguided in:

*"regarding the native minds as so many jugs only requiring to be emptied of stuff which is in them and refilled with the particular dogma he is engaged in teaching, in order to make them the equals of the white races."*

Kingsley was also not convinced of the merit of converting Africans to Christianity, so that they were forced to abandon their own traditional religion. In her opinion, the new missionary converts had become *"the curse of the Coast"*. They may have adopted European manners and customs, and started to wear European clothes. But in her opinion, that had only resulted in the new converts being disliked on all sides. Her overall assessment was that: *"the pagans despise them, the whites hate him."* Nevertheless, despite these reservations, at the end of her journeys Kingsley concluded that:

*"Taken as a whole, the missionaries must be regarded as superbly brave, noble-minded men who go to risk their own lives, and often those of their wives and children, and definitely sacrifice their personal comfort and safety to do what, from their point of view, is their simple duty."*

# Legacy

Early missionaries in West Africa were dedicated single-mindedly to their cause. They earnestly believed that they could convince the local population to turn its back on what were widely viewed in Europe at the time as heathen practices, and to embrace the Christian way of life and beliefs. They were determined and uncompromising in their effort to introduce the concept of One God to the local people, to make the Bible available to them, and through education to implant their own ideals of good government, equitable justice, and legitimate trade. They did not seek to impose their ideas by force but by preaching, and it was only after the 1870s that Europeans resorted to military conquest to impose their ways.

However, it is also true that early missionaries varied enormously in the contribution they made to the welfare of the local people with whom they lived and worked. Most missionaries treated Africans as potential equals of Europeans and were convinced that Africans could achieve the same levels of education and perform the same jobs. Some were contemptuous of those they were endeavouring to convert, but others developed deep affection and respect for those with whom they worked and made a long lasting impression on their local communities. Mary Slessor was one such missionary, who spent over 40 years in Calabar, and her story is told in the next chapter.

The early missionaries were also courageous people. Disease was almost universal for them, and the cure for malaria came too late for most. In their relentless pursuit of their spiritual, educational, and economic agendas, they showed an astonishing disregard for their own safety or comfort. The average time on the West African coast and its hinterland was just a few years, and those who survived and returned home often endured recurring fever and ill-health for the rest of their lives.

They were impervious, but sadly not immune, to the ever present threat and deadly menace of malaria, yellow fever, and other killer diseases. Their time on African shores was fleeting, but their supporters back home firmly believed that that they had left behind an important legacy: a new religion for those they converted, new skills and knowledge for those they educated; and new medicines for those they treated. But perhaps the most remarkable feat of the early missionaries was that they established permanent homes in the 'White Man's Grave'. Until they did so, the only Europeans to stay ashore had been the dead resting in their graves.

# 9 MARY SLESSOR

*(1848-1915)*

Mary Slessor was born in Aberdeen in 1848 and moved to Dundee at the age of 11 when her family was looking for work. Her father was an alcoholic and had been dismissed from his job in a shoe factory. He eventually found work as a mill worker, and the family scraped a living on whatever money was left over after his drinking sessions. To make ends meet, Mary was sent out by her mother to work part-time in a local jute mill, working for half the day and attending the mill school for the other half. She was determined that her children should get a good education, and that they attend church regularly. It was her ambition that her sons would take up missionary work, but both sadly died young. As Mary grew up, she began to develop a strong interest in religion, and this led her to become involved with a local mission dedicated to teaching underprivileged children in her area. One famous story from this time is that Mary dared a gang of boys that she would not flinch as they swung a metal weight closer and closer to her face. She successfully stayed still, and the boys had to attend her Sunday School class as a forfeit. Mary Slessor's missionary work had begun.

Slessor was fascinated by the accounts of missionary work in Nigeria that were published in the *"Missionary Record of the United Free Church"*, and they fired her imagination. Initially she doubted her own ability to emulate their achievements, describing herself as *"wee and thin and not very strong"*. Eventually, however, she applied to the Foreign Mission Board of the United Presbyterian Church to be trained as a missionary. After a brief period of training in Edinburgh, she was enlisted to join the Scottish Presbyterian Mission at Calabar in the Delta region of eastern Nigeria. She sailed from Liverpool in August 1876 on the steamship *'Ethiopia'* and reached her destination in West Africa a month later.

From the very beginning she displayed the wry humour that would characterise her mission and endear her to the local people of Calabar whom she would go on to serve for the rest of her life. As she boarded ship in Liverpool, she spotted a large number of barrels of spirits being loaded from the wharf, and was overheard to make the rueful comment: *"Scores of casks of rum and only one missionary".* When she reached her destination and some of the old hands in Calabar saw her slight frame and bright red hair, they might have been excused for questioning whether she would see the end of the year out.

The Calabar Mission had its origins in Jamaica after the emancipation of slaves on the island. Many of them had come from the Cross and Calabar River areas of Nigeria and were anxious to return home. This gave weight to the emerging idea at the time of taking the Christian message to Africa. And so, in 1846 a party from Jamaica landed in Old Calabar, led by Hope Waddell from the Scottish Missionary Society. Progress was at first slow and church membership remained small. But in the 1880s some growth was evident, and the mission began a period of expansion, which included the appointment of Mary Slessor. The mission concentrated partly on education and partly on preaching, which they hoped would combine to introduce both religious and social change.

The Efik people living in the Calabar region traditionally worshipped the local god Abassi whom they believed to be the supreme creator. Their belief system was very relaxed, and they had no formal priesthood or organised religious institutions. Worship and ritual were carried out on an individual or family level, and had a number of practices which were abhorrent to Europeans and offended their Christian beliefs. Blood sacrifices were offered to fetishes on a daily basis, skulls were worshipped, and secret societies robbed and murdered under laws they made up as they pleased. Guilt was customarily decided by ordeal, either through poison, boiling oil, or red-hot knives. And when a chief died, his many wives were dressed in their finest clothes, made drunk and then strangled. Hundreds of slaves were also slaughtered to serve him in the spirit world, and anyone could be accused of causing his death and made to submit to ordeal by poison. Twin children were destroyed at birth and the mothers banished from the community. It was this last practice which touched Slessor most. She vowed that she would stamp it out, even if it took all her life to do so.

It was not long before Slessor infuriated the European missionary establishment by choosing to live with the local people, and worse still to *"live like an African"*. She learned to speak the local language of Efik fluently and used it to inject humour and sarcasm into her arguments. She had all the vocabulary, the idioms, and inflections of the language, as well as some of the characteristic gestures associated with it. Her command of the language explains the control and influence over the local people that she built up over the years. She also immersed herself in local customs and culture, and the day to day lives of those she served. This behaviour greatly assisted her missionary work and her promotion of women's rights, but it scandalised the genteel missionary society which she had entered. Quite unforgivably in their eyes, Slessor was observed to walk about barefoot, to cut her hair short, and to wear only thin cotton dresses. She dispensed with the usual corsets, shoes, hats, and veils expected of a Christian woman in her position. Exaggerated health precautions were the rule with most Europeans on the coast. Newcomers were warned not to put bare feet on the gound when leaving their beds in case they trod on the *'jigger'* fleas that are commonly found in the mud floors of homes in sub-Saharan Africa, and which burrow into human flesh to lay their eggs. Women were also cautioned not to lean out of an open window without a hat for fear of getting sunburnt.

Slessor's wilful character led to frequent conflict with the authorities and as a result she was posted ever further into the interior, where it was assumed that the crazy Scottish woman would either die of fever or be eaten by *'cannibals'*. Slessor, however, was a formidable force, and the locals literally never knew what hit them. She was known to push grown men over, grabbing them by the scruff of the neck, to stop them getting at the rum that was ruining their health. She would also give a thoroughly good smack to anyone who refused to drink any medicine that she prescribed. When she once walked into a village and witnessed a ritualistic gang rape in progress, she lashed out with her umbrella, bashing heads and stabbing bare flesh with its metal point. On another occasion, she threw herself between two fighting gangs and demanded that they laid their weapons down either side of her. The piles of guns and machetes ended up higher than Slessor herself.

Her reputation soon went before her, so that as she moved further north, the peoples higher up the river had already heard of her. She came to be respected locally as the white woman who lived alone and wanted nothing for herself. She would walk miles to bring medical help to people, and to rescue and care for what they regarded as worthless babies. Slessor saw the defence of women's and children's rights as one of her primary causes, and she went on to save many thousands from enslavement or death. She managed to convince the local people that the birth of twins was not a sign of coupling with devils and a reason for infanticide, but rather of male virility and therefore a cause for celebration. As the process of winning over the local people took some time, she personally adopted and housed in her own home a large family of rescued twins.

Slessor also ended the barbaric practices of slaughtering the wives and slaves of rich men who died, and of throwing orphans into the graves of their parents. When an infant could not be saved, the care she took in the dressing and burying of the dead body made a strong impression on any onlookers. Not only did she gain the respect of the locals, but she also even secured the approval of visiting Mary Kingsley, who reported how the red-haired Scottish woman's *"unbounded courage and industry"* had prevented the slaughter of a pair of new-born twins and their mother in accordance with local superstition:

*"Had it not been for the fear of incurring Miss Slessor's anger she would, at this stage have been killed with her children, and the bodies thrown into the bush".*

As it was, the mother was merely hounded out of the village.

In later years, Slessor's affinity with the local population was acknowledged, and she was appointed by the Colonial Governor as a Vice-Consul in the town of Okoyong. In this capacity, she presided over the local court and performed her duty conscientiously, but with her customary eccentricity. When a local man called Okpono came to court to sue his brother-in-law for a small debt, Slessor already knew that he neglected his children and regularly beat his wives, especially the wife who was the sister of the defendant. The defendant, on the other hand, she knew to be a decent man who had fallen on hard times. When the defendant confessed that he did indeed owe Okpono the money he was suing for, Slessor delivered a typically idiosyncratic verdict:

*"This court orders you to pay Okpono the money you owe him. I also order you to give Okpono a good whipping, here and now! Do it thoroughly too - or I'll fine you."*

Because she was fluent in the local language and knew the local laws through and through, her advice was sought on many matters. One British government official commented on his experience of visiting her in 1898:

*"All came to her in any kind of trouble. As interpreter she made every palaver an easy one to settle, by the fact that she could represent each side accurately what the other party wished to convey."*

Another strength Slessor possessed was her pioneering vision. As the mission was always short staffed, there was a concern as to how its work could be expanded further inland. So, in 1903 she proposed her own solution, which would involve the greater use of women. Her idea was that bands of two, three or four women could travel together as itinerant or travelling missionaries on brief but regular excursions into the interior. In her view, women were better suited for this work, *"as they could live simply among the people"*. The idea was rejected by the Mission Board in Edinburgh, but Slessor was not to be put off. Instead of going on leave, she spent the next six months exploring the area and conducting a detailed survey of it. Although her scheme was again rejected, Slessor carried on regardless and supervised the construction of a small school and church building as a first step in the development of the region. She would later be described as *"dragging a great church behind her into Africa"*.

By 1905, the first hospital up the Cross River had also been built, later to be named after her in her honour. The trading markets she had enthusiastically encouraged also soon began to attract visitors from the surrounding areas. And all the time Slessor was badgering the church authorities back in Scotland for funds to finance her operation. Gradually the money was forthcoming and, as new missionaries took over the posts she had created, she was able to move further inland to pursue her ambitions. The courage she showed in facing the hostile reception she sometimes met in making these incursions only served to increase her reputation both locally and abroad.

Slessor's letters home chronicle a period of colonial expansion, with new roads being opened into the interior and allowing military expeditions to make use of motor vehicles. She enthusiastically embraced these technological changes, but with typical humour. In one letter, half in jest, she urges that one expedition might usefully include a Maxim machine gun.

Slessor could see that the development of a road and rail network would facilitate the journeys of the missionaries and the spread of Christianity into the interior. In one letter she writes:

*"I told the High Commissioner he would not get a cheaper or safer way of steadying and pacifying and civilising the country."*

Less than a year before her death she was still thinking of expansion using modern means, by making use of a motor car devoted to missionary work to enable workers to get round quickly. She rejoiced in the thought that: *"in two hours I can do what takes me two days to do in a canoe."* In another letter, she also tells of her delight at having her voice recorded on an Edison Bell Phonograph, which a British government official had brought back on return from leave. Her pioneering spirit could immediately identify a number of possible uses of the invention in outreach, and immediately included it in her next Sunday service.

However, Slessor's bright personality and steadfast humour were unable in the end to withstand the rigours of forty years of hardship in a debilitating climate for Europeans. In the early years of the twentieth century, some medical remedies and prophylactics were becoming available, and Slessor herself was able to administer vaccinations against smallpox. But the cause of malaria was still a mystery, and like many other missionaries she succumbed to regular bouts of fever, forcing her on several occasions to return to Britain to recuperate. Her resilience is best illustrated in a letter in which she apologises for a delay in writing:

*"I had fever right on 3 or 4 times a week, all through January, and I have only twice been able to walk to church this year. But last Saturday I took quite a turn for the better and am now just myself again."*

But the recurring illnesses eventually took their toll. By 1915, her physical strength had greatly declined and the woman, who had once thought nothing of all-night treks through the rain forest, was finally reduced to travelling in a hand-cart pushed by one of her assistants. After an excruciating and prolonged bout of fever, Mary Slessor died. Her body was transported down the Cross River to Duke Town in Calabar for the colonial equivalent of a state funeral.

Even before her death she had become an extremely popular figure among the Christian community back home. The Victorian faithful had a voracious appetite for biographies of well-known missionaries particularly if, as with Mary Slessor, they contained some *'ripping yarns'*. Over the years her colleagues, friends, and acquaintances had faithfully reported her exploits to an eager audience. A few months after her death, based on these documents and Slessor's own letters, the Editor of the *"Missionary Record of the United Free Church"*, W.P. Livingstone, published a record of her life, which was aptly titled: *"Mary Slessor of Calabar: Pioneer Missionary"*. But perhaps the most enduring tribute to her life of sacrifice was from the local people she loved. They long remembered Mary Slessor as the *"Mother of All the Peoples"* or simply *"Ma"*.

# 10  EMPIRE BUILDERS

*"For two or three generations we can show the Negro what we are: then we will be asked to go away. Then we shall leave the land to whom it belongs, with the feeling that they have better business friends than us than in other white men."*

## The Rise Of European Imperialism

Towards the end of the nineteenth century, attitudes towards Africans in Europe, and particularly in Britain, took a marked shift in the wrong direction. In previous centuries Black Africans had generally been viewed by Europeans as noble savages, and Christian converts had been regarded almost as equals. But now indigenous peoples in West Africa came to be regarded as inferior, and were treated as subjects by the European invaders. Until the late 1870s and the so-called *"Scramble for Africa"*, the period when the great powers carved up the continent between them, Europeans were content to trade and preach, without their home government extending control over the areas in which they worked. Where European governments were established, they did not embark on military conquest, but were content just to introduce European systems of law and order.

The general policy was also to try to assimilate Africans into the local administration as far as possible. At Saint Louis in Senegal at the beginning of the nineteenth century there was a mixed community of white French, mixed race people, and black Africans. Indeed, the French government took pride that the local population there *"enjoyed up till now equal rights with the Europeans and…have the same privilege of having mayors chosen from among them."* In 1848, Durand Valentin the first Deputy to be elected by Senegal to the French Chamber of

Deputies was of mixed race. And by the time of the Scramble, the little colony of Senegal had the same representative institutions as a *'département'* of France, and both people of mixed race and black Africans held senior positions in both the administration and the army.

The British too, in their fledgling colonies in West Africa, accepted the principle that black Africans could undertake the work of white Europeans on equal terms. Former slaves from London, Nova Scotia, Jamaica, and other regions of West Africa were brought as immigrants to the coast of Sierra Leone, and a safe haven for liberated slaves was established in 1787 and a colony in 1807. The freed slaves were resettled in small communities that were modelled on English villages, and which were quaintly given names such as Waterloo and Hastings. Each settlement proudly boasted its own village church and school, and in 1827 Fourah Bay College was established in the capital Freetown as an institute of higher learning. During the course of the late eighteenth and early nineteenth centuries the intermingling of the newly free black and mixed race immigrants with indigenous African peoples, such as the Akan, Igbo, and Yoruba, led over several generations to the creation of an elite ethnic group, which became known as the *'Creoles'*. They became westernized in their manners and ingratiated themselves to the British administrations along the West African coast, becoming a dominant force in the religious and economic activity of the communities that grew rapidly around the British enclaves. The extension of their business and religious activities to neighbouring Nigeria in the late nineteenth and early twentieth centuries subsequently generated an offshoot in that country, called the *'Saros'*.

By the 1870s Creoles held half the posts in the civil service and were employed as officials in the British administrations in the Gambia, the Gold Coast, and Lagos. In this era, Africans were appointed to some of the highest government posts in the territories under British control. Leading figures included Samuel Ajayi Crowther, a Yoruba preacher, who in 1864 was ordained as the first African bishop of the Anglican Church. He had previously participated in the ill-fated Niger Expedition of 1841, and in 1843 returned to his homeland to set up a Christian mission in Abeokuta. His grandson, Herbert Macaulay, became one of the first Nigerian Nationalists and played an important role in ending British colonial rule in Nigeria. Africanus Horton, a Creole from Sierra Leone, became the first West African doctor to be commissioned in the British army. In addition, he wrote a number of books and essays, the most widely remembered of which is his *"Vindication of the African Race"*, published in 1868 as a response to some of the racist literature that was being published in Europe at the time. His writings look forward to African self-government and anticipated many of the events that took place in the 1950s and 1960s. He is often seen as one of the founders of African nationalism and has been called *"the father of modern African political thought"*.

Another Creole, James Parkes, in 1896 became the first Secretary of Native Affairs in the newly founded Protectorate of Sierra Leone, and subsequently Creoles were appointed as Chief Justice and Colonial Secretary. Further along the coast in the Colony of Lagos, in 1875 the Heads of the Police, Posts and Telegraphs, and Customs and Excise Departments, as well as the Registrar of the Supreme Court, were all indigenous Nigerians. In the Gold Coast, Africans even attempted to establish their own government, which was called the Fante Confederacy. Africanus Horton wrote the constitution, and other Africans assumed the chief administrative and executive offices of the new state, under the presidency of a traditional ruler. An army was created, taxes were collected and courts operating both the British legal code and African customary law were established. The confederation was short-lived, largely because the British were unable to stomach a government that was independent of the control of their newly created informal protectorate. Nevertheless, the recommendation of a Parliamentary Select Committee in 1865 was that British policy in West Africa should be:

*"to encourage in the natives the exercise of those qualities which may render it possible for us more and more to transfer to them the administration of all the Governments, with a view to our ultimate withdrawal from all except, probably, Sierra Leone."*

But despite this apparent French and British willingness to accept Africans as their equals, there was never any likelihood of real power being transferred. For, whatever the official policy might be at home, the administrators on the ground in West Africa took an entirely different view and were determined to expand the colonies over which they presided. Africans might hold high office within their administration, but they were definitely not going to receive any form of education and training that might prepare them for self-government. Colonial officials might have to accept Africans as professional colleagues, but there was no question of Europeans becoming subordinate to them. And so, although Samuel Crowther was elected as Bishop over all the missions of the Church Missionary Society in West Africa, his appointment was rejected by Reverend Henry Townsend, who was based at Abeokuta in Nigeria. Under pressure from Townsend and his supporters, the headquarters of the society in London felt obliged to remove Abeokuta from Crowther's jurisdiction, even though he had worked there formerly as a missionary.

The tide of public opinion in Europe was starting to turn. So, although a substantial French-speaking and English-speaking educated class of Africans had been created, they were soon to be elbowed aside. Between 1880 and 1904, the great European nations embarked upon the military expansion of their small settlements in West Africa, so that they became full-blown colonies. Consequently, in purely practical terms it was no longer thought feasible to offer the same educational and professional opportunities to the much larger population under the new administration. At the same time a less admirable and more sinister trend was also beginning to emerge, as racial theories claiming the natural inferiority of the *'Black Race'* gained ground in Europe.

One leading colonial administrator of the time, Harry Johnson, stated that it was:

*"the white-skinned sub-species which alone had evolved the beauty of facial features and originality of invention in thought and deed."*

This view seemed to be given credence by the Europeans who began to make their way into the interior from the coast. There they came across a variety of peoples in different stages of technological development, and apparently therefore on different rungs of the evolutionary ladder. As a result, Africans who had participated in government before 1880 were reduced to the status of mere subjects. The educated African elite had been effectively disinherited and disenfranchised. Yet, these same educated Africans would return to haunt their colonial masters, as they became the leading spokesmen of the opposition and resistance to colonial rule. Unwittingly the European authorities had already sown the seeds of their own destruction.

## Background To The Scramble

The new European empire in West Africa was based upon the patent superiority of Europe's professional armies and advanced equipment. Military muscle enabled European officers, in command of African foot soldiers, to overcome the mightiest empires of West Africa. This supremacy was largely due to the invention in the second half of the nineteenth century of rapid fire guns, such as the Gatling and the Maxim. The introduction of quinine as a prophylactic against malaria also made the Europeans less wary of venturing inland from the coast.

However, initially the strategic objective was more economic than military, either to prevent another European nation from establishing its own trading monopoly in a particular area, or to bring to heel a local African leader who was an obstacle to the expansion of European trade.

Both the French and British administrations in West Africa were designed with the precise purpose of promoting trade and opening up access to the rich resources of the interior. Between 1850 and 1880, there was relatively little military activity by the colonial powers. In the 1850s, Britain's interests were confined to Bathurst at the mouth of the Gambia River, Freetown and its peninsula in Sierra Leone, and to a string of forts along the Gold Coast. The use of British troops in the tropics was far from popular. Victorian military strategists generally condemned the use of white soldiers in the tropical rain forests, on the grounds that white men could neither brave a hostile climate, nor withstand exotic diseases.

There were some exceptions, such as the repeated campaigns in the nineteenth century on the Gold Coast against the kingdom of Asante. Military invention in that instance was deemed necessary because ongoing wars between the Asante and Fante, two indigenous peoples, had led to instability and was impeding the so-called 'legitimate' trade. In October 1873, Colonel Garnet Wolseley became Governor of the Gold Coast and Sierra Leone. As Governor of both British Territories in West Africa, he also had charge over the colonies of Gambia, Gold Coast and Western, Eastern and Northern Nigeria. In this capacity, he took command of a major new expedition into the interior against the Asante people. He was accompanied by a company of Royal Engineers, whose immediate task was to convert the single file track that led to Kumasi 260 kilometres away to the north into a road that was suitable for troop movements. The labour was sourced locally, but sickness, despite taking quinine daily, claimed the lives of many European engineers. The military force arrived in January 1874, and the expedition comprised of 2,500 British troops and several thousand Caribbean and African troops (including some Fante).

Wolseley had long campaigned for more comfortable clothing for a hot climate, and for this campaign he managed to get his troops kitted out in a more suitable uniform. Medical as well as military instructions were also issued to all the soldiers. In addition, Wolseley was able to complete the campaign in two months and to re-embark the troops for home before the unhealthy season began. Nevertheless, despite precautionary measures, there were still 55 British casualties from disease during the campaign, in addition to the 18 soldiers who died in combat. The expedition was celebrated in Britain as a major miltary victory, and Wolseley became a household name. Subsequently, to provide greater protection and security against future Asante raids, the territory was annexed by Britain to create its first major colony in West Africa.

However, elsewhere along the coast there were as yet no similar territorial ambitions. For a larger part of the nineteenth century the defence of British interests depended largely on the Royal Navy. Their squadrons patrolled the shoreline to protect traders offshore from pirate raids, or to intervene to resolve any trading disputes on the shoreline and in the adjacent river estuaries and creeks. In the Niger Delta area, the Consul for the Bights of Benin and Biafra interfered regularly in the affairs of the palm oil producing states, both to facilitate trade and to suppress the slave trade. If necessary, from the safe distance of his base on the island of Fernando Po, he could summon the navy to quell any insurrection with a salvo of its guns. As far as possible, any military intervention was kept at arm's length, with only the occasional punitive expedition on land. The British army's presence in West Africa was restricted for the greater part of the century to the West India Regiment, whose dark skinned soldiers were assumed to have greater resistance to disease and cheaper to maintain than white Europeans. In addition, there were a few other small local forces which included the Lagos Constabulary, the Sierra Leone Frontier Police and a constabulary retained by the Royal Niger Company. In terms of size, none of these combined forces amounted to much, and the Sierra Leone Frontier Police only had 17 officers, 23 NCOs, and 300 men.

The fact was that, throughout the whole of this period, the British government remained deeply opposed to any major colonial occupation of West Africa. The region was considered by the Colonial Office to be *"expensive and troublesome"*. When Lagos was acquired for the Crown in 1865, it was viewed as *"that deadly gift from the Foreign Office"*. Colonies were regarded as neither helpful in the fight to end the slave trade, nor in the promotion of trade. The British traders on the coast applauded this policy, as they were not keen for their activities to be exposed to the gaze of a resident administration. The missionaries too resented government interference, since their preference was for small self-governing states, such as the one that had been established at Abeokuta in Nigeria. The only people who were in favour of territorial expansion were the administrators on the ground, such as John Glover in Lagos and Arthur Kennedy in Freetown, who were frustrated at trying to run their colonies without being able to interfere in the affairs of the surrounding peoples.

Even by 1880, Britain had a sizeable official presence solely in Gold Coast. Elsewhere in West Africa it had more informal commitments, most significantly in the Niger Delta and in Yorubaland, based around the other main colony at Lagos. The only place where the Britishmanaged to penetrate any distance into the interior was in the Niger region, where the entrepreneur George Goldie was determined to stake his own territorial claim. In Yorubaland, by contrast, it was the missionaries who were the driving force. From their bases in

Abeokuta and Ibadan, they claimed the region for their parent church organisations back home and decreed it to be a Christian state. The British government could not at the time see any justification for major occupation of any part of West Africa. A prime consideration was the potential cost of imposing and then maintaining a local administration, which they knew that the local African population would not accept willingly. In addition, received wisdom at the time was that European settlement would be impractical on health grounds alone.

The export of slaves had been reduced to a trickle, and the new products that Europe now demanded could be exported with relative ease. There was only the occasional need for the despatch of a gunboat, in order to intervene in a dispute between Europeans and Africans over terms of trade. There was some concern over the continuance of domestic slavery in Africa, as slaves were now being employed in the production and transport of the palm oil or groundnuts that the British or French traders now required for their home markets. But that was not enough to persuade the governments to take a more interventionist approach.

The overriding concern of both British and French administrations at the time was to gain ascendancy over their rivals in territory acquired and to open up commercial channels in the interior. There was a race to get there first on the Senegal and Gambia Rivers in the West and the Niger, Cross and Benue Rivers in the East, and to negotiate new treaties and commercial arrangements with the rulers of the ethnic groups that populated the riverbanks. Once this objective had been secured, a string of trading stations could be established at strategic points on the river network to register a national claim to the territory. Initially the governments were content to delegate this work to the larger European trading companies that were beginning to emerge.

But all this was to change dramatically between 1880 and

1885 for both economic and political reasons. Traders were becoming more adventurous and acquisitive, and competition between the rival trading companies of different countries had forced up prices at the coast. And so, some traders hoped to be able to access cheaper sources of supply inland. They remained largely ignorant of the geography of West Africa and imagined that the great waterways of the Niger and Senegal were highways to much richer markets in the interior. Their ambitions were fuelled by the tall tales of travellers in the Western Sudan, such as Heinrich Barth. But they were not prepared for the fierce resistance they encountered from African middlemen, who naturally resented this invasion into their own private monopoly. Resentment led to conflict, and progressively traders began to look to their home governments for military protection.

In the Niger Delta, the British trader George Goldie was also agitating for the British government to give his company a charter, so that he could take control of the waterways. A further concern for governments was their growing fear of protectionism. Britain and Germany were both anxious to ensure that the Niger River remained open to free trade. The French too were concerned, if they could not gain control over the river, that it should remain open to all-comers. Theories of the racial superiority of the white man, endorsed by explorers' and missionaries' tales of the backward state of the peoples of West Africa, also fuelled a growing public campaign for occupation. In the end, these pressures on governments in Europe became irresistible. Mutual antagonism and deep suspicion of each other's motives reached fever point. Countries were no longer prepared to put off military intervention, for fear of being left behind. It was a matter of who blinked first. When Britain occupied Egypt unilaterally, after joint Anglo-French control had broken down, the Scramble for Africa began in earnest.

Initially, the British government of the day was reluctant to become directly involved in any military action in West Africa, preferring instead to adopt a more hands-off approach. Its approach was to stand back and allow an invisible empire to develop through a secret network of trade, supported by the informal power that the British Consul and naval gunboats exercised along the coast. Conventional wisdom at the time was that an informal empire was sufficient, and that direct government intervention on the ground would be more of a hindrance than a help to commercial interests in the region. The high death toll of Europeans in West Africa and the experience of the Asante campaigns were other factors that would have weighed heavily on official minds before committing further troops on the ground. A more interventionist approach might follow in due course, but only once the local situation had become complex enough to demand formal sovereignty, and when business was large enough to bear the costs. For the time being, traders kept life simple and business was flourishing in the political vacuum.

Moreover, the British Foreign Secretary Lord Granville cared little for Africa, and especially for the disease-ridden west coast from Gambia to the Congo. He was only too happy to delegate West African affairs to his deputy, Charles Dilke, a decision that rebounded on him when Dilke became embroiled in controversy by siding with the local British Consul, Richard Hewett. Hewett was an impetuous man and in 1882 had rather impertinently sent a letter to the Foreign Office demanding that Britain should impose a formal protectorate over the whole area of the Oil Rivers, the coastal strip that stretches for 500 kilometres from Lagos in the east to the Niger Delta and Cameroon River in the west. Hewett's plan had been summarily dismissed by the Colonial Secretary Lord Kimbolton, and yet Dilke proceeded on his own initiative to ask Hewett to build a case for the protectorate by drumming up local support for it. Hewett duly asked the most prominent of the local African leaders to write letters to the British authorities. Their response was to write a *"loving letter"* to Queen Victoria begging her to intervene, followed by a similar appeal to the Prime Minister William Gladstone.

*Acqa Town*
*Cameroon*

*Dearest Madam,*

*We your servants have join together and thoughts its better to write you a nice loving letter which will tell you about all our wishes. We wish to have your laws in our towns. We want to have every fashion altered, also we will do according to our Consul's word. Plenty wars here in our country. Plenty murder and plenty idol worshippers. Perhaps these lines of our writing look to you as an idle tale.*

*We have spoken to the English consul plenty times about having an English government here. We never have answer from you, so we wish to write to you ourselves.*
*When we heard from Calabar River, how they all have English laws in their towns, and how they have put away their superstitions, oh, we shall be very glad to be like Calabar now.*

*We are, etc.*
*King Acqua*
*Prince Dido Acqua*
*Prince Black*
*Prince Jo Garner*
*etc.*

The Foreign Office was unmoved by this appeal and unwilling to alter its policy, although the Queen herself is said to have been charmed by the letter.

While the shape and direction of British colonial expansion was largely dictated by their traders, it was the navy and army that directed French policy. The Marine Nationale was still recovering from defeat by the British navy and the French army was still smarting after its defeat by the Prussians in 1871. Both were keen to compensate for their humiliation by expanding France's overseas empire, and the French government was also under considerable pressure from public opinion to take action to restore national pride. And so, in 1879 it announced its intention to build a railway eastward from the upper Senegal River, and proceeded to acquire vast tracts of land in West Africa to establish the new colonies of Senegal, Soudan, Upper Volta, and Niger.

However, the quantity of land acquired seemed to be greater than its quality. Lord Salisbury was later to comment sarcastically that France had merely gained *"a lot of sand in which its cockerel could use its spurs".* But the conquest of West Africa offered the French army a golden opportunity to earn promotion and military honours, and soon it converted the government initiative into a war of conquest against the Umarian Empire. Once in motion, this process was to continue for more than twenty years, as the French engaged in a prolonged series of local wars. The French strategy was to link their coastal settlements with their new colonies inland, and to occupy the Niger until they arrived at the point on the river where a navigable passage could be made to the sea. At the same time, their traders had established bases on the coast in Guinea, Ivory Coast and Dahomey.

Meanwhile, on the Niger River British traders were having to contend not only with the African middlemen, who still maintained a monopoly of the Niger Delta trade, but also rival French trading companies that wanted to achieve the same dominance on the lower and middle reaches of the Niger that they had already accomplished on the upper course of the river and in Senegal. Goldie, who led one of the most British successful trading companies, was alert to the danger and realised that the only way to fend off his rivals was to create a monopoly on the river. He began by amalgamating his company with three other British firms to create a single more powerful enterprise, and consolidated his position by creating his own army, including a fleet of gunboats to patrol the river. When the African middlemen struck back and sunk one of his company's boats, he called in the gunboats to make a punitive raid on the local villages. This show of force gave the company effective control of the waterway, enabling it to strike deals with the local rulers and to establish a network of new trading stations along the Niger River.

But Goldie remained concerned about the French presence on the river that threatened to undermine his power base, as well as a potential new danger of incursions by German traders from their base in Cameroon. He knew that he needed to have more direct political authority and official support to secure his company's future in the long term. And so, he began to lobby the British government and made regular visits to the UK to make his case. In 1879 the British government accepted Goldie's plan for his National Africa Company and granted it a charter to assume control of the whole of the lower and middle Niger, and to govern it as its own private colony. The French were bought out in 1884, so that at the Berlin Conference on West Africa in 1885 Goldie was invited as the sole expert witness on all matters relating to the river. He was able to proudly announce to the assembly that on the lower Niger only the British flag was flying.

## Berlin Conference (1884-5)

European interest in Africa had increased dramatically in the early 1880s. Henry Morton Stanley's charting of the Congo River Basin (1874–77) had removed the last bit of terra incognita from European maps of the continent, thereby delineating the rough areas of British, Portuguese, French, and Belgian control. The powers raced to push these rough boundaries to their furthest limits and eliminate any local minor rulers that might prove troublesome to European competitive diplomacy. The European race for colonies made Germany start launching expeditions of its own, which alarmed both British and French statesmen. Hoping to quickly soothe the brewing conflict, the Belgian King Leopold convinced France and Germany that common trade in Africa was in the best interests of all three countries. Under support from the British and the initiative of Portugal, Otto von Bismarck, the Chancellor of Germany, called on representatives of 13 nations in Europe as well as the United States to take part in the Berlin Conference in 1884 to work out joint policy on the African continent.

In a series of meetings, Great Britain, France, Germany, Portugal, and Belgium proceeded to negotiate their respective claims to African territory, which were then formalised and mapped. The leaders also agreed to allow free trade among the colonies, and established a framework for negotiating future European claims in Africa. Neither the Conference itself nor the framework for future negotiations provided any say for the peoples of Africa over the partitioning of their homelands. No African representative had been invited to attend the Conference which took almost four months of deliberations to complete, from 15 November 1884 to 26 February 1885. At the conclusion, the European powers had neatly divided Africa up amongst themselves, drawing the boundaries of Africa much as they remain today.

The Berlin Conference gave international recognition and brought some sense of order to a situation in West Africa that looked as if it might rapidly get out of hand. The various powers were able to have their existing claims to territory ratified. France's territories on the Senegal River were now linked to the Niger. At the other end of the river, Goldie with the British government's blessing had amassed treaties in the Niger Delta area and as far north as the Sokoto Caliphate. Germany laid claim to Cameroun and Togo. And so, around the conference tables at Berlin West Africa was divided into the units that largely form the boundaries of the modern independent countries of the region. The outcomes of the conference were summarised in a General Act:

*To gain public acceptance, the conference resolved to end slavery by African and Islamic powers.*

*The properties occupied by Belgian King Leopold's International Congo Society, were confirmed as the Society's and hence Leopold's private property.*

*The 14 signatory powers would have free trade throughout the Congo Basin as well as Lake Malawi and east of it in an area south of 5° N.*

*The Niger and Congo rivers were made free for ship traffic.*

*Any fresh act of taking possession of any portion of the African coast would have to be notified by the power taking possession, or assuming a protectorate, to the other signatory powers.*

*Definitions were given of the regions in which each European power had an exclusive right to pursue the legal ownership of land.*

A '*Principle of Effectivity*' was also established that European powers could acquire rights over colonial lands only if they possessed them or had '*Effective Occupation*'. In specific terms, this meant that if a European country had negotiated treaties with local leaders, had flown itsflag there, had established an administration in the territory to govern it, and had recruited a police force to keep order, then it could also make economic use of the colony. This principle became important not only as a basis for the European powers to acquire territorial sovereignty in Africa, but also for determining the limits of their respective overseas possessions. It also served in some instances to settle disputes over the boundaries between colonies.

The Berlin Conference did not initiate European colonisation of Africa, but it did legitimise and formalise the process. In addition, it gave fresh momentum to the increased interest in Africa. Following the close of the conference, European powers began a rapid expansion of their operations, so that by the start of the twentieth century European states had claimed nearly 90 per cent of African territory. By 1895, the French had mapped out and occupied well over half of its future empire in West Africa, and Britain was in danger of being left behind in the race. It was the appointment in the same year of Joseph Chamberlain as Secretary of State for the Colonies that led to a more dynamic policy for Africa. Even so, the colonisation of British West Africa was driven forward less by government will, but more by the ambition and determination of individuals. At the forefront of the drive were George Goldie and Frederick Lugard in Nigeria, both adventurers with a thirst for glory and a burning desire to write their own page in history.

Superficially, the two men could hardly have had less in common. Goldie was the playboy, with a personality that could charm the birds from the trees, and a massive ego to go with it. He tended to act by instinct rather than design, and to manipulate rather than command. Lugard on the other hand was a military man to the core, the very model of the Boy's Own hero, with the stiffest of Victorian stiff upper lips. But, despite their different characters, both Lugard and Goldie were fired by the same burning ambition and inspired by the same romantic ideal of Empire.

They also shared a common contempt for the Foreign Office establishment, whose instructions they by-passed at almost every opportunity. Both men were vain in the extreme and showed themselves to be both arrogant and intolerant in the single-minded pursuit of their own personal glory and fame. Yet, it was the drive and determination of these two men that was almost entirely responsible for the Britain's imperial expansion in the area of West Africa that became initially the colony and ultimately the nation of Nigeria. A fuller account of their relative contributions is given in the next two chapters.

# 11 GEORGE GOLDIE

*(1846-1925)*

George Goldie was born in 1846 in the Isle of Man. His family had a distinguished military pedigree, and so it was no surprise that he should be educated at the Royal Military Academy, Woolwich. For two years Goldie held a commission in the Royal Engineers, but he was never cut out for a conventional military career. Indeed, he was later proud to admit being blind drunk when he passed his final examinations. So, when a relative left him a small legacy, he left all his worldly goods behind and took off for Egypt. There he lived for three years with a local Arab girl in what he was later to describe as his *"Garden of Allah"*. But it was also there that he heard tales from pilgrims to Mecca of the Niger River far to the west. This inspired him with a glorious vision of British rule from the Niger to the Nile.

When Goldie returned to England, he again defied convention by seducing the family governess, thus offending both the accepted social class structure of the time, as well as its strict code of sexual morality. This time he ran off to Paris, where the couple became marooned when the city was blockaded by the Prussian army after the surrender of Napoleon III in 1870. When they were able to return to England in the following year, they found found themselves in a compromising situation and had to arrange a hasty marriage. Goldie's notorious reputation now preceded him in public, and he was shunned by polite society. To make matters worse, he subsequently declared that he had become a devout atheist. Moreover, Goldie was also not an easy man to know or like, and he had a terrible temper. Like many others who were to lay the foundations of the British Empire around the world, he was a social misfit and the black sheep of his family. He had already abandoned a career in the army and, despite a private income and a wealthy family to back him, he had no hope of pursuing a public career as a civil servant or in politics. The only avenue available to Goldie seemed to be commerce. But even there his prospects did not seem bright, as he did not seem to be the sort of individual who would be prepared to work his way up from the bottom.

It was therefore with some relief to all concerned that an opportunity presented itself for Goldie to return to Africa. Through family connections, and still only 29 years old, he took over the running of Holland Jacques, an ailing trading company on the Niger River. His first plan was predictably idiosyncratic. With his younger brother Alexander, he took a boat up the Niger, in order to follow the caravan track of Muslim pilgrims in the general direction of Mecca across the Sudan to the Nile. The plan collapsed when Alexander nearly died in the town of Nupe, not far beyond the tropical forest zone of the Niger. But Goldie had seen enough to confirm his diagnosis of what was wrong with the Niger trade. The problem, in his view, was that there was too much competition, and that too many traders were chasing too little palm oil. His conclusion was that only a monopoly would restore the Niger trade to health.

On his return to England, Goldie reorganised his company into the Central African Trading Company, giving it power to merge with other companies. By 1879, Goldie had amalgamated his own firm with three of its rivals into a new venture, the United Africa Company, later to be called the National Africa Company. He achieved this coup through the sheer force of his personality. He was able to cajole the hardened Liverpool and Glasgow ship owners to accept the logic of his commercial strategy for the Niger trade. He convinced them that their trading houses in the Delta would be immeasurably stronger by pooling their resources, as they could conspire together to hold down the price they were paying for the oil.

Goldie recognised that the chief threat to the profits of the leading trading houses on the Niger was paying too high a price to the African producers and middlemen. The Industrial Revolution had created a huge twin demand for palm oil in Europe. Firstly, it was needed to make lubricants to keep the wheels of the new factories turning. Secondly, it was the vital ingredient to make soap to keep the new generation of factory workers clean. However, European manufacturers were not prepared to pay exorbitant prices for their oil, and there were also alternative sources of supply. By ending competition among the British traders, Goldie had figured out how he could save the Niger traders from pricing themselves out of world markets.

There remained the threat of competition from African middlemen, who still maintained a monopoly of the intermediate trade in parts of the Niger delta and in the other important rivers along the coast to the east. Their business was also secured by the commercial treaties that they had negotiated with the British traders. But to Goldie these were mere details, and the contracts were not worth the paper they were written on. He assembled an impressive fleet of gunboats, and armed his constabulary to the hilt, each man being issued with a Snyder rifle and bayonet. His new company then established arsenals at strategic points across the Niger territories, where it housed larger weapons, including machine guns, five-pound mortars and a twelve-pound cannon. This show of force gave the company effective control of the waterway, enabling it to strike deals with the local chiefs and to establish a network of new trading stations along the Niger riverbanks. When the African middlemen struck back and sunk one of the company's boats, the British traders called in the gunboats to punish the natives and to raze their villages to the ground.

However, Goldie recognised that such punitive measures would not be the long term solution, and that he needed to have more direct political control. He was also alarmed by the presence on the river of two large French trading companies that enjoyed the full backing of their government. They threatened to create a monopoly for French trade on the lower and middle reaches of the Niger, as they had already done on the upper course of the river and in Senegal. In order to prevent this disaster and to confirm a British rather than French monopoly, Goldie and his fellow directors sought an audience with the Foreign Office in January 1883.

There then began a protracted process of persuasion and argument that ultimately led to the British government's acceptance of Goldie's plan for the National Africa Company to take over the whole of the lower and middle Niger, and to govern it as its own private colony. The Berlin Conference had agreed to place the Niger coastline under British protection. This gave Goldie the opportuity he had been waiting for. Capitalising on his vast network of local agents and intermediaries, Goldie succeeded in negotiating over 400 treaties with the chiefs of the lower Niger, as well as the Hausa states to the north. The British government had no option but to relinquish authority for the area, and so in 1886 an official charter was granted to Goldie's company, which changed its name for the third time to the Royal Niger Company.

Goldie then adopted a more aggressive and overtly political stance, and lost no time in declaring his new company to be the effective government of the whole Niger region. The centre of command in this new administration was the Board of Directors in London, and Goldie in particular. On the ground, the backbone of the administration was its network of District Agents, who were in fact the company's European trading agents in a new disguise. They reported to an Agent-General, who was in command of local military forces, as well as a court of first instance, empowered to hear all cases except those involving foreigners or sums over £50. The shape of the administration and the spirit behind it were to affect not only the whole area of present-day Nigeria, but ultimately the whole of the British Empire.

Goldie had unconsciously established the basis for the system of administration that was later to become known as Indirect Rule, based on the idea of working in tandem with the existing legitimate African rulers. In Goldie's own words, the company would follow a policy of *"interfering as little as possible in the internal laws of each native state or tribe."* Behind these noble sentiments, the reality was that Goldie did not want to become overcommitted. He realised the limitations of his operation and was acutely aware of his lack of funds and resources. Back home, Goldie's authority and integrity were under constant assault from disgruntled Liverpool traders. He was also threatened by the attempted insurgency of both French and German traders on the Niger River. But Goldie was the consummate wheeler-dealer and managed to outmanoeuvre all of the opposing forces and maintain an iron grip on his territory. He achieved this not just through his extensive network of agents and officers, courts and judges, but by a constricting web of commercial regulations.

The true character of his administration is revealed by his very first action on the day after the company charter received its seal. With immediate effect, Goldie imposed tariff and licensing regulations to which all foreigners had to submit. These stipulated that any *"vessel, boat, canoe or other craft"* coming from outside the Niger Territories must clear customs at Akassa at the mouth of the Niger and obtain a certificate from the customs authorities there. Vessels could only trade at listed ports of entry and export, and at no other places. At Akassa, import duties would have to be paid at the rate of two shillings a gallon on spirits, sixpence on a pound on tobacco, a shilling a hundredweight on salt and 100 per cent of value on any war materials. If officials suspected fraud, they were empowered to purchase the goods by force at cost price plus 2 per cent.

If the importer intended trading up the river beyond Lokoja, where the Niger meets the Benue River, then he had to go through a second procedure, and pay a second set of duties, either at Akassa when he entered the river, or at the custom house at Lokoja. Exports were also taxed, but only once. Duties were levied at the rate of two pence a hundredweight on palm oil kernels, a penny a gallon on shea butter and palm oil, and a shilling a pound on ivory. Any attempt to defraud the revenue would be met with a hefty fine of £500 or a penalty not exceeding five times the amount lost to the revenue; and both vessel and goods would be confiscated. On the same day as the tariff regulations were issued, the company established a system of licences for trade. Every foreigner wishing to engage in barter or retail selling was obliged to obtain a retail selling licence costing £100. If in addition he wished to trade in spirits, he needed a separate licence also costing £100.

These regulations excluded competitors in two ways, firstly by making them pay, and secondly by using the administrative machinery to create difficult conditions for trade. Worst hit were the African traders, most of whom were not literate enough to complete the new documentation. Besides, they were barter traders, unused to expressing values in currency, and possessing no English coinage with which to pay the duties. And even if they surmounted these obstacles, the system of licences, needing an upfront outlay of £200, was quite beyond their means. In fact, Goldie had deliberately designed the licensing system to exclude African traders whom he condemned (somewhat outrageously even for the racist attitudes of the time) as:

*"the worst enemies of civilisation in Central Africa...disreputable*

*coloured men (in the past they were generally inferior clerks, dismissed for peculation) who...lived by surreptitious dealing in slaves...stirring up the natives to discontent and bloodshed... under a mask of ardent piety."*

For the European traders, the licences and customs duties were not impossible obstacles. Much more serious to them was the restriction on ports of entry and export. These places were naturally those at which the Royal Niger Company possessed stations and had already established a flourishing trade, and the battle for trade would thus be fought on the company's terms. Moreover, the company claimed property rights in all these places to the land on both sides of the river and would not sell any of it for wharves and warehouse. It was thus impossible to land, moor, set up business or put up stores, without the company's blessing and assistance. Naturally, these measures were not seen as exactly fair play, let alone fair trade, and provoked a wave of protest.

The exclusion of the African traders of the neighbouring Oil Rivers area struck at the heart of the Liverpool palm oil trade and restricted it to the area immediately behind the coastal towns. But initially opposition was muted, since paradoxically the Liverpool traders liked what Goldie had done and wanted to repeat his successful formula in the Oil Rivers. They were ready to abandon their uneasy alliance with the African middlemen and push up the rivers to trade directly with the producers. They considered that the best way to do this was to have a charter of their own. So, the basic ground of their grievance against the Royal Niger Company was cut from under their feet. What followed was a lot of bluster and hot air aimed in Goldie's direction, and then a deafening silence. For Goldie had craftily opened up secret negotiations with the Liverpool traders on a partial or total amalgamation of Niger and Oil River interests. This was based on mutual agreement to fix prices, and on a combined campaign to persuade the British government to grant the Oil Rivers control of their region by extending the Royal Niger Company's charter over it.

This pact soon became public, and outraged the larger shipping lines, such as Elder Dempster, which faced ruin if the amalgamation plan succeeded. The traders would then be in a position to dictate freight charges. They could also exclude from the deal the traders in Lagos and Freetown, from whom the shippers collected passage money and freight charges. They could even start up a rival shipping line of their own, assured of the constant freight of their own trade. The ship owners were a powerful lobby and attacked the Royal Niger Company's charter as being anti-competitive, allowing the company to exploit and abuse its monopoly position. Goldie accused them in return of being primarily motivated by the profits they derived from the liquor trade. He also immediately terminated all the Royal Niger Company's agreements with the shipping companies and threatened to set up a new shipping line if their opposition did not cease. This put the wind up the Foreign Office, which did its best to conciliate. But, as the British government did not wish to take over the administration of the Niger and Oil Rivers directly, it was at the mercy of Goldie and his fellow traders, at least for the time being.

The critics of Goldie's regime were not only domestic. Soon they were joined by the opposition of the German government. At the Berlin Conference, the strongest guarantees against monopoly were contained in the international agreements which Britain had concluded with the other European powers, especially Germany. Goldie had driven a horse and cart through them. His ingenious and mischievous interpretation of the Berlin Act was that it referred only to navigation on the Niger. According to Goldie, navigation simply meant moving on water, and all ships were free to do so without any interference from his company. But should they touch the banks of the river, they would cease to be simple navigators. They would be deemed to have entered the company's territories and must submit to its laws and pay its taxes. Only vessels sailing though the Niger territories to places beyond could claim free passage. And even this freedom was illusory, since in reality any ship sailing the length of the Niger and Benue Rivers would be forced to land to take on fuel and provisions.

The Anglo-German Agreement of 1885 presented a greater obstacle, as it was less ambiguous and clearly stated that taxes could only be levied to cover administration costs. But the ever resourceful Goldie was able to exploit loopholes in the legislation, which he neatly sidestepped through creative accounting. Essentially, he was able to bamboozle the authorities by muddying the waters between administrative and commercial expenditure. After all, his political agents were also the company's traders, the trading steamers carried the constabulary on punitive expeditions, and the stations on the rivers were both administrative and commercial outposts. Even a treaty-making expedition could do good business on its journey. Goldie was therefore able to massage the company finances at will, and not surprisingly the accounts submitted to the Foreign Office regularly showed an excess of administrative expenses over revenue.

The building of Nigeria as a British colony had to be carried on in the face of further opposition from Germany, which had established its own colony in neighbouring Cameroon, as well as attempts by the French to establish a foothold in the Royal Niger Company's territories. Various attempts were made to stir up trouble in the occupied parts of the company's territory, and *"to burst up the charter"* as one German envoy put it. In 1887, a German trader, Jacob Hoenigsberger, tried to test the company's hold over the Emir of Nupe by informing him that the company not only levied duties on traders within his kingdom, but also claimed a protectorate over it. After smoothing things over with the Emir, Goldie had Hoenigsberger summarily arrested, swiftly convicted of *"promoting and attempting to promote strife and disorder"*, and promptly deported. This enraged the German government, which already had its knives out for Goldie. And when in 1889 a French military officer was attacked by local people as he sailed up the Niger to make a treaty with the Emir of Yola, the French government accused Goldie of instigating the attack. Pressure was put on by both governments for the British government to bring Goldie to heel, and to assume responsibility for the local administration. The Germans reasonably argued that *"a clerk and a warehouse did not constitute a true administration."*

Despite the growing animosity towards Goldie both at home and abroad, he vigorously resisted all further intrusions, and the frequent uprisings of the local people were swiftly put down. In order to secure a stable commercial environment and a reliable profit stream, Goldie relentlessly extended his company's control over the hinterland. The company had a total of 40 stations, mainly concentrated in the palm oil belt. The company's buildings at Akassa, the depot station at the mouth of the Niger, covered 35 acres. They included customs houses, wharves, engineering shops, offices, and houses for employees. The commercial headquarters at Abutshi covered 50 acres. The administrative headquarters at Asaba was almost as large and included the only prison in the Niger Territories, a prefabricated building of wood and iron which was the grandest house in the country (and the residence of the Chief Justice), the barracks of the constabulary, and a botanical research station covering eight acres. The whole area of the lower Niger was covered with a network of smaller stations, which gave effective control over the creeks and tributaries leading into the Niger.

Few of the Africans living near the riverbanks could have been unaware of the company's power. If they had a surplus to trade, they found that their outlets had narrowed down to the company's posts, as the visits of other traders, African or European, became less and less frequent. If the chiefs and elders intrigued against the company, attacked the company's stations, formed alliances with other tribes, or invited other traders in, the company's reprisal would be swift and merciless. A gunship would arrive, with uniformed African soldiers and British officers on board. Local houses would be burned down, and the local area devastated. Aside from rebuilding homes, there would be a fine to pay, and much trade without goods in return. Any more formal dispute with the company would end up in the company's courts, with the threat of potential imprisonment.

The courts themselves were often irregular in their judgements. The most notorious of these was what became known as the *'Zweifel Affair'*. Zweifel, an official of the company, together with William Wallace, the Agent General, had taken a party of Sierra Leonean labourers up the Niger to explore the possibilities of gathering rubber. When the party arrived at Lokoja, the labourers refused to go any further, saying that they had come to cut rubber, not *"to walk in the bush for nothing"*. Zweifel singled out the ringleader and shot him dead. In the ensuing melee Wallace gave orders to the soldiers to shoot, and a further six labourers were killed and 28 wounded. The company's Chief Justice conducted an inquiry into the affair, and duly exonerated Zweifel and Wallace. Despite demands for a prosecution both at home and abroad, Goldie somehow managed to hush the affair up, and both men continued in their employment with the company.

But time was running out for Goldie and the Royal Niger Company. The protests at home became more and more strident, particularly from the steamship companies, which had begun to win over some of the traders to their side. It was also beginning to dawn on the British government that the chartered company had served its purpose and could no longer be expected to control the vast territories which it now governed. This made the area vulnerable to foreign competitors, especially the French. A British government official wrote home that:

*"It is hardly realised in England how very slight the control of the RNC is over the interior districts...It is nil five miles from the river."*

Goldie's unbridled ambition and high-handed attitude also provoked the need for an imperial official to control the company on the spot. The British government began to treat the plan for extending the charter to the neighbouring Oil Rivers area with increasing caution.

In 1889, as a first step to rein in Goldie's unbridled ambition, a Special Commissioner was appointed to inquire into the Royal Niger Company's administration. The findings of the inquiry were ultimately shelved, but nevertheless they had registered to the British government that it was relinquishing its responsibilities by delegating power to a chartered company. Opposition to Goldie began to mount and unite, especially after it became known that his idea of a charter for the Oil Rivers had been rejected. Behind the scenes, resentment was brewing in the areas around the towns of Brass and New Calabar as the inhabitants saw their trade dwindling month by month until their own food supply was in danger. They began collecting weapons and plotting to take revenge against the company that had ruined their livelihoods and taken away their traditional markets.

When an outbreak of smallpox ravaged their territory, the men from Brass could wait no longer. In January 1895, led by the ruler of the Nembe-Brass people, King William Koko, they steered their canoes at dawn into the compound at Akassa. The African employees inside were ruthlessly slaughtered as they slept in their huts. All the workshops and machinery were wrecked, and particular care was taken to trash the engines of the despised steamers. The stores and warehouses were looted and torn down. The Europeans only escaped with their lives through the providential arrival of a mail steamer, which prompted the Brass men to retreat. They later claimed that they withdrew only because it was the Queen's ship, and they had no quarrel with the Queen. They also later repented in a letter to the Prince of Wales, blaming systematic abuse by Goldie' company for their actions, alleging that it was:

*"grievances and sufferances here under the Royal Niger Company, which have driven us to take the law into our own hands by way of revenge in looting the company's factories at Akassa, and attacking its officials for which we are now very sorry indeed, particularly in killing and eating parts of its employees...We now throw ourselves entirely at the mercy of the good old Queen knowing her to be a most kind, tender hearted, and sympathetic old mother."*

Goldie's first reaction to the news of the massacre was one of shock and amazement, stating that: *"We always looked on Akassa as being as safe as Piccadilly."* But his mood soon turned to anger when he realised that public opinion had rallied to the side of the Brass people, and that in consequence the Royal Niger Company's monopoly and even its charter were in jeopardy. His demands for a swift reprisal were met with a blank response. Instead, in March 1895 the government set up yet another inquiry under Sir John Kirk. His report was pretty much a whitewash. But it did contain the important recommmendation that the Royal Niger Company should only be allowed to keep its charter status if it gave up its trading interests and concentrated exclusively on its administrative role.

Goldie seized on this proposal and became its greatest advocate. Indeed, he may have invented it himself. He was tired of the persistent criticism of his company's activities from Liverpool shipowners, and perhaps saw the report as a way out of his difficulties. He also wanted more than to be remembered just as commercial opportunist, he wanted a place in history. Like many previous adventurers on the West African coast, vanity got the better of him. He informed his shareholders:

*"I am not content that the sacrifice to a national object of all the best years of my life…should result in my name being remembered only as that of a monopolist, who blocked the road to civilisation and commerce in the Niger Basin."*

Goldie wanted desperately to join the colonial club at the top table, but the tide was moving against him. Kirk's scheme was duly rejected.

When Joseph Chamberlain became Colonial Secretary in 1895, events gathered pace. Chamberlain was a staunch imperialist and had his own agenda for West Africa. The time in his view had come for the British Empire to take a firmer hand on events, and to bring more military discipline to what was a still quite lawless region. In his own words:

*"You cannot have omelettes without breaking eggs; you cannot destroy the practices of barbarism, of slavery, of superstition… without the use of force."*

In truth, the Royal Niger Company made only pretence of governing territories under its royal charter. It remained a trading company, more or less confined to the banks of the river. It did not have the resources to fight wars or to occupy unprofitable territory. In addition, Chamberlain was getting fed up having to field complaints being levelled against the company from all sides. The era of military occupation and conquest had arrived, and an injection of fresh talent was needed to mastermind campaigns.

The Royal Niger Company would be allowed to limp along for another five years. By 1896 it had succeeded in securing for Britain complete control of the navigable stretch of the lower Niger, as well as a dominant presence in the Hausa states of the North West. In 1897 Goldie consolidated this position by commanding another expedition against the Muslim states of Nupe and Ilorin. Meanwhile, the British government had extended its *"sphere of influence"* in the East through agreements

in 1886 and 1893 with Germany. In 1890 it had also successfully negotiated a demarcation line with France in the North
East at Lake Chad. The only open boundary left was in the West
with Dahomey (now Benin) and the adjacent Borgu State.

Goldie thought he had made a treaty with the Borgu rulers, but
France still harboured its own imperial ambitions in that area
and refused to recognise it. In 1884 the French government
mounted a well-equipped expeditionary force to seize control
of Borgu. Goldie had to act fast to outmanoeuvre the French
forces, but he was beginning to recognise his own limitations
as a military commander. He was aware of Frederick Lugard's
growing reputation as a successful military commander in
East Africa and identified him as the ideal man to lead an expedition north to Borgu to sign a treaty with the local ruler
before the French did. But any successes were short-lived. As
soon as the company's forces withdrew, the French would return to reassert their territorial claims.

Goldie realised that a more powerful authority was needed,
and one less besieged by critics. In a typically economical
phrase, he wrote:

*"An Imperial Administration may steal a horse, while a Chartered
Company may not look over a hedge."*

Goldie knew that his days were numbered, and he was in any
event growing tired of West Africa. It was also becoming evident that it was impossible for a chartered company to hold its
own against the state-supported protectorates of France and
Germany.

And so, in 1900 the Royal Niger Company finally lost its
charter status and transferred its territories to the British
government for the sum of £865,000. Lugard was promptly
appointed as High Commissioner for the newly created Protectorates of Northern and Southern Nigeria. Each had its own
administration, with its own High Commissioner or Governor
and its own civil service. Indeed, as if to seal their separ-

ate identities, each new administration issued its own set of postage stamps. Meanwhile, although the Royal Niger Company lost its regal adjective, it continued to trade in Nigeria as the single biggest British commercial company, with stores in every small town selling everything from pots and pans, to sugar and soap, and matches and hoes. Their agents bought up the cotton, palm oil or groundnuts produced by their customers. In 1920, W H Lever bought up the company, and in 1929 it was amalgamated with his other companies into the United Africa Company (UAC).

Thereafter Goldie played little part in public life, rejecting various offers of colonial governorships, and turning down an offer to take control of the British South Africa Company after Cecil Rhodes's death. He died in 1925 and is buried in London. He had devoted almost a quarter of a century to his work on the West African coast and its interior. During that time, he had endured a hostile climate, defied the ever-present threat of disease, and survived the deaths of many of his colleagues. He seems to have possessed a robust constitution, and at the age of 51 was still leading his troops into battle at Bida and Ilorin on his final military campaign.

George Goldie was one of the last of the world's great merchant adventurers. In many ways his career was similar to that of Cecil Rhodes elsewhere in Africa, but he lacked Rhodes's thirst for publicity. Both men possessed the same domineering personality, ruthlessness, and energy. Their primary motivation was to achieve great personal wealth by building up a successful commercial empire. But after 1886, when Goldie and his fellow company directors became agents for the imperial cause, he also became the driving force in Britain's 'Scramble for Africa' on the West Coast. In that role he enjoyed being a major player on the world stage and relished the Machiavellian negotiations that took place behind the scenes at the Berlin Conference. He also seemed to enjoy the cut and thrust of his constant wrangling with the Colonial Office and the Foreign Office, as well as his intense rivalry with the Liverpool traders.

Above all, Gorge Goldie was a formidable competitor and was utterly determined to give no ground or quarter to his international rivals, most notably the French. And yet, although his fame and reputation at home for his exploits in West Africa may have equalled that of Rhodes in South Africa, he differed from him in his preference for anonymity. Before he died, Goldie destroyed all his personal papers and pronounced a curse on any of his children should they write about him after his death. He was content to have achieved the national and international status and reputation he desired.

His elevated status and ranking in society was recognised when he was made a KCMG in 1887, the Order awarded in the nineteenth century to those who had performed distinguished service in the colonies and protectorates of the British Empire, and it was confirmed when he became a Privy Councillor in 1898. In 1905 he was also elected President of the Royal Geographical Society and held that office with distinction for three years and was awarded the Livingstone Medal for his contribution to Geography in the following  year. Other honours included Honorary Degrees from the Universities of both Oxford and Cambridge and Fellowship of the Royal Society. All his hard work and sacrifice had been rewarded, and he had come a long way from his modest beginnings in the Isle of Man. Sir George Goldie proudly ended his life as a fully paid up member of the British Establishment.

# 12  FREDERICK LUGARD

*(1858-1945)*

Frederick Lugard was born in 1858 of British missionary parents in India, and educated in England at Rossall School and the Royal Military Academy at Sandhurst. He obtained a commission in 1878 and returned to India, where he participated in the Afghan War of 1879-1880. In 1885 he accompanied the Indian contingent to the Sudan, joining the Suakin campaign to relieve Khartoum, and in 1886 he joined military operations in Burma. After this promising start, his career was derailed when he fell in love with a twice married British divorcee he met in India. When he learned that she had been injured in an accident, he abandoned his post in Burma to join her in Lucknow, and then followed her to England. When she deserted him, Lugard decided to make a fresh start in Africa.

In 1888 he took up a position with the African Lakes Company and led a successful mission to Lake Nyasa to relieve a trading station besieged by Arab slave traders. His next enterprise in 1890 was to open up a trade route to the kingdom of Buganda for the Imperial British East Africa Company, one of the chartered companies that preceded imperial annexation in Africa. Within eighteen months he had achieved this objective, in the teeth of constant warring between the religious factions in the country, which was being fuelled to some extent by the presence of French missionaries who had entered the country from the south. When he heard that his company was thinking of closing its business in Uganda because of mounting debts, Lugard immediately packed his bags to return to England and launch a political campaign designed to convince the government to annex Uganda. In England, Lugard found that he had fallen out of favour with officials in the Foreign Office, who were disconcerted by rumours of his alleged involvement in the mysterious deaths of some French missionaries in Uganda. Therefore, in 1893, to defend his own reputation and to promote his imperial vision, he had published *"The Rise of Our East African Empire"*, an autobiographical account of his activities in Nyasaland and Uganda.

East Africa was very much Lugard's first love, and he was a reluctant recruit to the imperial cause in West Africa. In 1894, without a job and impatient for action, he accepted a commission from George Goldie to lead a Royal Niger Company mission to the north of Nigeria, where the French were busy furthering their claim to the disputed territory. The plan was to take the French by surprise, and to outflank them by securing a treaty with the kingdom of Borgu. The expedition was accomplished successfully, but its course of events reveals much about the personality of Lugard himself. With typically military gusto, Lugard set off at breakneck speed on a hundred mile dash to Bussa, one of the key centres of the Borgu kingdom. As he said himself, *"I rather overdid it – am not sure if I was not spitting blood…and was played out."* But after protracted negotiations, Lugard realised that any contract with Bussa would not guarantee a treaty with the whole of the Borgu federation. His temper was not improved by the fact that he had been kept waiting for an hour in the blazing sun by the local ruler and made to wear local African clothing. Lugard was singularly unimpressed by this affront to his dignity:

*"I brought the scarlet coat emblazoned with gold lace and stars and foolery, but I wrapped it in a towel and only put it on at the door. I detest this mummery, it is more irksome to me to dress myself up like a Punch and Judy show than to visit a dentist."*

He did, however, eventually manage to secure safe passage to Nikki, the main centre of Borgu. There, the king initially refused to meet him, because the local shamans had told him that he would die whenever white men came to Nikki. Lugard responded by threatening to go elsewhere if the king did not see him within two days. The bluff apparently worked, and the treaty was sealed the next day.

Lugard cabled Goldie with the good news when he reached the company's headquarters at Akassa in January 1895. Two days later came Goldie's reply:

*"If Lugard Akassa, where is expedition? What date treaty? French says theirs dated November 26."*

Lugard responded that his treaty was dated 10th November. Back came Goldie's terse reply:

*"Bravo Lugard."*

But nothing in West Africa was ever straightforward for the British colonisers. It was the very next day that the Royal Niger Company's headquartes at Akassa had been ransacked and burnt down by local rebels. Added to that, far from admitting defeat, the French had pressed on beyond Nikki to the Niger itself. It had needed a further expedition led by Goldie himself to re-establish Britain's imperial claim to the territory. He was exhausted by this effort and reluctant to commit his company's resources any further, since he was already convinced that its charter was going to be revoked.

At the same time, the Colonial Secretary Joseph Chamberlainwas becoming increasingly concerned at the deteriorating situation. He decided that it was time to establish a more regular military presence.And so, in1897 he set up the West African Frontier Force (WAFF), a 3,000 strong imperial force of soldiers drawn from the local population, but with British officers in command. Its immediate object was to cope with small-scale local disturbances, such as the hut tax revolt in Sierra Leone in 1898. But the force was also to assume a wider imperial significance, as a general service in West Africa against the assumed French threat.

For this purpose, Chamberlain turned to the old imperial warhorse, Frederick Lugard. His mission was to infiltrate behind

French positions in Borgu, and to plant the Union Jack alongside the tricolour. So, for every village that was supposed to be French, there would be another village that could be shown to be in British hands. It was an ingenious plan to make a mockery of the French occupation, without actually starting a war. Chamberlain had called the French's bluff and it worked. Soon after, the French officially surrendered Borgu to the British.

Lugard's reward was to be made High Commissioner of the Protectorate of Northern Nigeria, a position he held until 1906, and during which he earned his reputation as the model colonial administrator. He was a tireless worker, and renowned for putting in exceptionally long hours. His greatest failure was his inability to delegate to others. Moreover, he was dismissive and unappreciative of the efforts put in by his subordinates. He was also a stern disciplinarian, intolerant of others and exceedingly difficult to get on with. Lugard's correspondence reveals not just his meticulous attention to detail, but also his unhesitating punishment of anyone who did not adhere to his rigid ideas of personal and professional behaviour. His decision to sack an official on the spot for shooting three giraffes without a proper licence might seem today to be warranted. But there are many examples of summary dismissal for more trivial offences.

A District Officer in Lugard's administration had a thankless and often lonely task. They would often be posted to a remote location with no railway or telegraph communications. Many would die of fever, some from hostilities and a few from wild animals. A significant percentage were always sick with fever or on leave, so Lugard was frequently short of staff. The danger of catching a fatal disease was always present, and Lugard himself had recurring bouts of malaria. He gives graphic accounts in his diaries of the debilitating effects of fever and his own fear of imminent death. But that did not perturb him or distract him from his own personal goals. Nor did he relax the relentless regime he imposed on his officials.

Although the area of Northern Nigeria was vast, the area under effective British control was small. Lugard's task was made even more difficult by the refusal of the Emir of Sokoto and many other local rulers to honour their treaty obligations. The government back in Britain wanted to subdue the north, but not by force of arms. However, Lugard was determined to make himself master of the whole Protectorate, which he regarded as the only way to rescue the country from slavery and open it up to more legitimate trade. This meant systematically undermining the independence of the Fulani emirates in the north, whose wealth and power depended on raiding their non-Muslim neighbours for slaves. He had no wish to destroy these states, only to bring them and their rulers to heel. He would then impose the same kind of indirect rule administration that the British had pioneered in the princely states of India.

But his military action to achieve this goal was brutal in the extreme, and his troops showed no quarter to any resistance. The North capitulated in the face of this assault for a variety of reasons. The local emirates were politically divided and fought constantly against each other. Some pragmatic rulers even sided with the British forces because they believed this would give them local ascendancy. But their main disadvantage was military, since their outdated tactics were based on the use of cavalry charges as the front line of attack, and walled cities as the main means of defence. Neither of these were effective against the sophisticted military hardware of the British army, especially its heavy artillery.

In 1902, when Chamberlain had his back turned, Lugard launched a lightning strike on the Emirate of Kano. The Colonial Office was outraged when it found out. As Lugard later wrote:

*"The government were in an insane funk re Kano...censured me for*

*going at it "without asking Mamma" as the Pall Mall puts it."*

Undeterred, Lugard gazed with satisfaction as his artillery tore great holes in the ancient mud fortifications of the city. Over 1,200 Africans perished as a result of this assault, while Lugard later claimed to have lost only one of his soldiers. The British expeditionary force next attacked the northern city of Sokoto, which surrendered without a fight, as the defenders' swords and spears were no match for Maxim guns. Within the space of only a few years, Lugard had subdued all the Fulani emirates in the north.

There remained only the small a matter of dealing with the Munshi tribe, who had dared to challenge his authority by burning down one of the Royal Niger Company's trading posts on the Benue River, temporarily closing it for traffic. Lord Elgin, the new Secretary of State for the Colonies, and his deputy, Winston Churchill, had by then become nervous about Lugard's brutal tactics. They were adamant that there should be no punitive expedition, at least not without their express approval. Churchill noted at the time that:

*"The chronic bloodshed which stains West African seasons is odious and disquieting."*

Lugard was ordered to advance only as far as was needed, in order to safeguard company property and to clear the river for navigation. But Lugard had other ideas, and was preparing to strike when he received even more serious news of defiance. In the small village of Satiru near Sokoto, Mallam Isa, a self-styled Mahdi, had led an uprising that had killed two local white officials and a military officer, as well as 70 black African troops. Lugard was over 400 kilometres away and powerless to intervene. He could see his whole empire collapsing like a deck of cards. However, the local emirs disowned Mallam Isa as a troublemaker, and kept faith with their treaties. With their backing, Lugard was able to march to the north and wreak his revenge on the people of Satiru. What happened next not only demonstrates his steely resolve, but it also reveals his brutal and uncomprimising approach as a military commander.

Lugard was at heart a racist and had scant regard for the lives of the ordinary African. He would later summarise his own stereotype of the African:

*"In character and temperament the typical African … is a happy, thriftless, excitable person. Lacking in self-control, discipline and foresight. Naturally courageous, and naturally courteous and polite, full of personal vanity, with little sense of veracity, fond of music and loving weapons as an oriental loves jewelry. His thoughts are concentrated on the events and feelings of the moment, and he suffers little from the apprehension for the future or grief for the past. His mind is far nearer to the animal world than that of the European or Asiatic, and exhibits something of the animals' placidity and want of desire to rise beyond the State he has reached."*

He also thought that education damaged the health of Africans and made them less fertile and more prone to:

*"disabilities which have probably arisen from in-breeding among a very limited class, and to the adoption of European dress".*

He was obsessed with what he genuinely believed to be the intrinsic evils of *"primitive people"*. In his own words, he had no truck with any *"negrophile kow-towing policy"*, preferring to rule with a rod of iron.

In Lugard's view, what the average African needed, when they fell out of line, was a salutary lesson to act as a deterrent. According to his code of coduct, the villagers of Satiru had misbehaved like naughty children and needed to be taught a lesson in good manners. The lesson consisted of gunning down 2,000 of the villagers, who were armed only with hoes and axes. Not content with this atrocity, Lugard proceeded to execute all prisoners and put their heads on spikes. For good measure, he razed the whole village to the ground. This was sadly only one of many punitive expeditions that Lugard was to mount during his tenure, and which were usually regarded by his soldiers as an open invitation to rape, kill and maim. His officers were alleged to have finished off the wounded with sporting rifles, and to have hacked off limbs for the sake of their bracelets and anklets.

Back home, the Colonial Office was horrified at what Churchill was later to call this *"butchery"*. They were also tired of Lugard's belligerent attitude towards them, and his refusal to brook any criticism. There was an almost complete breakdown in relations, and a lack of understanding between both parties. The last straw was when Lugard applied for the right to administer Northern Nigeria for six months every year from an office in London. This was so that he could spend more time with his new wife Flora, who had been unable to withstand the rigours of the West African climate. This preposterous scheme for what Lugard euphemistically called *"continuous administration"* was turned down flat. Lugard promptly resigned, and after a year in London was offered the Governorship of Hong Kong, which at the time was a bit of a dead end for an empire builder.

But Nigeria had not seen the last of Frederick Lugard, and in 1912 he returned in triumph as the newly appointed Governor of both the Northern and Southern Protectorates. His main mission was to complete their amalgamation into a single colony, and to extend the policy of Indirect Rule which he had developed in the North to include the Southern Protectorate. The system of Indirect Rule was designed to allow the colonial authority to delegate the day-to-day running of the administration to the indigenous rulers and their traditional institutions. The system was not popular or effective with all the indigenous peoples and their diverse traditions. And yet by 1919, when Lugard retired as Governor General of the then combined Colony of Nigeria, the territory was well on the way to becoming a unified administration. This achievement confirmed Lugard's reputation as the empire's leading exponent of the policy of Indirect Rule.

And so, on his return to England in 1922 Lugard published *"The Dual Mandate in British Tropical Africa"*, a manual which soon became regarded as the authoritative guide to the administration of Britain's overseas territories, and essential reading for all new recruits into the colonial service. In the book Lugard set out in detail his own concept of Indirect Rule and advanced his belief that Britain had a responsibility to support the social, political, and economic development of its African dependencies. He never resumed his service overseas, but he remained active in political life until his death in 1945. He was appointed to the Privy Council in 1920 and given a peerage in 1928. He served on several national and international commissions dealing with Africa and was a member of the Permanent Mandates Commission of the League of Nations from 1922 to 1936. To the end of his life, deeply saddened by the death of his wife in 1929, he worked tirelessly in relative seclusion on a survey of matters affecting the interests of indigenous peoples across the British Empire and beyond.

Lugard continued to promote his racial theories, holding on to his belief that black Africans were essentially different from white Europeans. And yet, at the same time, he was a passionate advocate for Africans to rule themselves. He reasoned that Africans were more likely to follow someone who looked like them, spoke their languages and shared their customs. Therefore, in his view, the most prudent and practical policy would be for indigenous rulers effectively to become the middle management tier in any colonial administration. His theory was that only a system of Indirect Rule would allow the British Empire to continue to prosper and not succumb to local revolt and insurrection.

The Scramble for Africa had launched a new era of imperial aggression on the continent and a series of military skirmishes between the leading European nations. In West Africa, the expeditions were no longer led by commercial entrepreneurs keen to exploit the region's natural resources, but by a new cadre of professional soldiers with an appetite for military glory and national renown. The home audience was eager to hear of the exploits of its soldier heroes and to watch British imperial ambitions grow relentlessly under their command. Frederick Lugard was applauded for his successes as a military commander in the field, and the acquisition and control of large swathes of territory in the British name. He was also praised for being the first to recognise how equally vital it was to British interests that an efficient and enduring administration was installed to govern it. For these reasons, Lugard gained a reputation with the Victorian public back home as the country's leading colonial figure, and was regarded internationally as the empire builder par excellence.

His career, however, was not without its frustrations, and his singlemindedness regularly got him into hot water with British government officials at home and abroad. In a similar fashion, he was often at loggerheads with the traditional rulers in West Africa over whose lands he was trespassing. His harsh disciplinary code also made him few friends among those who worked in his official service or who were employed locally by him. And yet he had a magnetic personality that enabled him to persuade and cajole everyone into a common endeavour. Lugard was a man of his time, and his dreams of glory were perfectly tuned to the imperial ambitions of the Victorian era.

# 13 COLONIAL ADMINISTRATORS

*"A virgin could walk from Lake Chad to Sokoto*
*with a bowl of eggs on her head and neither the*
*virgin nor the eggs would be spoiled."*

The French and British colonial regimes adopted different models of administration, although initially they shared a similar ambition to assimilate Africans into European civilisation and culture. The key difference was that the French policy of assimilation was a policy of direct rule through appointed officials, whereas the British policy of assimilation evolved into a policy of indirect rule. In French West Africa, the colonies were integral parts of the metropolitan country, and were also considered overseas provinces. West Africans were regarded as subjects of France and, like children, were expected to have patriotic duties to their mother country. The French adopted a policy of assimilation which sought to civilise the indigenous peoples and gradually turn them into *'Petits Français'* or junior Frenchmen. The highest-ranking of these juniors were the *'évolués'*, or evolved ones. They were colonial subjects trained to work in administrative positions.

*'Évolués'* served two purposes, firstly to cut down on costs by replacing French manpower, and secondly to create the illusion that the local people somehow profited from becoming civilised. West Africans that were deemed civilised were rewarded by having the privileged status of French citizenship conferred upon them. Like the British, the French divided their colonies into regions and districts. The colonies were divided into *'cercles'* under the *'Commandants du Cercles'*. Cercles were

divided into subdivisions under *'Chefs du Subdivision'*. Subdivisions were divided into cantons under local African rulers. The key differences from the British model was that the local African rulers were not local government authorities, could not exercise any judicial functions, and did not have a police force or maintain prisons. African chiefs were not leaders of their people. They were mere functionaries, supervised by French political officers.

During the nineteenth century British colonial policy in West Africa originally had a not dissimilar policy of assimilation. This had created a western class of black Englishmen, especially the Creoles who graduated in the larger communities of Freetown, Accra and Lagos to important positions in the church, commercial firms, and even the colonial government. However, this western educated African elite soon found that it was increasingly discriminated against inside the administration. The colonial regime gradually began to import British administrators to fill positions previously held by Africans. Indeed, by the beginning of the twentieth century it had had become the official policy of the British Colonial Office that white British should be preferred to black Africans in all senior positions. However, the problem was that there were not enough white British prepared to serve as colonial administrators in West Africa because of its reputation as a hostile and potentially lethal posting. Therefore, the colonial administration was forced to reverse its recruitment policy. In its place it introduced the new administrative system of Indirect Rule. This enabled the colonial regime to operate on a more arms-length basis, and to integrate the local African elite more discreetly into the administration.

## Indirect Rule

Frederick Lugard was very much the architect of the new system of dual government, which in his own words:

*"came about partly because in various parts of Africa we had bitten off more than we could chew."*

He had been maturing his theory of Indirect Rule since his early days as High Commissioner of the Northern Protectorate, and outlined the principles of the system in *"The Dual Mandate in Tropical Africa"* published in 1922. In the book he argued that, in order to ensure that British economic interests were protected, you had first to establish political control.

Nigeria contained a number of ancient highly developed kingdoms, especially in the North. The South had been under British influence for centuries, and a loose system of dealing directly with the local population had been established. As a result, there developed over time a marked division in style between the administrations in the North and South. In the South, the government was conducted through direct rule, and British District Officers were in full charge. In the North, by contrast, Britain decided that it would be more efficient to work through the channels of government that were already in place. And so, Lugard was able to introduce his new experimental system of Indirect Rule.

Traditional rulers in the North continued to exercise authority over their own people, although admittedly under the close supervision of British officials. If the local emirs were prepared to accept British rule, abandon the slave trade, and cooperate with British officials in modernising their administration, then the colonial power would be prepared to keep them in office. But, although the emirs retained the trappings of power, their wings were clipped. They were fully accountable to British District Officers, who had the final executive authority. In addition, the emir's own advisers were transformed into salaried staff. They became in effect mere agents of the British authorities, responsible only for keeping the peace and collecting taxes.

Under the dual mandate system, the Northern Protectorate

required the supervision of only a limited number of colonial administrators scattered throughout the territory. Depending on local circumstances, they were relatively free to exercise their own discretion in advising the emirs and their local advisers. But the protocol was that all orders from the High Commissioner were transmitted directly to the emir. Although the High Commissioner possessed unlimited executive and legislative powers in the Protectorate, day to day government was largely undertaken by the emirs and their local administrations, subject always to British approval. There was also a dual system of law in operation, with Islamic sharia courts handling all matters affecting the personal status of Muslims. These included land disputes, divorce, debt, and slave emancipation.

Economic development was severely limited by the meagre revenues available to the colonial government. One of Lugard's initial acts, therefore, was to draw a clear dividing line between the general treasury of each emirate and the emir's own private income. Initially a quarter and later a half of all taxes collected by local officials was appropriated by the colonial regime to finance its operations. In the South, Christian missionaries did what they could to compensate for the lack of government expenditure on services for the local population. But in the North, Lugard and his successors restricted the activities of missionaries, so as not to disturb the Muslim hegemony. As a result of this policy, educational and medical services in the North lagged behind those in the South. However, some progress was made in economic development, when a railway was constructed to transport tin from the Jos Plateau in the middle of the country, as well as groundnuts and cotton from the far North, to the ports on the coast.

The peoples in the South had been exposed to European influence for much longer than those in the North. European traders had been active along the coast from the fifteenth century, and Christian missionaries had begun the invasion of both the South-West and South-East of Nigeria in the early nineteenth century. The result was that in the Southern Protectorate British rule was more direct, with the higher posts in government being entirely filled by white British officials. This was particularly true in the South-West, where the British presence was deeply entrenched.

In the South-East, where the British had found little in the way of organised government structures to work with, they somewhat arbitrarily nominated their own local chiefs to assist in the local administration. This drove a cart and horses through the traditional system of village democracy. As one village elder later recalled:

*"Before the coming of Europeans we had no chiefs, but when they came they installed chiefs. When they waged war against any village, the person that stayed behind and did not run away was installed chief."*

Another commented:

*"When asked who was their Chief, the people sometimes put forward a man who was the most important in their village; sometimes (most often) they just looked blank; and sometimes they put forward the village idiot to see what happened to him."*

These new chiefs became rich and powerful. But for the average local resident, colonialism meant only forced labour, the loss of land and heavy taxes.

The system of Indirect Rule was exported to the South when the two Protectorates were combined to form a single colony. There it met with fierce resistance, most strenuously in Yorubaland. In particular, the powers of direct personal taxation now given to traditional rulers were quite alien and bitterly resented. In the south-east the new policy led to widespread discontent, including most famously the riots of female traders in the market towns of Aba and Owerri. The disruption soon spread as far as Calabar and Opobo in the Niger Delta area, enflamed by the false rumour that the colonial government was about to impose direct taxation on all adult women. In Opobo the riots were so fierce that the police had to open fire on the crowd, resulting in 32 deaths and 31 wounded.

Even when the North and South had been amalgamated, they continued to develop as if they were separate nations. Both were oppressed, but in different ways. Indirect Rule in the North secured British interests, but patently failed to benefit the local population. If a ruler in the North was loyal to the British administration and paid his dues on time, it did not matter if he was corrupt or brutal to his own people. Western education was prohibited in the Islamic North, whereas in the South, where government and commerce required English-speaking employees, schools flourished. Indeed, educated Southerners became indispensable to the British administration, in order to perform the routine functions of government.

Another key difference was that there was no system of direct taxation in the South, but instead a standard currency was introduced in which all taxes had to be paid. To acquire this currency, every family had either to work for wages or produce cash crops. Under whichever system they lived, the local population bitterly resented the burden of these taxes. They knew full well that half of all revenues collected went to pay for the white officials, whom they had not invited into their lands, and who now lorded it over them.

In their own defence, European officials employed in the colonial regimes of West Africa would have claimed that they were bringing the benefits of new transportation and communication systems, as well as the innovation of Western education and technology, to what they regarded as *'backward nations'*. But the reality is that the roads and railways were only built by the colonial authorities in order to ship raw materials to service European industries. The German adminstration in Togo rather revealingly named all its new railway lines after the products that they carried: Coconut Line, Cocoa Line, Cotton Line, Iron Line, and Oil Line.

The infrastructure of all the European colonies in West Africa was not developed primarily to support the local economy, but rather to serve the interests of the mother country. The colonial system, primarily through taxation, forced African farmers to concentrate on export crops to the detriment of their subsistence crops. The most glaring example of this was in the Gambia, where peasant farmers were encouraged to produce groundnuts to the exclusion of rice, with the result that the colony had to import rice from abroad. Similar artificial shortages were created in Senegal by the focus of the colonial administration on the production of rubber. The large foreign-owned companies which imported and processed the raw materials, or which manufactured the goods exported to Africa in exchange, were the principal beneficiaries of colonial rule. And in some respects they were the real empire builders.

## European Trading Companies

In the early years of colonial rule, there was still room in the expanding economy for the African trader, despite increased competition from European businesses. But European traders, with their access to greater capital resources, were soon able to edge Africans out of business in the main centres of the interior. Some enterprising African farmers then tried to open up new markets by migrating to a neighbouring agricultural area where there was no established European trading post. But even then they might find themselves dispossessed by the arrival of a new and highly competitive rival. Lebanese traders had begun to infiltrate the Nigerian market, and were gradually taking over the Africans' role as middlemen between the large European trading company and the local farmers.

Moreover, across the whole of West Africa economic power was becoming increasingly concentrated in the hands of a few major European commercial houses: United African Company (UAC), John Holt, and Paterson Zochonis in British West Africa; Societé Commerciale de l'Ouest Africain (SCOA) and Compagnie Française de l'Afrique Occidentale (CFAO) in French West Africa. These giant corporations created effective monopolies for themselves in their own domains. Not only did they control the companies that produced the commodities that the Africans wanted, but they also owned the shipping lines that transported them, the shops in which they were sold, and the factories in which the cash crops they bought would be processed.

Initially, these foreign-owned enterprises preferred to recruit high cost European company officials, rather than to train lower cost African employees to replace them. Their only problem was that it was becoming more and more difficult to attract Europeans to work in one of these commercial companies, or to serve in the colonial service in West Africa. The region remained an unpopular posting, and one which was slow to lose its reputation as the *'White Man's Grave'*. The British government became very concerned at the situation, and feared that it would no longer be able to fill all the vacancies in the different colonial administrations. It therefore announced that, with immediate effect, it would no longer recruit new administrators by examination for West Africa.

Fortunately, there were enough Europeans who were inspired by the examples of empire builders like Goldie and Lugard. They saw an opportunity to better themselves and to achieve a status in life denied them at home. They imagined that in Africa they could become aristocrats, and that their white skin would be sufficient to set them apart as a privileged minority.

## The Thin White Line

Colonial rule for the local rulers of West Africa represented the loss of their sovereignty to a new group of chiefs, the European *'bush administrators'*. Although they might be able to retain at least some of their former powers, the fact remained that ultimate authority was now in the hands of the white man. Local authority was vested in the District Officers or Residents in British West Africa and the Commandants du Cercles in French West Africa, who were appointed as the colonial government's local agents. They not only exercised powers that had previously been the exclusive preserve of the African chiefs, but also new powers delegated to them by their home government. On the back of military conquest, these administrators moved in to keep the peace, and to maintain law and order in his designated area. The colonial governments, at their headquarters in the capitals of Europe, were a distant concept to the average African inhabitant. The District Officers and Commandants du Cercles alone represented the authority of the new regime.

It is somewhat of a mystery how the imperial mission in Africa survived for so long, since the officials who administered it were extremely thin on the ground. It is estimated that only 1200 administrators, 200 judges and legal officers, and 1000 soldiers and police were able to control 43 million people across the 5000 square kilometres of Britain's dozen or so colonies in Africa. It is equally remarkable that someone straight from university could be put in charge of an area the size of Wales. Any major insurrection could easily have overwhelmed this *'thin white line'*. However, the British government was alert to this threat, and devised an ingenious plan, and what was in effect a two-track approach.

The central strategy of the British Colonial Office was to consolidate the national position by adopting a policy of collaboration with local elites. The second overlapping strategy was to bolster British prestige by imposing white superiority. Keeping up appearances was the stuff of Empire. Come what may, the colonial administrator needed to present a bold front. District Officers always dressed for dinner, even in the stifling heat of the tropical rainforest. Everything was done to elevate the rulers above the ruled, and to demonstrate them to be a separate and superior class. An imperial hierarchy was established, with each man enjoying his own status and privilege according to rank. At the pinnacle was the King or Queen in Britain, and every colonial official had their own share of the divine authority supposed to flow downward from the monarch. The colonisers believed that their administration was omnipotent, and that it was their duty to personify its majesty in their own local area.

Indeed, so much effort went into the display of supremacy that it was often at the expense of efficiency. Soldiers would march up and down on military parades, with great ceremony and in their full colours. Yet they were far less professional and impressive in the execution of their basic soldiering duties. Military practice also did not keep up with the times, as there was a stubborn in-grained resistance in the higher ranks to change. So, when advanced mechanised equipment became available, local regiments in West Africa were often slow to take advantage. Indeed, when they were issued with modern self-propelled artillery guns, they succeeded only in slowing down the firing rate by sticking resolutely to the elaborate procedures in place for controlling horses, which of course were now absent.

## An Unhealthy Posting

Nevertheless, although colonial officials may have embarrassed themselves at times with their focus on ceremony and show, they took real pride in their administration and demonstrated great courage in suffering stoically the rigours of a hostile climate and at times perilous environment for European immigrants. Even in the early years of the twentieth century West Africa was still an unhealthy posting for newcomers. Mortality rates remained high, and there was a constant threat of debilitating illness from malaria, yellow fever or blackwater fever. Rarely did a month pass, without the need for a European resident to attend the funeral of some other member of the white community. Official statistics for the time record that one in five new recruits to West Africa were either dead or repatriated through ill health within their first year.

There was also a wide variety of other less deadly but uncomfortable afflictions that could strike the unsuspecting European. First there was the *'guinea worm'*, a waterborne parasite that laid its eggs in water. If the water was not boiled and filtered properly, the egg would subsequently hatch out inside the body. Its worm would then circulate until it became lodged in one of the extremities, usually the leg. This would create a nasty swelling on the surface of the skin, until gruesomely the worm eventually tunnelled its way out. A second threat was the *'tumbo fly'*, which liked to lay its eggs on the grass where clothes were put out to dry in the sun. Its worm would reveal itself in a large unsightly boil. Thirdly, the worm of the *'filaria fly'* would travel around the body until it lodged in a vulnerable spot such as the wrist. Not only would this result in an egg-shaped lump, but the fingers would blow up like a rubber glove. Sometimes the only way to remove the worm was to pick it out with a needle if it was spotted crawling across an eyeball.

Understandably, therefore, there was not a flood of applicants to join the various fledgling administrations in West Africa. Indeed, when one new recruit landed at Lagos in 1912, he was taken aside by the first European he met and asked where he had arrived from. When he replied that he had come from England, he received the somewhat unsympathetic response: *"Well, why don't you go back there?"*

## New Cadets

The vast majority of West African administrators were drawn from the middle classes, and the great majority had been brought up in the British tradition of service that was part and parcel of public school education. There was also a tradition of family service that made a career in one or other of the imperial services almost mandatory. *"My family believed in service overseas,"* wrote one colonial officer. In Nigeria the sons of four Governors enlisted as District Officers. But there were others, especially in the army, who were motivated by more pressing financial concerns. Army officers were not well paid at the time, and yet were expected to live in some style. It was quite easy therefore for them to fall into debt. Mostly this was to their bank, but sometimes it was to their tailor since regimental tailors were able at the time to give officers unlimited credit.

The very first generation of British administrators was in fact drawn largely from the ranks of the army or from local paramilitary forces such as the Royal Niger Constabulary. Many had seen service in the Boer War. In the nineteenth century military men were also often selected to serve as Governors of the new colonies in West Africa. The Colonial Office preferred to appoint ex-officers, because it thought that they would be better adapted to life in a hostile and dangerous environment. One prospective Governor in West Africa asked his interview panel whether his return fare would be paid for, and received the somewhat alarming reply that the question had simply not arisen before. In Sierra Leone alone, eight Governors and three of their wives died between 1805 and 1887.

However, by the turn of the century medical science had advanced, and local sanitary conditions had improved substantially. The Colonial Office was therefore able to reverse its recruitment policy. It had progressively become irritated by the ex-military administrators, who had proved not to be ideal bureaucrats, as well as to be incompatible with civil service rules and traditions. A new breed of Governor therefore emerged, who owed their appointment to promotion up the civil service ladder, a process that was usually a combination of seniority and good luck, rather than of talent and qualification. Critically, all new recruits had to undergo a selection process in London.

The British initially did not insist on any specific educational qualifications for the Colonial Service, and recruitment was not done by competitive examination. Indeed, the selection panel was largely one man, the formidable Ralph Furse. Furse was the very incarnation of snobbery and treated the Colonial Office as his personal domain. Legend has it that he even played cricket in the Colonial Secretary's room, bowling from the direction of the great door towards the fireplace as the wicket. Furse had been educated at Eton and revelled in the old public schoolboy network. Indeed, public schools provided over a quarter of those joining the Foreign Office in the 1930s, with a strong bias towards men whom Furse considered to come from what he regarded as *'good stock'*. Preference was also given to outstanding sportsmen and athletes.

However, the overriding considerations for Furse were a man's character and demeanour. Failure to meet the grade could be displayed in a number of ways. The Colonial Office's own *"Appointments Handbook"* stated that:

*"Weaknesses of various kinds may lurk in a flabby lip or in averted eyes, just as single-mindedness and purpose are commonly reflected in a steady gaze and a firm set of the mouth and jaw"*.

Monocles were apparently no impediment to a steady gaze, but Furse took a dim view of *"the spectacled chap"*. His blinkered opinions were shared by many in the political establishment at the time, who thought that the Empire was best managed by well-bred, patriotic chaps, who could strap on their pads and *'play the game'*.

During the Victorian era, many men who volunteered to serve the British Empire were motivated less by the prospect of financial rewards than by a sense of patriotic duty. Some were inspired by the mission of delivering Civilisation and Christianity to the ends of the earth. Colonial service also offered others a unique opportunity to prove themselves to their peers, and to pursue professional careers that might not have been open to them at home. It promised them an extraordinary measure of individual responsibility at an early age, and the freedom to act without the constraints of a more routine job at home. Many were also attracted by the appeal of the great outdoors, and by the seemingly endless opportunities for open air sporting activities such as hunting, fishing, polo, and horse racing. All of these sports became major features of colonial life in West Africa and dominated its social calendar.

Reports of daring deeds in West Africa had also fired the public imagination. The explorations of Mungo Park and the conquest of the Ashanti attracted those with a spirit of adventure. The impact on young minds of the thrilling stories of Edgar Wallace, H. Rider Haggard and G.A. Hendy was also considerable. Equally influential was the *"The Boy's Own Paper"*, which regaled readers with tales of *'derring-do'* in far-flung lands. Rudyard Kipling cast his own particular spell, with his emphasis on service and the need for the rulers of the Empire to endure deprivation, hardship, and danger in strange lands. His vision was that by doing so they would not only give *'backward'* people the blessings of peace and modern government, but they would receive in return a sense of purpose, and perhaps acquire a meaning to their lives that they could no longer find in a humdrum city job in Britain. The majority of administrators lived up to these high expectations, and were industrious, honest, and responsible. But many were at the same time extraordinarily conventional and reactionary, and frequently the most terrible snobs. At home, critics such as H.G. Wells condemned the public schools for producing such a narrow-minded bunch of Philistines, committed only to the defence of the privileges of their class and race.

In the wake of the First World War, many army officers also

sought new careers in the Colonial Service. However, they proved to be poorly suited for the role, and by the 1930s a university degree became a mandatory entry requirement. Selection became exclusive, with recruits generally from the older and more prestigious universities and from the top public schools. British cadets then received one year's training at Oxford, where they were required to pass examinations in Law and African Languages.

The British colonial service was also almost uniformly white, with only a few exceptions. In the Gold Coast, for example, an African Solicitor General held office during the 1930s. But in Nigeria the first black African Assistant District Officers were not appointed until as late as 1951. By contrast, the French recruited on a more open and competitive basis. Entry into their colonial service was normally dependent on passing through the *Ecole Coloniale* (later the *Ecole National d'Outre Mer*), a specialised institution established to train colonial administrators. Yet, despite an ostensibly more open selection policy, very few Africans were appointed by the French, even though provision was made for them to be assimilated as French citizens. In practice, the quality of education offered to Africans in French colonies was so poor that hardly any managed to become assimilated, let alone to enter the dizzy heights of the colonial service.

A major problem for colonial administrators was continuity of employment. District Officers were not allowed to settle in one place, and were quickly moved on to a fresh posting, even if they had spent time learning the local language and studying the local culture. The British did, however, make it a general rule not to transfer an official from one colony to another. The French, on the other hand, systematically posted officials from one part of their empire to another, as well as from one *'circonscription'* to another within the same colony. Indeed, this became such a deliberate policy that it became known in

West Africa as *'rouage'* (a cog in the wheel). Its main object was to prevent officials from becoming corrupt by too close an involvement in local affairs. However, this regular rotation of staff was inappropriate in British territories that were governed by Indirect Rule, since this system required administrators to develop a deep and detailed understanding of their local area. Promotion in the British colonial service was also to some extent dependent on progress made in acquiring a vernacular African language.

A normal tour of duty would last between a year and eighteen months. Due concession was made for the hostile climate in West Africa, and leave allowance was generous compared with other colonies. The ratio was one week's leave for every month's service. Salary conditions varied according to length of service and rank. But a bachelor in a rural posting, drawing all his allowances, could expect to have saved a lump sum by the end of his tour. Married couples were generally less content with their conditions, as they were faced with the cost of bringing up a family, and possibly of maintaining two homes and paying school fees in the UK. The normal age of retirement was 55, but there was an option to retire at 45 in West Africa because of the hardship of the posting. Life insurance was also highly recommended for West African recruits, although this was not paid by the government. One colonial officer later observed that:

*"one of his abiding memories of his year at Oxford before sailing to Nigeria was warding off the salesmen ready to quote terms for the White Man's Grave".*

In the early days, new recruits had to take everything with them - clothing, food and drink, and almost all their furniture. The bulk of the luggage would consist of *'chop boxes'* containing enough supplies to last a full tour of eighteen months. These were generally packed and supplied by firms with such splendid names as Whale and Company and Griffiths McAllister. Nothing was left to chance, and the contents of the boxes were finely calculated in line with the average load of 56 pounds that an African porter was reckoned to be able to carry. A District Officer was entitled to 80 porters during his tour of duty, and therefore eighty loads of 56 pounds in weight.

A typical list of provisions included: 18 four-pound tins of loaf sugar, 36 seven-pound tins of flour, 2 half-pound tins of cloves, 6 half-pound bottles of curry powder, 2 small tins of Oakey's knife polish and three plum puddings. Even as late as the 1950s a cadet heading for Nigeria was advised to be sure that he packed enough marmalade, toilet rolls and saddle soap to last for 15 months, as well as a year's supply of soda-siphon refills. There would also be camp equipment to take, such as a chair, stool, bed with cork mattress, and an ingenious tin bath with a canvas cover in which to keep all toiletries. Other required items included kerosene lamps and mosquito nets. Optional items included wind-up gramophone players and portable lavatory seats. A sporting rifle was also a common purchase.

Clothing would be made to measure, and a record kept by the tropical outfitters to meet a customer's subsequent re-order. The shop assistants would also be able to advise the raw recruit on specialist tropical gear, such as a *'Bombay bowler'*, a white *'Minto pith helmet'* or a khaki *'Cawnpore sola topi'*. Spine pads to protect the back of the neck from sun, and cholera belts to prevent a chill on the stomach, also continued to feature in recommended kit lists up until the 1930s. A lightweight linen suit would be recommended for formal wear. A cadet was not entitled to wear the white Colonial Service uniform until he had been confirmed as an Assistant District Officer, usually after three years of service. No small expense was then involved, since the full uniform came complete with *"Class IV gorgets, white gloves, dress helmet, ceremonial sword and gold bullion knot"*.

On the outward journey to West Africa aboard ship, passengers would automatically split into different groups by their destinations and would eat at separate tables. Everyone was expected to dress for dinner, the men wearing dinner suits, with officers in the Colonial Service sporting cummerbunds of different colours – green for Nigeria, blue for The Gambia, red for Sierra Leone and gold for Ghana. There was little contact between the different groups, and some were even openly contemptuous of each other. Officials going to the North and South of Nigeria in particular would rarely speak to each other. The Northerners were accustomed to a healthy outdoor life of polo and horse riding. They viewed the Southerners as *'softies'*, who were accustomed to be carried around in hammocks. The Southerners were also known to start drinking at six o'clock, whereas the ostensibly more sober Northerners waited until at least six-thirty.

But perhaps the strongest division of all was between the *'first-timers'* or *'first-tour men'* and the *'old coasters'*. The sea passage to West Africa took two weeks, and the coastline that the ship passed had become known as the *'Elder Dempster Boneyard'*, after the leading shipping line. And so, old coasters would take delight in alarming first-timers with chilling tales about life (and of course death) in the *'White Man's Grave'*. Two or three days before the ship reached its final destinations in West Africa, custom and practice was to send a telegram to the ship as it travelled down the coast, which gave advance information on the postings for the new recruits. A list would then be posted on the ship's noticeboard, which would give the old coasters fresh ammunition. The old hands would take turns to unnerve the new boys by offering commiserations on being posted to the *'cholera belt'*, or sympathetic good wishes that they would have a luckier tour than the previous incumbent, who had gone to an early grave. Typically, one Northern Nigerian cadet assigned to the town of Yola was consoled:

*"Oh dear, a punishment station. What did you do wrong on the Cambridge course, old boy?"*

When a new recruit disembarked at his final port, he would only receive a brief orientation course on shore before being be smartly despatched to his station up country. In Nigeria, before the development of a road and rail network, access to the interior would generally be by river on a steamship called a *'stern-wheeler'*. This was later described by Sylvia Leith-Ross, the wife of a British transportation officer, as two sardine tins laid on top of each other:

*"Although this was for official transport only, the lower deck was usually crammed with Nigerian passengers, all dimly related to the crew or fulfilling some obscure nautical function. Women, children, babies, goats, fowls added to the babel...The loads were neatly stacked in separate mounds on the stern-wheeler's upper deck, the deckchairs were put up, the boys brought teapots and the traditional tins of 'Rich Mixed' biscuits, the stern-wheeler shook herself, gave a warning hoot to the clustering canoes, the giant paddle-wheels turned in a welter of yellow foam and slowly we headed up the Niger River."*

The journey to the final destination might take over a week to complete, and when the waters were low it would be necessary to transfer to small steel canoes that could be poled further up-river. For some obscure reason, the captains of stern-wheelers were often from Sweden, which led to the rumour that they were all Counts in the Swedish aristocracy. The pilot happily was always an African expert, who knew the river and could navigate with ease through the seemingly impenetrable labyrinth of mangrove swamps and creeks. But the stern-wheeler was not the most stable of vessels and tended to vibrate alarmingly from bow to stern. It was vulnerable to any sudden change in river current or direction and seemed ready to fall apart whenever a partly submerged tree trunk glanced against the side. The interior of the ship would have seemed suffocating, especially after the bracing sea voyage. Even on deck, any fresh breeze coming from the river would have been stifled by the combined stench of rotting vegetation on the riverbanks and the acrid smell of cooking in palm oil below.

For the new recruit this journey would have been a forbidding entry to the *'dark continent'*, and it would be with considerable relief that he finally arrived at his posting. But although some would be given a warm welcome, others would be flummoxed and unnerved by the cool reception given to them by their District Officers. On arriving at his first station in the Gold Coast, one new recruit was told by his DO, who was so drunk that he could hardly stand up, that *"he had never heard of me and didn't want to."* On plucking up courage the next morning to ask the DO his name, he received the gruff reply:

*"My boy, have no illusions, this is a bloody awful country. The birds have no song, the flowers no smell, and the women no virtue – so don't be bloody starry-eyed."*

## The District Officer

Every province in a British colony in West Africa was sub-divided into districts. Each district was administered by a District Officer, who was supported by a number of Assistant District Officers. Together they supervised a system of dual government, which operated to a greater or larger extent through various forms of local authority. In the Muslim states of Northern Nigeria there was a form of partnership with local emirs, whereas in the pagan regions of Southern Nigeria local chiefs acted in a subordinate role and had to acknowledge the absolute authority of the District Officer. However, whether he had to establish his authority indirectly through negotiation and persuasion, or directly by government mandate, the District Officer reigned supreme. In addition to working in the courts as a magistrate, he was in sole charge of prisons, road building, tree planting, tax collection, trading licences and all matters relating to hygiene and health. As a symbol of this authority, the DO had the privilege of flying the Union Flag on a tall flagpole in his garden, which was formally raised at sunrise and lowered at sunset by a uniformed policeman accompanied by a bugler.

In Northern Nigeria, the British concept of Indirect Rule introduced a system of government whereby all external, military and tax matters were controlled by the British, while almost every other aspect of life was delegated to the local pre-colonial elites who had sided with the British during their conquest. The British colonial administrator had no formal executive role in these so-called *'Native Authorities'*. The District Officer or Resident acted largely as a local consultant and as a watchdog for the central administration. As far as possible, he performed his tasks through the agency of his local Native Authority. His job was to ensure that the administration ran smoothly, that there were no abuses of the system. He was there to offer advice on local government affairs when it was sought, or when he deemed it necessary.

In addition, the District Officer coordinated the administration of the various local authorities under his control and acted as magistrate in cases which did not fall within the jurisdiction of local courts. The Native Authority was largely autonomous and left to its own devices. Its main responsibility to the central administration was the collection of taxes, a certain proportion of which was returned to the local treasury. The great emirs in the north retained their own courts, where customary law was applied, and even had the power to impose the death sentence. Native Authorities had their own police forces and prisons and were similar in operation to local government bodies in Britain at the time. They were also responsible for roads, hospitals, education, water supplies and sanitation. Most important of all, they were the legislative authorities of local government.

This general strategy worked smoothly in areas such as the great emirates of the north of Nigeria, where the emirs remained very much in charge of their peoples, despite a reduction in their powers. The emirs received minimal interference from their District Officers. Even where direct orders had to be given, the British authorities bent over backwards to make them appear as if they had been issued by the emirs themselves. They were the court of last resort and would only accept applications when all other avenues had been exhausted. They remained aloof from the daily routine of government and from the resolution of trivial disputes and reserved their interventions to only the most serious matters of state. As a result, the District Officer was generally held in awe by the local population, and some could be said to have acquired an almost divine status.

However, this policy ran into trouble in the south of Nigeria where societies were not used to direct taxation, or where authority was decentralised or shared between several groups. It led on occasion to riots in protest at the imposition of local tax regimes among both the Yoruba and Igbo groups. The policy had a particularly rough ride in Yorubaland in the south-west. Although the Oba was nominally in charge, decisions were often drawn out by protracted negotiation between a large number of local political factions. The Igbo in the south-east had no actual chiefs, and so willing participants or collaborators were recruited and given 'warrants' to act as local representatives of the British administration among their people. These Warrant Chiefs exercised considerable authority, and their abuse of this power and their lack of traditional authority led to a revolt against them and the British administration in 1929. As a result, the British were forced to abandon the experiment, and tried thereafter to work as best they could through a multiplicity of local political structures, strangely and rather incongruously often basing their decisions on detailed anthropological research of the local communities.

One common attribute shared by all colonial administrators in West Africa was the arrogant belief they knew more about their *'subjects'* than any other Europeans, with the honourable exception perhaps of the local Christian missionaries. Yet the reality was that few ever came close to acquiring the intimate information which gave local African rulers control over their own peoples. In order to address this situation, District Officers were incentivised to learn local languages. It became British government policy that all newly appointed colonial officials should pass a standard language examination within a specified period. Success brought with it an increase in salary, whereas failure could result in dismissal from the service. But it was not easy to become proficient in local languages, with neither the time nor the grammars and dictionaries with which to master them. Moreover, District Officers were regularly re-assigned, as a result of staff shortages, ill-health and gaps caused by home leave. This instability served to discourage colonial officials from learning local languages, despite the bonuses and promotional incentives on offer.

As a result, on the whole colonial administrators had difficulty in understanding Africans and were unable to put across their policies except through interpreters. Since many interpreters were either incompetent or dishonest, it is no great surprise that misunderstandings and injustices were commonplace. This inevitably led to tense relations and occasionally some friction with the local community. Even if a District Officer did manage to master the local language, he still relied for information and local intelligence on African intermediaries.

District interpreters, clerks, and messengers were the backbone of the administration, and were ostensibly reliable individuals. They were usually hand-picked for the job by the District Officer, and often acted as personal servants or bodyguards. But some exploited their District Officer's ignorance to their own advantage and accepted bribes from Africans, who either wanted them to intercede with the District Officer on their behalf, or who threatened to expose local rulers who had something to hide. It was in the interest of these intermediaries to keep the truth from their employees, and there was a stock joke of a white administrator telling a local audience one thing, while his interpreter deliberately mistranslated it to mean something completely different.

To familiarise themselves with their local area, District Officers were also expected to make regular tours. It was thought by senior administrators that a District Officer could only truly get to know his territory by going from village to village, talking to the local people, looking at their crops, and taking their tax census. Sometimes District Officers would complain that excessive bureaucracy kept them pinned to their desks and unable to travel away from their offices. On the other hand, communications up to the end of the 1930s were so rudimentary that officials in distant stations experienced relatively little interference from their superiors. They could simply ignore an instruction by pretending to be away on tour when a message had arrived, in the secure knowledge that no one would be any the wiser.

But the greatest drawback of the job was the isolation and loneliness. The only cure, apart from alcohol, was to keep busy. The main escape route from boredom was to take a tour through the district, *'going to bush'* or *'going on trek'* as it became known. In West Africa, it was customary to travel from one rest-house to another, rarely camping under canvas. In Northern Nigeria, the travelling was mostly done on horseback, accompanied by the emir's representative to act as intermediary.

Since the effectiveness of the District Officer depended very largely on his power to influence and control his Native Authority, a good working relationship with the local rulers was essential. Another important local personality with whom the

DO had to have a good relationship was the African shaman who often had a considerable influence in local villages. But good relations were not helped by the fact that many Europeans were accustomed to using more disparaging terms such as *'witch-doctor'* or *'medicine-man'*.

Nevertheless, after several tours, many District Officers became closely identified with their own districts and inhabitants. Some even began to regard themselves as natives of the district and would stand up for the district against anybody, including the Colonial Governor. Although it was officially frowned on, they would use such terms as *"my district"* and *"my people"*. One or two became so comfortable with colonial life that they even refused promotion to a more senior desk-based position in the Colonial Office back home. One retired DO later obseved in his memoirs that he preferred to be *"sole lord of his inaccessible domain to serving in a more bureaucratic and less individualised post."*

District Officers were therefore very much their own masters. But in their splendid isolation some developed an exaggerated sense of their own self-importance. They resented any direct orders from central government, picked fights with fellow officials, and sometimes even took the law into their own hands. Some were determined to leave their own indelible mark on their territory, and so became obsessed with their own specific enthusiasms such as agriculture, road building, water supplies or health measures, and even, in one case, latrine digging. The District Officer's loneliness and frequent illnesses also sometimes led to erratic or eccentric behaviour. Some even deliberately cultivated an image of being known as 'characters' and gloried in nicknames such as *'Rusty Bucket'*, *'Mr Chat-Chat-Chat'* and *'Marmalade Joe'*. However, the majority of District Officers were weighed down by more serious matters and an immaculate sense of duty to the Crown.

# Keeping The Peace

A prime function of all administrators in colonial West Africa was to maintain law and order in their areas under their supervision. However, the way in which they performed this role differed greatly in the French and British colonies. In French West Africa, an administrator had immense legal authority over the local population, which were regarded as his subjects or *'sujets'*. The *Commandant de Cercle* was free to impose summary punishment for a multitude of crimes, ranging from murder to disrespecting the French nation, its symbols, or officials. The most potent legal weapon possessed by the French administrator was the power of summary imprisonment for up to fourteen days of local Africans under the *Indigénat* legal code. He could also impose fines without trial. In addition, any African accused of what could loosely construed as a political offence could be imprisoned for up to ten years.

In British West Africa, legal powers varied widely from territory to territory. In general, the District Officer was a magistrate and had supervisory powers over the administration of local justice. But in Northern Nigeria the emirs' courts continued to try cases for which there was no right of appeal. Even serious offences, including those involving the death sentence, came before the emirs' courts, and were judged according to sharia law. The colonial administration merely inspected the courts, reviewed cases, and approved appointments. Where District Officers were unhappy with proceedings, they also had the authority to transfer cases to provincial courts, or to suspend sentences. But they had no right to reverse a decision, only to order a retrial

Until 1933, the resident British administrators of Northern Nigeria presided as judges of the provincial courts, which tried cases deemed to fall outside the remit of the customary courts. In 1933, the provincial courts were replaced by magistrates' courts, and the administrators lost their judicial function, although they retained the right to review cases. Under the new system, there was usually a right of appeal from the customary to the British courts. Authority to act as a magistrate came in the form of an official warrant from the Chief Justice of the colony, which was handed over in a ceremony as solemn as a marriage. One Chief Justice in Nigeria offered a new recruit the benefit of his wisdom and experience:

*"When you give your judgements never give your reasons. Your judgements will probably be right, but your reasons will probably be wrong."*

The District Officer had to be judge, prosecutor and defence counsel all at the same time. Very often, without proper legal advice, he was operating in the dark. There was little respect among the African community at large for the majesty of British law. It was standard practice for false accusations to be made, and bribery and corruption were widespread in the courts. One African defendant in a court case in Nigeria is alleged to have asked a European colleague for advice on whether he should send the British judge a gift of six cattle. His friend replied that such a gift would be frowned upon and would certainly lead to him losing the case. The defendant promptly sent the cattle to the judge as a gift, but in the name of his accuser.

The tradition of gift giving was a particularly tricky area, and government officers were instructed to accept any gifts offered to them in case refusal would give offence. But they were required to give back in return a gift of equal value. Faced with this situation, officers took the precaution of taking with them supplies of tobacco or objects suitable for presentation as gifts. In order to discourage this practice, one District Officer in Nigeria took the rather extreme action of publicly burning a £5 note he was offered as a bribe, in order to expedite the issue of a motor vehicle licence.

But perhaps the most serious problem for law officers was the sheer volume of paper involved, which made it almost impossible to comply with the requirements of court procedure. Faced with a mounting backlog of court cases, some officers tended to take a more flexible approach when it came to handling the less serious cases. Written records of such cases were kept to the bare minimum, with only a brief note of the accused's guilt or acquittal recorded.

Another more unpleasant duty was the requirement of district magistrates to witness punishments ordered by the court, perhaps in the form of six or twelve strokes of the cane, but very occasionally the hanging of a condemned man. Such events had to be witnessed in the company of a medical officer: *"to see that all was tidy"*. Assistant District Officers were also frequently appointed as superintendents of the local jail, and in this capacity would be required to see the prisoners turned out to work in gangs every morning and sent off to do various jobs about the station, such as cutting grass, digging ditches, and emptying the *'thunderboxes'* from the bungalows.

A central part of the job of the District Officer was dealing with appeals and petitions on all manner of local disputes. Not only did the law have to be upheld, but public order also had to be maintained. The two most common flashpoints in otherwise peaceful and law abiding districts were disputes between villages or neighbouring tribes over land, and quarrels over succession to chieftainships. In Ghana, the Ashanti tradition was that a chief remained in power only if he retained control over his people. Otherwise, they would find a good reason to *'destool'* him and to find a successor. This inevitably led to intense rivalries between those who favoured retaining their chief in power and those who campaigned to replace him.

Sometimes disturbances of the peace were directed at the government authorities, but often they were conducted in a rather half-hearted manner. Once in Southern Nigeria in the 1920s a large crowd gathered outside the offices of the Lieutenant Governor. When asked what they wanted, they replied:

*"Please, sir, we are riot."*

To which the Lieutenant Governor is said to have responded rather tersely:

*"I'm too busy for you to riot today, you must come back tomorrow."*

At which point, the crowd dispersed and duly turned up the following morning when the dispute was calmly resolved.

## Tax Collection

An equally important role exercised by the administrators was that of tax collector. In all the British colonies in West Africa local African inhabitants were taxed directly by the colonial administration, with the local elite often acting as the regime's intermediaries or agents. However, there did not exist a universal and consistent tax regime that was applied across all the colonies. In some areas of Nigeria local Africans were not taxed until the late 1920s, and in the Gold Coast direct tax was not generally introduced until after the Second World War. Nevertheless, taxation was vital to the colonial economy, not only to cover the cost of administration, but also to finance capital projects such as the building of roads, railways, and ports to facilitate the expansion of trade.

The home countries at the time gave little financial assistance to their colonies, and the modern concept of aid to developing countries did not exist. Development was largely financed either by direct or indirect taxation, or by loans from overseas investors. Direct taxation was never as important as indirect taxes on exports and imports. But direct taxation forced Africans to grow crops for sale, so that they could earn the cash to pay their taxes. It also forced them to work on the farms of white settlers or in mining industries. In the French colonial territories of French Sudan and Upper Volta, where no cash crops were grown, high levels of taxation left local farmers with no option but to abandon their land, and to seek alternative employment in the groundnut fields of Senegal or the cocoa farms of the Ivory Coast.

Another option open to the colonial administrations was to impose forced labour on the local African community. In British West Africa, maintenance of local roads was supervised by colonial officials, but executed by means of compulsory work enforced by the local chiefs. Similar conscription was used in Nigeria up until 1933 for railway construction and other public works projects. In French West Africa, all non-assimilated Africans had to undertake twelve days labour for the colonial administration, which they could redeem for a few francs per day. In addition, French administrative officials could recruit workmen for public works projects in return for a modest payment.

The most common uses of forced labour were on the construction and maintenance of the main arterial roads in a colony, and on large government construction projects where a workforce was difficult to source locally, such as on certain stages in the development of a railway network. In French West Africa, many African soldiers were also conscripted into the French armed forces. The largest compulsory recruitment campaign took place during the First World War, when the French government ambitiously attempted to recruit a black African army of a million men to join its military forces engaged in Europe. In the end, however, it failed to raise anywhere near that number.

In addition to drafting labour for government projects, administrators in some colonies occasionally acted as recruiting agents for white farmers, European commercial companies and mining industries. In Nigeria during World War II, when

Britain was cut off by the Japanese from tin supplies in Malaysia, the colonial administration supported the war effort by mobilising local African workers for the tin mining industry on the Jos Plateau. In French West Africa, the most significant example of compulsory conscription of this kind was in the Ivory Coast, where a large labour force was needed on the European cocoa and coffee farms.

## Daily Life

One seasoned colonial official, Charles Temple, in 1918 painted a rather depressing picture of an administrator's daily routine in Northern Nigeria:

*"In the morning he is called and fed by native boys who are nearly always out of touch with their own people.*

*He goes to work, which is done in pens, ink and paper, or possibly with various tools: in the course of the work he may come into contact with a few native clerks in European clothes or with skilled native artisans, a special class entirely out of touch with the natives generally.*

*He is fed at midday and returns to his work. In the evenings he takes his exercise for the sake of his health with other Europeans. He is fed again and goes to bed.*

*This he does for 365 days and then gets on a steamer and goes home. He spends his leave recruiting his health, occupying his mind with matters as little connected with official duties as possible. This goes on for eighteen years. He retires."*

The Colonial Office back in London was well aware of the debilitating effects of working in the tropics and went to great pains to recruit persons whom they thought could be self-reliant and resilient. In particular, a candidate's athletic records would be scrutinised, as evidence of a healthy and robust character, and as an indication of potential leadership qualities. The objective was not to select the most intelligent or imaginative young men in Britain at the time, but rather men most likely to survive the physical and psychological challenges ahead.

Loneliness and a sense of intellectual isolation were the main hazards. Many young officers would spend months on end in a distant posting unable to converse with anyone else in his native language. Living successfully in the *'bush'* was as much a matter of mental as well as physical well-being. Boredom and loneliness were exacerbated by the oppressive heat and humidity, the ubiquitous insect life and the ever-present threat posed by venomous snakes. To make matters worse, if any man was unfortunate enough to fall sick, there was little in the way of medical support available to him. Doctors and nurses were few and far between, and at best a dentist would make an annual visit. The nearest hospital might be a day's journey away by car, or up to a week away by horseback in those areas where as yet there was no road network.

Official statistics of the officers who had died or were invalided out on colonial service in West Africa, particularly in the early decades of the twentieth century, were a stark reminder to the Colonial Office of the continuing perils of the *'White Man's Grave'*. The principal dangers to health were malaria and sunstroke. The white Europeans were prey to mosquitoes in the evening, even though everybody was still expected to dress formally for dinner and would not have dreamed of doing otherwise. Imperial standards had to be maintained. There were divergent opinions about the best ways to keep healthy, but it was universal practice to take a daily dose of five grains of quinine, usually with a drink at midday just before lunch. If anyone failed to do so and subsequently fell ill, his salary was liable to be stopped.

It was also virtually compulsory to wear a helmet if you made an expedition into the full sun. Another essential item of clothing was a *'spine-pad'*, which was a key part of military kit used by the British Army when on service in hot climates. It was a piece of cloth, often quilted, designed to protect the spine from heat from the sun. Women, on the other hand, were expected to wear a *'double terais'* (two wide-brimmed felt hats placed one inside the other lest the sun penetrate a single layer) and a veil hanging down the back of their necks. For men, the official white uniform had to be worn on special occasions but was otherwise to be avoided at all costs. For the most part, District Officers preferred to wear an open-neck bush shirt, with khaki shorts and stockings up to the knee. They dressed for comfort, rather than to display their office or status. Their white skin was the only badge of office that they felt was required.

Living conditions in the early days of colonial administration in West Africa were rudimentary, with no luxuries and few home comforts. The standard housing was a bungalow shipped out from Britain, and then assembled on site by the Public Works Department using local labour. When the prefabricated building had been assembled, it was then mounted on iron stilts about four feet off the ground for protection from vermin and damp. Standard issue consisted of a line of three square rooms, with a wide veranda all the way round. The house would be served by a number of servants, including a cook, a gardener and, in northern areas, the horse-boys. All servants were called *'boy'* regardless of age.

Water had to be boiled and filtered. Meat had to be eaten almost at once, and was stored in a meat safe, which was a large box with muslin sides suspended from the ceiling. Tinned butter or drinks were kept cool floating in the large earthenware jars in which the water was collected. All food had to be kept away from a wide variety of insect life, with ants being the greatest pests. It is said that the arrival of refrigerators, initially powered by kerosene and then by electricity, did as much to improve the health of District Officers in West Africa as the discovery of quinine as an anti-malarial drug.

Individual postings or stations varied in size, from the well-staffed Secretariat in the capital city to the one or two man headquarters up country, where being out on trek was an almost daily requirement to cover the territory. A typical Divisional HQ would be staffed by the District Officer, perhaps with one or two Assistant District Officers and half a dozen government colleagues from various professional departments. Some of these would be married, and so boost the numbers of the small community of Europeans. In a Provincial headquarters, almost every department would be represented: Education, Police, Engineering, Forestry, Veterinary Science, and Agriculture. There would often be a Medical Officer and a Nursing Sister or Midwife. Besides a Resident, there might be a senior District Officer, one or two other District Officers and several Assistant District Officers.

Towards the end of the colonial era, in the larger District Offices many of the European officials might be married, so that the government community could number between 20-40 Europeans. There would be a thriving Colonial Club that provided a social meeting place for the expatriate residents in the station, as well as a place to talk shop and to iron out any personality or policy disputes. Above all, the club offered facilities for sport and physical exercise, which were thought to be indispensable for a healthy life in the tropical climate. Relaxation after a day's work was a welcome relief from the daily routine. There might be a tennis court or golf course, and in larger stations the opportunity to take part in team sports. In Northern Nigeria, polo was not only played to a high standard, but also allowed the local elite and the District Officers to meet off duty.

However, especially early in their careers, colonial administrators would be posted to more isolated and lonely stations. There recreation and leisure opportunities for District Officers were virtually non-existent. As a result, many would welcome any opportunity to go on tour, where they might take their rifle to shoot game, or explore the local scenery on foot. Otherwise, they would have to be content in the evenings with ambling around their village, viewing a local dance display, or clambering up a nearby hill. Some would fill their time more productively with hobbies such as bird watching or sketching. Others such as Joyce Cary, the author of *"Mister Johnson"*, would write up their experiences either in novels, or in patriotic articles for the popular *"Blackwood's Magazine"*. Another enthusiasm for the more academic-minded was the study of local history, language and anthropology. In most British colonies the shelves of the official library were also full of historical accounts of the founding of the colony compiled by District Officers of that period.

In the early days of colonial rule, there would have been hardly any white women present, and not a single white child. The consequences of this shortage of European female company were predictable, and many officials had an African girl living with them. She would not have meals with the officer and would rarely be seen in the house during the day. She would live in her own hut at the back, along with his servants and the servants' wives, and only come into the house after dark. This practice became controversial, and divided local European opinion. This dilemma for the colonial administration was highlighted by the two *'Secret Circulars A and B'* that were issued by the Secretary of State for the Colonies in 1909. The first circular declared that:

*"It has come to His Honour's attention that a certain number of government officials were living in a state of concubinage with native women and a very serious view would be taken of people living under these circumstances."*

There was an immediate uproar from within government service, and a hurried Circular B was sent round saying:

*"With regard to my last Secret Circular A, it now appears that not such a serious view will be taken of government officials living in a state of concubinage with native women."*

In the main administrative centres, where there were a number of Europeans in residence, and especially where there were wives present, colonial society created its own hierarchy, customs, and codes of conduct. Because the society was small, deviation from the norm was frowned upon. Thus, one French official noted on an official's dossier:

*"Mixes with the natives. Even receives them at table. Not cut out for colonial life."*

Once wives appeared on the scene in the healthier conditions of the 1920s and 1930s, bachelors also had to be more cautious about their relations with African girls. However, one activity which was indulged in without disapproval was excess drinking, even though *"The West African Pocketbook"*, compiled on behalf of the Secretary of State for the Colonies, warned in bold letters:

*"Heavy drinkers should not go to West Africa, moderate drinkers should be very moderate there, and total abstainers should remain so."*

As colonial society developed and wives became a more regular part of the expatriate community, the observation of protocol became of vital importance to those in government service. New recruits in Nigeria would be taken soon after their arrival in Lagos to sign the Governor's Book, the Chief Justice's Book, and the Chief Secretary's Book. Furthermore, on arrival at one's station not only did you have to sign the local Resident's Book, but you had to leave visiting cards at the right addresses within the local European community. Any married couple was to have two cards, but it was not obligatory to drop cards on married men who had not got their wives with them, or alternatively bachelors without wives. But, this custom of dropping and returning of cards was not without purpose, as it resulted in a considerable number of invitations to drinks and dinner.

This overt display of status and seniority was maintained through the medium of the Staff or Civil Service List, known irreverently as the *'Stud Book'*. This listed every official in the territory in order of seniority, together with details of salary, age, qualifications, and present posting. All formal entertaining was largely conducted with the Staff List in mind. The administrators regarded themselves as a cut above the commercial members of the European community, and also looked down on anyone employed in a junior or middle management role within the civilian administration. They were particularly dismissive of the Europeans working in more practical roles such as foremen in the Public Works Department, railway engineers or civil contractors, who were usually out on short term contracts.

## The District Officer's Wife

There was a traditional condition that was known as feeling *'end of tourish'*, whether the tour lasted one year or three. Towards the end of tour most people felt run down, and the only remedy was the generous and extensive period of leave that they yearned for. Not only were the District Officers able to recuperate their health and recharge their batteries, but it was also often during such leaves that the men found, and in due course, married their wives. But in the early years, marriage for colonial officerswas largely discouraged. One of the contractual terms was that one simply could not marry, without first seeking the permission of one's Governor or District Officer. The absence of married quarters was a common excuse for encouraging officers to delay marrying, or at least not to bring their wives with them to the tropics. Other practical considerations were also advanced, such as the need in the early years of a posting to make regular tours into the bush, in order to become familiar with the district.

Wives were in fact officially discouraged right up until the end of the Second World War, when new recruits coming out of the armed forces had been married for several years and could not be expected to abandon their wives. Although they were still expected to ask permission, in practice this was never refused. As late as 1952 the Colonial Office policy, while ostensibly encouraging young officers to take their wives and children with them to their posting, was qualified by a number of caveats such as *"a lack of suitable accommodation for a married man"* or *"the need for extensive travelling in undeveloped areas"*. It was considered that such shortcomings *"may make it undesirable that an officer should be accompanied by his wife and family"*. The normal course of events therefore was for young officers to become engaged after their second or third tour, and to marry on the next leave. This conveniently would often coincide with their promotion from Assistant District Officer to District Officer, so that officers returned to West Africa not only with a new bride but also to take over the adminstration of their first full district.

Not surprisingly quite a few colonial officials married within the tribe, finding their wives from among the sisters of fellow officers, or more typically from among those families where the tradition of colonial service was well established and understood. Such partners knew to some extent what they were letting themselves in for. Even so, the sea passage to West Africa could be a daunting journey in itself, particularly as the new bride's female passengers would relate grim tales and dire warnings of what to expect, and what not to expect, as a District Officer's wife. This was compounded by the arduous journey up-country following disembarkation, and the shock of seeing her new house for the first time. It did not help that some members of the expatriate community would make it crystal clear that a woman's presence was not welcome, and children even less so. One officer in Eastern Nigeria was even accused by his Resident of *"criminal irresponsibility"* in risking having his children in Warri.

There were a number of other challenges facing the new District Officer's wife, and which made it difficult for her to settle in immediately to her new life. There was often little advice on hand as how to behave, and in particular how to pass the time during the long mornings when her husband was away at work. One of the most widely read books in the life of a District Officer's wife was Emily Bradley's *"Dearest Priscilla"*, which attempted to answer all the burning questions that every District Officer's bride was likely to be asking herself on arrival in Africa. In 17 chapters Bradley sought to set out *"all you ought to know about marrying an Empire Builder"*. There were useful tips on servants, what to wear and when, race relations, committees, children, health and living off one's pay. The chapter entitled *"The Silent Partner"* also offered cautionary advice on social occasions, such as:

*"one must never, never talk shop to senior administrative officers who hold the keys to transfers, promotions, leaves"*

*"one of the most difficult lessons for a wife to learn is to know a great deal of what is going on and then forget it."*

Readers were also encouraged to combat loneliness by pursuing a hobby such as gardening or keeping a diary.

In the towns and on larger stations, new wives had an easier and less traumatic introduction to colonial life. Communications improved rapidly in West Africa during the inter-war years, with new ports and harbours constructed along the coast and with better road and rail links into the interior. From 1930 there was even an Imperial Airways service to West Africa. But deep in the *'bush'* on remoter stations, life changed very slowly. There was no refrigeration, no electricity, and no viable means of keeping food fresh for any length of time. There was real excitement, therefore, when the boat train arrived once a fortnight, delivering newspapers and mail from home, and providing perhaps the opportunity to buy fresh butter or real English sausages. Sadly, in general, colonial wives barely adapted their cooking to accommodate local produce, and instead relied on the culinary wisdom of such works as *"Chop and Small Chop: Practical Cookery for Nigeria"* by Norah Laing, wife of the Senior Resident of Zaria in the early 1920s, which studiously ignored all local produce and contained such salutary warnings as:

*"Groundnut oil is at the bottom of a great deal of indigestion."*

When the new European wife arrived at her new home she would meet her local African staff for the first time. For some this could be a culture shock, and there was the additional problem of some workers being reluctant to take orders from a woman. There was also a language barrier to overcome and enormous room for confusion, as many of the staff were relatively untrained. This gave rise to a rich vein of apocryphal stories, which were embellished and exaggerated over time as they did the rounds of the local European community. Patronising and mocking tales would quickly circulate whenever a member of staff made an unfortunate blunder: such as cleaning the family silver with Vim scouring powder; pounding delicate silk underclothes with pestle and mortar; decorating the top of cakes with toothpaste; or commenting on a dropped plate that *"its day had come"*. Yet, despite this undercurrent of racial prejudice and the constant war of domestic attrition between the two cultures, a bond of trust and affection did over time develop between mistress and servants in many households.

Although some District Officer's wives might complain of being cooped up indoors while their husbands toured the countryside, in the larger stations especially there was the compensation of an active social life. This was centred very much on the Colonial Club and the various sporting and social entertainments that were held there. The social calendar for the privileged European community was an endless round of dances, fancy dress parties, amateur theatricals, cricketing weekends, gymkhanas, and polo weekends. In addition, there were private dinner parties and suppers, with their rounds of *'toasties'* and *'small chop'*, and grand weekend luncheons.

There were some wives who never adapted to the climate and conditions, and who were the real casualties of colonial life. Some hated being parted from their children, and to being left alone for long stretches. But for other  wives the most rewarding aspect of their induction to colonial life was becoming involved in their husbands' work, especially the social side. They were more than content to play the role of the first lady of the station, the person to whom other wives would turn in moments of uncertainty or anxiety. They took the lead in official functions and advised on dress and matters of protocol.

It was a standard joke of the time that the most important book of reference in the District Officer's wife's library was the Staff List. This allowed her not only to locate all residents and any visitors in the hierarchy of government, but also guided her on precisely how to lay places at the dinner table. Colonial society considered that a major contribution of a District Officer's wife to her husband's career was to organise in an accomplished manner his entertaining of visitors for lunch or dinner, whether socially on the station or officially for visitors passing through on tour. Indeed, the Colonial Office in London came to regard successful entertaining of a husband's colleagues as a benchmark of success as a District Officer's wife. As one Whitehall mandarin once commented:

*"The woman who could not entertain, could not manage a cook or steward and was not interested in gossip, did not really fit into the scene".*

There were, on the other hand, examples of District Officer's wives who were more independently minded and self-reliant.

In 1907, a year after Sylvia Leith-Ross first arrived in Zungeru in Northern Nigeria as a young bride, she lost her husband from blackwater fever. She had to leave Zungeru after her husband's death, since there was no provision for the residence of white widows in such a distant station. But instead of turning her back on abandoning the land that had caused her husband's death, over the next sixty years she returned there again and again in different capacities. In 1910 she was allowed to return to stay with her brother, who was the District Officer in charge of Muri Province on the Benue River. There she began a study of the language of the Fulani people, which culminated in the publication of a Fulani Grammar in 1919.

Later, Leith-Ross was appointed the first Lady Superintendent of Education in the country. But after a spell in the Education Department of the Northern Provinces she was invalided out in 1931. Undaunted, she returned three years later at the age of 55 to make studies of Igbo women in the aftermath of their riots that had so disturbed the government in 1929. She returned on many more occasions, most notably in 1956 to make a collection of Nigerian pottery at the museum in Jos, upon which she devoted her indomitable energy over the next decade. She left that assignment in 1960, but was to make eight more visits to Nigeria, her last in 1968 at the age of 85. She may not have been a District Officer's wife for long, but she definitely helped to break the mould.

## Class And Prejudice

During the colonial era there was one matter upon which most Europeans could agree: that in their society the African was a second class citizen. Lugard summarily dismissed the notion of equality between African and European with the following spurious argument:

*"However true from a doctrinal point of view, it is apt to be misapplied by people in a low stage of development, and interpreted as*

*an abolition of class distinction."*

He was admittedly a dreadful snob, but his expression of racial superiority was a common presumption. The Europeans segregated themselves from the African community for health reasons, thus reinforcing the feeling of remoteness from it. The Liverpool School of Medicine gave its students the following advice:

*"It is usually very dangerous, and often deadly, to live or sleep in houses occupied, or recently occupied, by natives."*

The French tended to move all Africans out of the centre of towns. The British, on the other hand, established *'Reservations'* or *'Governmental Residential Areas'* on their outskirts. In Hill Station, the European reservation in the Sierra Leone capital of Freetown, no African children were allowed. Each white resident also had to comply with the government regulation that only one African sleep on their compound at night. As a result, colonial officials became detached from any intimate contact with the African, except through their servants. One senior official gloomily concluded:

*"It is a point not to be lost sight of that few Europeans working in a native protectorate are in a position to learn anything about the native population, even though they may spend a lifetime there."*

And yet, perversely, the records and notebooks of many District Officers are filled with detailed anthropological observations on their local communities, which clearly fascinated them at the same time.

With such minimal engagement with Africans, it is not surprising that European attitudes to them were very strange and bore little relation to reality. Some Europeans considered the African degenerate, over-sexed, lazy, dirty, and intellectually inferior. Such ignorant and prejudiced observations can be found ad nauseam in colonial writings, even those of Christian missionaries. One missionary wrote of the *"mental dishonesty, habitual deceit and apparently ineradicable lying"* of one Hausa man he was trying to convert. In similar vein, a colonial wife in Freetown as late as the 1950s felt obliged to make her own ice cream for dinner parties, because:

*"You just can't depend on these people at all. I find it's best to get on with things myself."*

The majority of British administrators believed that colonialism was an instrument of social reform. The ordinary District Officer thought of himself as a kind of adult prefect, dedicated to a noble career of service in the reform and improvement of his inferiors. Africans were like children and had to be helped slowly to climb the ladder of civilisation. The role of colonial officials was to ensure that the natural evolution of Africans took place with minimal interference, and of course at a manageable pace. Such trusteeship notions were also linked with racial stereotypes prevalent at the time. Racial categories came to be widely applied in Africa. The so-called *'higher'* races arrogated to themselves a kind of aristocratic status, but all members of the race supposedly shared in its virtues by reason of their common descent, rather than by individual merit.

Such notions went hand in hand with the equally prejudiced view that Africans needed protection from exploitation by lower class Europeans, such as traders, mechanics, farmers or entrepreneurs, men whose living depended on their ability to profit from selling their goods or labour. The ambition and drive of these *'commercial johnnies'* was viewed with suspicion by colonial officials, who often shunned their company and excluded them from social events on the station. British colonial officials were equally disdainful of the *'educated native'*. They had a particular dislike for the *'mission boy'*, whom they regarded as arrogant, self-important, and bent on success at all costs.

Lugard was even more bigoted, and absurdly claimed that Europeanised Africans were *"less fertile and more susceptible to lung trouble and other diseases."* In 1909, an official committee of enquiry into the liquor trade in Southern Nigeria roundly condemned the heavy drinking of Christianised local rulers and concluded that they must have learned *"the bad habits of the lower class of Europeans"* in mission schools. The world of the District Officer and his wife had become a closed community, deeply suspicious of anyone whom they perceived to be beyond the pale, and paranoid about the steady erosion of their previously unchallenged and superior status in society.

District Officers were not only the key figures of the colonial regimes, but they and their wives also served as models or reference points in matters of dress, etiquette and behaviour not only for other Europeans, but also for aspiring middle class Africans, often with sad results. They were the last group of Europeans to be replaced by Africans, and with independence they were swept away entirely. While some Europeans continued to serve as Permanent Secretaries in Ministries, or as senior officials in the central administration and technical services of government, African governments could not tolerate the continued existence of *'bush administrators'*. They were, after all, the symbolic representatives of the colonial regimes.

And yet retired colonial adminstrators would claim with some passion that they were also the loyal servants of Empire, who devoted their careers and risked their health and well-being in its cause. The concept of dedicated service is a prominent theme of their diaries and memoirs. It is also reflected on the memorial plaque in Westminster Abbey erected to honour those who represented the crown in colonial territories. The simple inscription reads:

*"And whosoever will be chief among you,*
*let him be your servant."*

The majority of British administrators were fiercely proud of what they managed to achieve in challenging and sometimes perilous conditions. Yet in the final analysis they may have left a far weaker imprint on the local population than the agents of European businesses or the many European medical, technical, and agricultural specialists in government departments, whose commercial enterprises and development schemes substantially changed African life and the prospects for the local economy to develop. Nor did the white administrator arguably have the same personal impact on the indigenous population as the average European missionary or teacher.

# 14  THE SUPPORTING CAST

*"The wealth of a territory depends not only on the riches of its soil, but also on the character and well-being of its people. The promotion of better nutrition, better health and better standards of education is as important, therefore, for the development of our Colonial Empire as the building of new roads or the introduction of new crops."*

In the early history of the colonies in British West Africa, some consideration had been given by the Colonial Service to the need for effective transport, communication, education, and medical care. However, the emphasis was always on command and control, rather than on development. Railways were built to promote agricultural or mineral exports, or to facilitate the movement of soldiers and policemen. Major roads were laid out to assist the military and administrative arms of government, as well as to promote trade and the marketing of crops. Post Offices, telegraphs and telephones gradually formed communication networks that helped to tie together various administrative units of the colony. Printing departments or government printers became responsible at an early stage for the publication of laws, ordinances, and regulations. Agriculture, forestry, and livestock all required their own administrative arrangements, and government also had responsibility for the essential work of providing surveys. Teachers and lecturers were needed to populate the burgeoning number of secondary schools and the virgin university campuses. Doctors and nurses also had to be recruited to staff the fledgling health service.

In each colony, therefore, there were hundreds of specialists, male and female, in Agriculture, Forestry, Medicine, Veterinary Science, Nursing, Education and Police. Their contribution to development was in many ways more appreciated at the time by the local peoples, and more long-lasting in its impact, than the work of the colonial administrators. Before the Second World War, they had largely been treated as bit-part players by the colonial administration. But the Colonial Development and Welfare Acts of 1940 and 1945 brought them into centre-stage. The Acts signaled a dramatic shift in British government policy and a belated commitment to the development of its colonies, rather than to their control and exploitation. And so, in the 1950s Britain attempted to expand rapidly its development schemes, for which the foundations had been laid in the early part of the century by a band of committed and dedicated pioneers. Up until that point, their achievements had largely been unheralded, and their projects had been substantially underfunded.

## Public Works

Among the first government units to be set up by the colonial authorities were the Public Works Departments. These were responsible for the construction of the new colonial infrastructure, including government buildings, roads, railways and bridges. Within each department there would normally be a number of specialist sections responsible for areas such as transportation, distribution, mail services, water supply and electricity. The most labour intensive of these was Transport. Given the prevalence of disease, animal carts could rarely be used successfully. So, both traders and administrators were forced to rely on human porterage. Porters remained indispensable until the advent of the railways and the development of minor roads. The largest transport operation in West Africa was the Gold Coast Transport Department, which started life as a transfer company, employing gangs of porters to take supplies inland. At its peak, it had a permanent staff of four Europeans, supported by a larger team of locally recruited clerks, mechanics, drivers, and messengers, as well as around 300 porters. Illness, death, or promotion caused frequent changes in the European staff.

The introduction of railways at the beginning of the twentieth century initiated a period of radical change. The development of an extensive road and rail network transformed the economies of the larger British colonies of the Gold Coast and Nigeria. In the Gold Coast, it opened up the main gold fields to exploitation. When the railway line from the port of Sekondi to Tarkwa in the north of the country was completed in 1903, its construction was primarily driven by the need to provide labour for the gold producers in the remoter areas of the territory that had previously been served by road. At the same time, it facilitated water transport, transferred mail to and from railway stations, and supplied porters to commercial companies and local river boat services. But, although the construction of the railway was primarily instigated by mining interests, it did serve the subsidiary purpose of improving military communications with the recently subdued Ashanti region. This combination of economic and political considerations led to the extension of the line to Kumasi in 1909.

Similarly in Nigeria the railway built from Port Harcourt on the coast to Enugu in the east of the country accelerated the exploitation of Nigeria's coal deposits. This line was later extended to the tin mining area of the Jos Plateau in the north. As a result, supplies as well as mining machinery could be transported swiftly up country. The distribution of other natural resources such as timber could also be expedited. In the cocoa and palm oil plantations, the improved roads increased the productivity of the local workers by enabling them to roll the produce over the surface in round barrels, and at a later date for consignments to be delivered even more quickly to the ports by trucks and truck drivers.

The construction of the railways was in itself a major technical achievement, as all the building material had to be imported from abroad. They were often constructed in remote locations and over difficult terrain. The problems of tropical forests, bad weather, and harsh living conditions took their combined toll on the health and well-being of Europeans employed to manage the projects. As a result, Europeans on the railways were commonly engaged for shorter tours of service than their counterparts in government administration. But, although railway officials did not have the same social standing as District Officers, their compensation was that they were generally better paid. The Nigerian Railway became a major employer of African labour, and at its peak had nearly as many senior and middle grade officials as an entire district administration. By 1917, in addition to 124 European managers, it employed over 800 African technicians, foremen, interpreters and junior administrators, as well as almost 18,000 labourers.

As the road and rail network developed, investment in the local industries were expanding at the same pace, leading to a major increase in the numbers of European managers and local labourers they employed. By 1911, it is estimated that a total of 19,000 men were working in the mines on the Gold Coast, and the booming cocoa industry had an estimated workforce of 185,000 people. Several thousand labourers were also required for a growing number of government construction projects. At the same time new skilled jobs developed to support the sawmills, brick and tile factories, processing plants and other light industries that were springing up around the railway terminal at Sekondi on the coast. In Nigeria too export trade in coal, tin, cotton, and groundnuts was stimulated by the railways, and the export of palm oil and palm kernels, cocoa and hides was vastly expanded.

## Agriculture

Opening the export market for tropical goods was a major

stimulus to agricultural development and technical change in West Africa. Colonies which failed to develop an export crop or a mining industry remained poor and relatively under-developed. Cheap transportation facilitated the rapid development of tropical export markets, as sailing ships were replaced by the faster steamships that carried three or four times as much cargo. Macgregor Laird's development of a small, shallow-draft steamboat revolutionised river transport and opened up the Gambia, Niger and Senegal river valleys to economic development.

The newly industrialised cities of Europe began to clamour for tropical African export crops, such as cocoa, coffee, tobacco, groundnuts, sisal, rubber, palm kernels and oil. African societies, spurred on equally by missionaries, commercial concerns, and colonial governments, responded to this demand by increasing their cultivation of export crops. The period from 1880-1913 was especially productive. Gold Coast exports grew from £0.4 million in 1882-4 to £5.4 million in 1913, an average growth rate of 9 per cent. Southern Nigeria's economy expanded even faster, with exports rising from £1.6 million in 1899 to £7.1 million in 1913, an average yearly increase of 12 per cent.

Export crops created a net surplus in farming output, and in general food cultivation kept pace with population growth. A glaring exception to this pattern was the French colony of Senegal, where the cultivation of groundnuts led to a decline of food supplies and to the need to import the basic staple of rice. However, it proved difficult in the longer term to increase the productivity of agricultural systems that were traditionally based on shifting cultivation. It was difficult to collect, process and transport produce grown on small plots for only a year or two. Agricultural improvement was also not easily achieved on communal land. Plant and soil diseases further slowed down development.

The British Colonial Office gave little financial support to agricultural research in its West African colonies before 1895. It occasionally issued a circular on a subject such as animal husbandry, but by and large the initiative was left to local officials. Some tried to introduce new crops, or to encourage local agriculture by supplying seeds and seedlings, grading produce, and opening new markets. But with limited resources at their disposal, their efforts had little effect. Some Christian Missions also tried to introduce improvements in farming methods. One of the most significant early projects was based in the Gold Coast, where the Basel Mission set up an agricultural station at Akropong, and cocoa from the Caribbean was grown for the first time.

However, in the early colonial period, although there were some experiments with new crops, little effort was made to alter traditional agricultural practices. Only gradually were specialist Agriculture Departments established that would begin to revolutionise farming methods. Thereafter, although use was still made of traditional farming methods, a number of significant technological innovations were introduced, such as ploughs, fertilisers, crop rotation, and irrigation. Experimentation in the cultivation of new crops was also accelerated. In general, local African farmers responded well to such initiatives and adapted to a variety of new crops, including maize, manioc and tobacco. They also helped to develop an extensive export trade in cocoa, groundnuts, and palm kernels.

It was the pioneering work of early botanists that would play a major part in developing economic cash crops in West African colonies. Botanical gardens in countries in other parts of the British Empire, such as Singapore and Sri Lanka, came to the assistance of African territories, not only by supplying new crops and seedlings, but also by providing training for agriculturalists. However, the most influential institutions were the Royal Botanical Gardens at Kew and the Imperial Institute in

London. They were at the forefront of training colonial staff, supplying the colonies with advice and plants, and carrying out investigations into the qualities and possibilities of tropical products. Cotton and tobacco were given their start in many West African countries as a result of their research. Moreover, whenever minerals were found in any colony, they would send out experts to survey and examine the deposits. This professional support gave birth to the tin mining and coal mining industries in Nigeria.

However, the problems of operating at a distance and of addressing the wide variety of local needs ultimately persuaded the colonial administrations that they would need to set up their own technical and scientific units. And so, from the 1890s onward colonies in West Africa began to develop their own experimental farms and botanical gardens. They recruited and appointed their own management teams, although initially the majority of them had been trained in England. Senior staff were also expected to travel extensively, in order to advise farmers in their villages on the most suitable approaches to adopt in their own locality.

This research was accelerated under Joseph Chamberlain, who realised that the development of new crops and resources would provide new wealth to the indigenous peoples, open markets to British industrialists, supply more jobs to British workmen, and provide colonial governments with useful additional revenues. Shortly afterwards, in order to coordinate the various initiatives, the Colonial Office created the post of Superintendent of Agriculture in British West Africa. Thereafter the main focus for agricultural development in the region would be on cotton, cocoa, palm oil, and jute.

As part of this effort, the British Cotton Growing Association was formed in 1902 to develop cotton production within the Empire, so that British textile companies would be less dependent on American supplies at a time when prices were escalating. The association was a private enterprise, founded by the shipping magnate Sir Alfred Jones. Its aim was to increase cotton acreage by providing seed, lending money and tools to cultivators, and then buying back the crop and providing ginning facilities. The result was that cotton production in the British colonies, including West Africa, doubled between 1906 and 1913. Efforts to establish cotton failed to a large extent in Sierra Leone and the Gambia, but the crop took hold in Northern Nigeria and the Northern Territories of the Gold Coast. Overall West African exports of cotton tripled from £1.5 million in 1905 to £4.5 million in 1913.

In 1902, the Southern Nigerian Protectorate set up its own Agricultural Department, followed by the Gold Coast in 1903, Lagos in 1904, and Sierra Leone in 1906. In Nigeria a succession of Governors promoted the experimentation and testing of plants to demonstrate their economic potential and viability. Local farmers were supplied with seed, seedlings and saplings from the colony's own botanical gardens and experimental farms. Plants and cattle were imported from the Caribbean, and American experts in cotton growing and stock management were invited to come to Lagos. There were also experiments with jute, castor oil, bananas, maize, and groundnuts. However, not every experiment prospered, and there were some notable failures such as tobacco, mangoes, tropical spices, and firewood plantations.

In addition to developing new export crops, colonial officials planted new trees, in an attempt to conserve and develop forest resources. Deforestation had become a serious problem and continued to gather pace. Forest reserves urgently needed to be demarcated and then protected for development. The first step was usually to recruit men to guard the forests. Surveyors then marked out the areas to be covered by the proposed forest reserves, which allowed forestry experts to undertake controlled experiments with different tree varieties. Nigeria appointed its first Conservator of Forests in 1905, and Sierra Leone set up a Forestry Department in 1912. A number of colonies experimented with rubber trees, and by 1912 rubber plantations in the Gold Coast and Nigeria had replaced wild rubber.

However, these colonial innovations in agricuture have to be reviewed in the context of the long term impact they had on the local people and their environment. The imperial ambition of the colonial powers was impelled to a large extent by an economic drive to increase European profits and markets. Initially, this was accomplished through the uprooting of people to satisfy the global market for slave labour. But subsequently the focus switched to the extraction of natural resources to fuel the engine of Industrial Revolution in Europe, and to feed the growing appetite of European consumers.

In agriculture, the most significant negative impact of colonialism was the overemphasis on single cash crop production. This was compounded by the fact that the plantation systems introduced by the colonial regimes were unsustainable and seriously degraded the environment. Cotton in particular severely reduced soil fertility in areas of West Africa that were dominated by cotton plantations. Local farmers found themselves unable to switch to more profitable crops, or even to produce food because of the depleted soil. The rural economies of many West African countries are still affected by this negative legacy of the colonial era.

## Medicine

The new developments in agriculture attracted a volunteer army of British and European physicians, veterinarians, foresters, and botanists. The most pressing problem that had faced all white pioneers throughout the history of colonial West Africa had been how to preserve their own lives, and health conditions at the end of the nineteenth century remained grim. In 1898, an article in the Lagos Standard pulled no punches:

*"There is no doubt that something should be done to relieve the grave-diggers from the strain of work to which they are constantly subjected. The demand of a constantly increasing death-rate, which has caused the cemeteries to be enlarged, makes it necessary that the number of grave-diggers should be increased. No holidays. At it from 6 am to 6 pm, every day, Sundays included, for the Grim Reaper is ever busy."*

Sadly, this was no exaggeration as the official statistics for the period show. During the 1890s it is recorded that almost a third of the 150 Europeans living and working in Lagos died over a 15 month period, and in Accra almost a quarter of the 200 resident Europeans died in 6 months. Moreover, there was still a considerable time lag between breakthrough medical discoveries and their practical application. As late as 1907, when the root causes of malaria were identified and well known, many communities in West Africa still suffered heavy losses.

The medical revolution in West Africa dates only from the turn of the century. The service was initially quite small, and most were doctors from the Royal Army Medical Corps, recruited to support the military on their campaigns. In 1864, there were no more than 35 army doctors in all the scattered forces in West Africa, including some Africans, mostly graduates of Edinburgh University. And so, in 1902 Joseph Chamberlain invited a Scottish physician Patrick Manson to reorganise these disparate medical services into a single body, the West African Medical Service.

It is a sign of the racial attitudes prevailing at the time in Britain that the local African doctors were at that point summarily dismissed from the service. In Sierra Leone, even the Chief Medical Officer, Dr Renner, was replaced purely on the basis of his African parentage. This flagrantly racist policy was linked in part to the military expansion into Northern Nigeria. The crude argument of the military top brass was that, since Europeans clearly could not be expected to serve under the orders of Africans, African doctors could not permitted to participate in military expeditions.

The first duty of a Medical Officer in colonial West Africa was to look after the welfare of the administrative officials, policemen, soldiers, prisoners, and labourers in government employ. He had to travel long distances to cover his district, and at the same time to supervise a clinic staffed usually by an African pharmacist and hospital attendant. Station duties were diverse and included treating a wide variety of diseases, organising vaccination campaigns, compiling meteorological observations, enforcing sanitary precautions, attending executions, and responding to the constant stream of demands from the Secretariat for accounting and other records.

On tour in his district, the Medical Officer, like the District Officer, travelled by horse, hammock, bicycle, or foot. He was expected to attend sick people, carry out vaccinations, supervise local hospitals, and sometimes supervise the evacuation of villages in areas stricken by an outbreak of disease, particularly of *'sleeping sickness'*. Sleeping sickness is a widespread tropical disease caused by parasites transmitted by infected *'tsetse'* flies, which remains endemic in 36 sub-Saharan African countries. Between 1921 and 1956, French colonial governments organized medical campaigns to treat and prevent sleeping sickness. Villagers were forcibly examined and injected with medications with severe, sometimes fatal, side effects.

But perhaps the most important work of the Medical Officer was not in curative medicine, but in rural sanitation. In the larger towns and cities the first successes in improving public health were also in preventative medicine. The British colonial administrations in Lagos, Accra, and Freetown all established Public Health Departments to enforce new regulations in sanitation, water purification and epidemic control. From 1900 to 1944, public health was a pillar of the French colonial project in French West Africa.

The Governor of the colony in Lagos, Sir William Macgregor, established the Lagos Board of Health and made it an immediate requirement that all hygiene courses in schools should be delivered by trained Medical Officers. He also set up a Ladies League to work with local children. But his greatest contribution to improving public health was to provide funds to reclaim the Lagos swamps and to dig a drainage canal across the island on which the city was built. At about the same time, after a major epidemic in the Gold Coast in 1908, another Scottish medical expert, William Simpson, was commissioned to conduct a detailed survey of sanitary conditions across the whole of British West Africa. His investigation revealed that the only towns with a public water supply were Freetown and Calabar. The rest of the urban centres depended on shallow wells, water-holes, ponds, rain barrels and tanks. As a result of his report, improvements were gradually introduced to local water supply systems, in order to prevent the spread of dysentery and other diseases.

At first, despite their enthusiasm and expertise, little progress was made by Medical Officers and their staff in the struggle against endemic infection. Sadly, the majority of the tropical diseases that they came across were as yet incurable. Quinine was available to treat cases of malaria, but doctors could do little for such illnesses as dysentery, typhoid, or sleeping sickness. Medical Officers were still relatively few in number, and it did not help that they were prone to be moved frequently from one district to another. Nevertheless, pay in West Africa was reasonable, and with wise management of his finances a man could save enough money in a few years to buy a small medical practice back in Britain. Life in the nursing services had no such rewards. Nurses from Britain needed an almost missionary sense of vocation, since the hospitals in the pre-war years were often primitive, and the work could invariably be hard and poorly remunerated.

At the beginning of the twentieth century, scientific and medical advances began to bring substantial improvements to working practices, and critically led to the development of new and effective treatments for tropical diseases. By 1914, progress had been made in identifying the underlying causes of malaria, which led to improved sanitation and other public health measures. Another major breakthrough came when smallpox vaccination became widely available in all the colonies. In the inter-war years, the successes of medical research multiplied, and happily more and more of West Africa's endemic diseases could be brought under control.

## Engineering And Surveying

Engineers were fundamental to the expansion of the British and French Empires in West Africa. Railway lines in particular transformed the infrastructure of the colonies, and gave the colonial administrations new levers of power. They were built primarily to exercise *'effective control'* in the Scramble for Africa, or to dispatch troops for better control of the local population. But, operating within limited budgets, the colonisers also expected railways to pay for themselves. Routes were therefore designed, not just with a military objective in mind, but also as part of a general plan to connect European trading companies on the coast to the rich agricultural areas and mineral deposits in the interior. Major roads and ports were also constructed to link the various parts of a colony to the outside world. At a more local level, engineers worked alongside District officials to put up bridges and dams, clear creeks and rivers, and construct irrigation channels. These allowed men and goods to move more easily and safely across the region, and to expand further the growth and sale of export crops and natural products.

Most of the work was done in the *'bush'*, the tropical rainforest, the mountains, and the desert areas. This meant having to endure months of isolation, living on short and often monotonous rations while camped in remote locations. Initially, living conditions in West Africa for European engineers in the field were tough. Disease was rife, and death was an ever-present threat. The majority succumbed to one form of fever or another, and most became heavy drinkers to alleviate their anxiety. Anyone who drank less than a bottle of whisky in a day was regarded as a rank amateur. The frequency of disease was hardly surprising, as stagnant mosquito-ridden pools were everywhere. The drinking water was foul, and therefore required filtration and chemical treatment. Thankfully living conditions gradually improved, and by the outbreak of the First World War engineers in West Africa could look forward to a reasonably healthy life and an income on a par with officers in the colonial army.

Victorian engineers were a diverse group. There were several routes to reaching the top of their profession, with opportunities for men from the workshop as well as a more academic background. But at the same time there was a well-established social and professional hierarchy. Some engineers were from British universities, particularly from Cambridge, and therefore from the upper ranks of Victorian society. Others were recruited from the Royal Military Academy at Woolwich, which gave opportunities to bright youngsters from aspiring middle class families. However, both groups considered themselves to be gentlemen rather than experts, and so deserved to be accepted into the colonial establishment. Indeed, several engineers graduated through the ranks to become Governors of colonies, such as Percy Girouard a Canadian engineer who played a leading role in the construction of the railway network in Nigeria, and Gordon Guggisberg, another Canadian-born British Army officer, who masterminded the development and extension of railways in the Gold Coast.

Engineers' duties were extremely varied, as they could find themselves deployed in the engineering branches of Post and Telegraph Departments, on the Railways, or in the Public Works Departments. The full range of their responsibilities included the building of roads, bridges, railways, public buildings, communications networks, and water works. Engineers were also in demand when the Colonial Office began to commission mineral surveys to encourage private investment in the emerging mining industries of various colonies. The task of mapping and surveying the target areas was an immense challenge, as the engineers had to travel across largely hostile and uncharted territory. Surveyors had to proceed with caution and to take the necessary precautions against the combined threat of insects, disease, and wild animals. But there were other less predictable hazards. On one unfortunate occasion, when a team of surveyors was working in the Cross River region of Nigeria, a local policeman on patrol to protect them suddenly ran amok in their camp. He proceeded to kill seven people, to injure several others with a machete, to slaughter all the camp animals, and to burn all the expedition's supplies and equipment.

There were also more mundane administrative issues to contend with. Some of the more complex surveys were difficult to negotiate and fraught with competing claims over land ownership. Timber and gold concessions in the Gold Coast became a major battleground, as *"The Aborigines Protection Society"* vigorously fought the colonial government to protect African landholdings. In order to cut down the number of boundary disputes, in 1900 the Colonial Governor, Matthew Nathan, initiated the process of surveying and mapping the entire mining area of the Gold Coast. This was no mean task for the European survey teams to accomplish, as they were unaccustomed to working in the stifling heat of the dense tropical rain forest. Without any medical support, they were also prey to the endemic diseases of malaria and blackwater fever. They could only dose themselves up with quinine and hope for the best. The life of a District Officer was snug by comparison.

In 1907, up to 40 European engineers were engaged on the mapping exercise, backed by a large team of about 700 African workers recruited from the local population. Despite their combined efforts, they could only manage to cut a path through the forest at the rate of one mile a day. In addition, the European engineers were only able to operate in the dry season from October to May, and were forced to return home to Britain in the rainy season. Nevertheless, by 1914 about 10,000 square miles of the Northern Territories had been mapped, and nearly 150 concessions and 10 towns had been surveyed.

## Education

The British government transferred the British educational system virtually unchanged to their colonies, but avoided interfering directly in its implementation. As public education in Britain had largely been pioneered by church bodies, the Colonial Office was happy to leave the early development of education in West Africa in the hands of the Christian Missionary Societies. As these varied enormously in their financial strength and their educational know-how, the result was that schooling developed in an uneven manner. This was not helped by the fact that each Missionary Society held sway over its own territory and showed little interest in exchanging ideas with colleagues in neighbouring areas or from other religious denominations.

Although missionaries in West Africa believed that education was an integral part of their mission, their priority was always to covert the local people to Christianity. In any event, most mission societies were not wealthy, and so could not support as many schools that they might have liked to. Consequently, with limited government support, most African children did not go to school during the colonial era. In fact, at the end of colonial rule, no colony could boast that more than half of their children finished elementary school, and far fewer attended secondary school.

Missionaries were convinced that the ability of African people to read the Bible in their own language was fundamental to the conversion process. They thought that basic skills in literacy and numeracy would be of little value to the local African children and their families. Many local farming communities even objected to sending their children to school, since their services would then not be available for domestic tasks such as herding livestock or weeding crops. Those African children who did go to school usually did not remain long enough to profit from their training, so that only a small percentage of those who stayed in class managed to progress beyond elementary level. Another issue was that pupils in remote village schools often had to receive their instruction from poorly trained African teachers, some of whom who were barely more knowledgeable than themselves. Standards therefore remained low, and even as late as 1927 in the Gold Coast less than 20 per cent of candidates were able to pass the civil service examination for African clerks, even if on occasion some students had managed to get their hands on the questions in advance.

Even when standards began to improve, the curriculum naturally reflected the background and interests of the British teachers and clergymen, rather than the varied cultures of their pupils. Later, when the British government attempted to introduce more practical courses, educated African parents objected that their children were deliberately being given a second-class education and being consigned to a subordinate role in society. They were opposed to the introduction of vocational and technical courses, because they believed that their children would be better paid and would have greater job opportunities with a more academic education.

The colonial administration also did not want a large class of semi-educated Africans dependent on the state for employment. Public funds dedicated to Education therefore remained low, and the burden continued to be passed to the Missionary Societies. As late as 1899 in Nigeria only 33 of the 8,154 primary schools, 9 of the 136 secondary schools, and 13 of the 97 teacher training colleges were government run. Similarly, in 1914 the colonial government of the Gold Coast was responsible for only 8 per cent of the schools. A mere £25,000 was allocated to so-called Native Education from a total government budget of almost £1.2 million.

And so, in the early days of colonial rule it is fair to say that the support for Education by colonial governments was driven more by practical considerations than by any enlightened ideas. There was only a limited demand at the time for educated and skilled workers, and so there was little pressure to expand the school systems. Indeed, Governor Hugh Clifford in the Gold Coast expressed serious reservations about the value of any secondary school education for Africans. He believed that primary schools could perfectly well provide the basic education that local craftsmen and farm workers required, and they were the kind of workers that the colony needed most. In his opinion, secondary schools only produced puffed-up 'black Englishmen', whom he suspected might in future have the audacity to challenge the colony's right to exist. In that regard, his judgement would prove to be correct.

Even though there were only a limited number of schools and training programmes for African children, they still turned out more skilled people than could be readily absorbed into the workforce of the various British held territories. Sierra Leone for many years saw its educated men move away to take jobs up and down the West African coast. Even a rapidly developing colony such as the Gold Coast had to export some of its skilled labour. Gradually, however, colonial governments began to realise that public funds would have to be used to supplement the limited resources of the church mission, and that African education was essential to the conduct of the administration. They started to subsidise missionary education and to appoint inspectors to enforce minimum standards. In addition, a number of government schools were opened to plug gaps in the missionary network.

By 1914, nearly all colonies had their own Education Departments, and the general pattern of education began to follow a set formula. A certain degree of uniformity was guaranteed by the common British educational background and by the British examination system for matriculation in the universities in England. Each colony, however, ran its schools more or less as local authorities saw fit. Policy was set by a Board of Education, and there were also local education boards to advise schools on problems in their own areas. Missionary schools continued to exist alongside government established schools and received some financial assistance. The development of colonial education began to follow a consistent pattern, but each territory proceeded at its own pace.

In the early period of colonial rule, the Sierra Leone education system was the most advanced in West Africa. Fourah Bay College, founded in 1827, provided higher education for the local elite, with a curriculum devoted to Theology and the Arts. In 1896, a school for technical education was opened, where local artisans were given free courses in the building trades. A teacher training college was also established in 1900 to supply qualified teachers to mission-run schools. Later the colonial administrators also needed educated African support staff to help run the so-called *'Native Administration'*. And so, a government school for sons of chiefs or their nominees was opened in 1906 at Bo in a remote area of Sierra Leone. The philosophy of the school was that labour was as important as reading, writing and arithmetic. So, students were given only the basics of an English education, with practical training in farming, carpentry, bridge-building, road-making, and surveying. European dress was forbidden, and the pupils lived outside the school compound in *'towns'* of round huts, each with a plot of land to cultivate.

In Nigeria, the government operated a dual system that reflected the divided nature of British policy. In Southern Nigeria, the government encouraged missionary work and subsidised a number of mission schools. These were supplemented by a number of government schools. European style education began with the arrival of the Wesleyan Christian missionaries at Badagry in 1842, and soon after about ten different Christian Missions had arrived and begun intensive missionary and educational work. A large number of primary schools were built by the different missions, and such was the competition that in some places the missions struggled for pupils. Most of the Christian Missions initially established primary schools only, and little attention was paid to secondary and higher education. But following representations from influential church members, rich businessmen and expatriates living in Lagos, the CMS Grammar School Lagos was established in 1857, and other secondary schools soon followed.

From 1882, the colonial government in Southern Nigeria became more directly involved, and introduced a raft of new regulations, guidelines and policies on the organisation and management of schools. The government also began to appoint inspectors and to make grants to schools to ensure quality. Higher Education in Nigeria started with the opening of Yaba Higher College English in 1932, which subsequently transferred to Ibadan, becoming University College, Ibadan in 1948. English was the natural choice as the language of instruction in these institutions, since their prime objective at the time was to help their students achieve the formal qualifications that would give them access to white collar jobs in government or commercial firms.

Western-style education developed faster in the South than in the North of Nigeria because of the scepticism of the Muslim areas about the impact of Christian missionary education. In 1914, it was estimated that there were about 25,000 Koranic schools already in existence all over Northern Nigeria. Unsurprisingly, therefore, the arrival of Christian education met stiff opposition. Missionary enterprise in the North was restricted mainly to the non-Muslim areas. There was some hostility too from British officials, who looked down their noses at educated African Christians for their humble origins and with their egalitarian ideas. Officials also feared that missionaries might provoke Islamic resistance and thereby start a holy war.

The colonial government's educational policy in the North also reflected Lugard's own prejudices. In his opinion, mission schools produced graduates who lacked integrity, self-discipline and respect for authority. He believed that the instruction that they received there led them to disrespect their elders, and to develop a deep-seated unwillingness to work on the land. In his view, local educational institutions would be better modelled on the example of the British public boarding school, where boys would be trained in character, play outdoor sport, and learn how to exercise authority in the manner of a  school prefect. Only then would they be able to qualify for service in the colonial administration.

In the Gold Coast, the initial demand in both business and government circles was that the local educational system should concentrate on training African clerks to work in their administrations. But, as in Sierra Leone, supply soon overtook demand and priorities changed. Concerns then began to grow in official quarters and the business community that the mission schools were turning out too many white-collar workers, and that there were too many clerks and not enough artisans in the local community. And so, in 1848, the Switzerland-based Basel Mission set up an experimental school that combined academic education with industrial training. It educated not only teachers and clerks, but also coopers, carpenters, blacksmiths, and wheelwrights. However, this was an isolated initiative, and overall development of Education in the Gold Coast followed a similar pathway to Southern Nigeria. During the later years of the colonial period, the country's educational system steadily improved, as the colonial government increased its financial backing for a growing number of both state and mission schools. In 1909, the administration established a technical school and a teacher training college in Accra, and in 1948 the country opened its first centre of higher learning, the University of Ghana.

In the French colonies in West Africa a similar pattern developed, with mission schools being the first to be established. Development of an educational system was equally slow. Although public or official schools appeared in Senegal between 1847 and 1895, the first such schools in Upper Senegal, Niger, Guinea, the Ivory Coast, and Dahomey were begun only from 1896 onwards. Only after 1900, with the organization of the federated colonies of French West Africa and French Equatorial Africa, was there a French colonial policy on Education. The primary objective throughout the colonial period was to expand the influence of the French language, in order to promote French nationality and culture in the local population. In the first two years of primary school the curriculum was rudimentary (basic French, Hygiene, and Arithmetic), and was aimed at preparing pupils for work in the rural cash economy. At upper primary school level, mainly in the urban centres of population, there was an elite programme of education for those students deemed to be capable of continuing their education. Its primary objective was to select and train suitable Africans to meet the personnel needs of European companies and the colonial administration for lower level staff such as clerks, primary school teachers, and medical assistants. No provision in French West Africa was made for secondary or higher education for Africans.

And so, right across West Africa during the colonial period the development of an educational system for the indigenous population was not only unsystematic, but also primarily dictated by the evolving needs of the colonial administrations and business communities. The practical demands of Empire trumped any consideration of local development. Recruitment of educational administrators and teachers followed a similarly erratic pattern. The Education Departments in the British colonies initially recruited men from the same British public school and university background as District Officers. But they later enlisted missionaries and some practising teachers as educational administrators. Despite their diverse backgrounds and experience, the overall contribution of the teaching profession to the development process should not be underestimated. For it was through British-style education that a new African elite gained the means and the desire to strive for Independence.

## The Military

The West African Frontier Force (WAFF) was a multi-battalion regiment created in 1897 by the British Colonial Office to protect the West African colonies of Nigeria, Gold Coast, Sierra Leone and Gambia. The decision to assemble this force arose mainly out of concern at French colonial expansion in territories that bordered Northern Nigeria. In 1901 there were six battalions in the WAFF, which were divided into 45 companies. The largest detachment was based in Northern Nigeria and was intended as an impressive show of strength. The total force consisted of two battalions of infantry with 1,200 African soldiers and over 200 Briitish officers. This was backed up by two batteries of artillery and a company of engineers. They were equipped with the most up to date weaponry, Martini-Enfield carbine rifles for the infantry and quick firing field howitzers for the artillery.

All the officers and the majority of the non-commissioned officers were British, while the regular troops were drawn from what the British considered to be *'martial tribes'*, mainly in the Muslim north. Most of these came from the lowest ranks of local society, including former slaves of the local elite. The commanding officers were usually transfers from the regular British army. But in the early years many of the junior officers were drawn from the local police forces and were unprepared for military life and discipline. There was no shortage of volunteers for officer ranks. Many wanted to see frontline active service, and to escape the boredom of garrison life. Some would have been enticed in particular by the opportunities that an overseas posting could offer for outdoor pursuits such as polo, horse racing, hunting, and fishing. Pay was also roughly triple that back home, and there was an additional *'bush allowance'*. Local servants and food were also relatively cheap. A job in the colonies would have appealed to many less well-off officers without an income of their own. The only British army officers in West Africa who became weighed down by financial problems were married men with children to educate back in Britain. Indeed there was a standing joke in military service at the time that *"lieutenants can't marry"*.

The European invading forces were generally small and easily outnumbered by any African forces that opposed them. Yet the Nigerian town of Sokoto was captured by only 600 troops, when they were resisted by over 30,000 Africans. European technical superiority made up for the great disparity in numbers. The WAFF had superior weapons, greater military discipline, and more sophisticated logistics. The British army adopted a square formation, with rapid fire rifles supported by machine guns and light artillery. Most African forces had to resort to using more primitive weapons such as spears, or bow and arrow. At best they were armed with highly inaccurate muzzle-loaded guns, with rocks or pieces of metal serving as gunshot.

Before 1890, Africa had been a dumping ground for obsolete European weapons. But the colonial regimes then clamped down on their export, and Africans had the greatest difficulty replacing their arsenal or keeping their existing guns in working order. In addition, few African states had standing armies, and invariably they failed to combine what forces they had against the common enemy. The conquest of West Africa would have been much more problematic, if some African peoples had not sided with the European powers against their own neighbours.

British military strategy was determined not just by the tactics deployed in the field by individual commanders, but also had to be adapted to suit the different systems of government adopted in the different colonies and protectorates. There was also a tendency for the colonial powers to divide countries into a non-martial South and a martial North. Differences of approach therefore evolved over time, and military campaigns increasingly reflected the politics of the different administrative areas. However, at least in the beginning, the guiding principle seemed to be that in the South the British flag would follow trade, whereas in the North it would advance well ahead of commerce.

In Southern Nigeria, under Ralph Moor's administration from 1896-1900, the British stepped up their influence and control in stages. In the first stage, small peacemaking expeditions were despatched to set up councils of chiefs in friendly towns, and at the same time to make an assessment of local economic production. The objectives in the second stage were to commission a detailed survey of the trading routes in local areas, to begin negotiations on the signing of binding formal treaties, and to resolve any burning local issues or complaints. Once these stages were complete, the colonial administration could begin to patrol the waterways, open up land routes, dispense with local tolls, offer protection to African travellers, and finally establish permanent posts, local courts, and local councils. The whole process was aimed at eliminating barriers to the peaceful development of commerce.

In Northern Nigeria, by contrast, the Governor Frederick Lugard relied purely upon military force and imperial prestige to establish control. In the dense tropical forest area of the South the terrain was ideal for ambush and guerrilla tactics, whereas Lugard's forces were able to operate in open country and to fight where he wanted to. His military commanders were able to adopt the same tactics in the field as the imperial forces had used in India, where Lugard himself had been trained. After conquest there was a similar focus on the pomp and ceremony of annual Durbar festivals, in order to impress and subdue the local communities with a show of Britain's imperial might.

The reality of service life, however, was much less glorious. Life in the field was tough in the extreme, and accommodation was both rudimentary and unhealthy. Despite the lessons of the successful military campaign against the Ashanti in the Gold Coast, the WAFF continued throughout the colonial period to suffer from sickness, especially from malaria and blackwater fever. An official report of the time grimly reported:

*"Timber for hutting had to be used to a great extent for coffins".*

The British officers and soldiers of the WAFF were sadly among the first and the last, as well as most frequent victims of the *'White Man's Grave'*.

Living conditions may have been grim, but the pomp of the military display was magnificent. The parade uniform of the

WAFF throughout its history was an ostentatious and highly distinctive one, in a rainbow of colours. Infantry units were issued with scarlet jackets with yellow piping, khaki drill shorts, and red fezzes with matching cummerbunds. The badge on the fezzes was a palm tree. Artillery units wore blue jackets with yellow braid, while the engineers had red jackets with blue braid. African warrant officers were distinguished by yellow braiding on the front of their jackets. In the field, the British officers wore khaki serge uniforms and *'bush hats'* with a green and black cockade.

The WAFF saw initial action during the occupation of the German territory of Kamerun (present day Cameroon) in 1914-1915. The experience gained by the troops during in this campaign, in difficult terrain against stubborn resistance, made them invaluable members of the British forces operating against the Germans in East Africa in the First World War. A single battalion of the Gold Coast Regiment arrived in German East Africa in 1916 and was soon joined by four battalions of the Nigerian Regiment. All remained actively engaged in the war effort until 1918. The WAFF also served with distinction during the Second World War in Italian Somaliland, Abyssinia and Burma. In the post-war period, the WAFF was made up of a Nigeria Regiment, a Gold Coast Regiment, and a Sierra Leone Regiment (including a company in The Gambia). The Nigeria Regiment by then consisted of five battalions, three of which were stationed in the South in Ibadan, Abeokuta and Enugu, and two in the North based in Kaduna). They were supported by a field battery of artillery and a field company of engineers.

Sadly, British military commanders were reluctant to commission African officers throughout the colonial period, and some were even hostile to the idea. This remained the case even during the years when the West African colonies were approaching their Independence. And so, when Her Majesty The Queen paid her first visit to Nigeria in 1956, only two African officers from the First Battalion of the Nigeria Regiment took any part in the military parade that welcomed her to the country. It is also indicative that both men had only risen to the junior rank of Lieutenant. In fact, the only African soldier at the time who had been promoted to the higher rank of Major was Johnson Aguiyi-Ironsi, who was later to become the first military ruler of Independent Nigeria.

## Commerce

British imperial expansion in West Africa focused on exploiting raw materials, minerals, and foodstuffs important to Western industrial development. Britain's twin strategy was to encourage tropical export crops in their colonies and to stimulate demand there for British manufactured goods. To achieve this objective, the colonies built railway networks between the 1890s and the Second World War, and constructed roads at an accelerating rate after the 1930s. These developments, along with the introduction of the pound sterling as the universal medium of exchange, encouraged a vibrant export trade in tin, cotton, cocoa, groundnuts, and palm oil. At the forefront of this economic boom were the established European trading companies and the generation of new national commercial enterprises into which they evolved. Some businesses established an early foothold in the market and were to develop popular local brands that endured right up to the era of Independence and beyond.

Slowly but surely smaller business interests lost market share and concentration increased. By 1930, it is estimated that three companies between them controlled between two thirds and three quarters of all West African trade - the French Compagnie Francaise de l'Afrique Occidentale (CFAO) and Société Commerciale de l'Ouest Africain (SCOA), and the British United Africa Company (UAC). The United Africa Company came under the control of Unilever in the 1930s and continued to exist as a subsidiary of Unilever until 1987, when it was absorbed into the parent company.

Unilever's own history in Nigeria dates back to 1923, when Robert Leverhulme opened a trading post in Nigeria under the business name, Lever Brothers. The company was primarily engaged in the trading of soap, and in 1924 changed its name to West African Soap Company. To capitalise on local demand, in the following year it opened a soap factory in the port of Apapa near Lagos, and was to open a second soap factory in Aba in the East of the country in 1958. The company later expanded into the production of food products and changed its name to Lever Brothers Nigeria in 1955. It continued to introduce new brands even after the colonial era had ended. Indeed, in the year of Independence in 1960, Lever Brothers Nigeria launched Omo detergent into the market. This new brand became so popular with Nigerian consumers that a new factory to manufacture it locally was opened in 1964.

By contrast, some of the other significant new commercial enterprises in West Africa at the beginning of the twentieth century had more modest beginnings, such as John Holt and Company. What developed into a giant business group was in fact the pioneering effort of one man. In 1862, John Holt, just under 21 years old with only £27 in his pocket, sailed from Liverpool to take up appointment as a shop assistant in a grocery store in Fernando Po (now Equatorial Guinea). Five years later, he bought out his employer and subsequently built up a substantial commodities trade with the Delta ports. Produce such as palm oil, palm kernels, rubber and cocoa were exported to England. In return, imports to Nigeria included textiles from Lancashire and bicycles from Birmingham. In 1897, John Holt's company was so profitable that he established his first business venture in Lagos.

Up to the Second World War, the focus of the business contined to be the distribution and export of local produce. A fleet of ships operated a fortnightly service from Liverpool to West Africa, and the company also had its own fleet of river craft. Apart from produce and merchandise, these river craft also carried cash. In places where there were no banks, John Holt's company used its strong rooms to provide a local banking service. Even after major international and national banks had become well-established local institutions, many Nigerians still preferred to deposit their cash with John Holt. In 1961 the company was incorporated in Nigeria as John Holt Limited, and became a public company quoted on the Nigerian Stock Exchange in 1974. By then the company had developed a diverse business portfolio in Nigeria, which ranged from the assembly and distribution of power generators, to boat building, and the manufacture of industrial and agricultural equipment.

Other less diverse European businesses capitalised on the traditional popularity in West Africa of particular export products. Guinness Stout was first exported to Sierra Leone in 1827 and soon was in high demand across the whole of West Africa. Even after Independence, Nigerians' thirst for the product remained unquenched. In response to increasing local demand, in 1963 the company opened a brewery at Ikeja near Lagos in Nigeria, which became the first location outside the British Isles to brew the iconic dark beer. The initial plant had the annual capacity to brew 75 million bottles or 150,000 barrels of beer. Two years later in 1965 Guinness Nigeria was listed on the Nigerian Stock Exchange. The company now proudly boasts that Nigeria is the second largest market in the world for Guinness. Indeed, it is sometimes said that many Nigerians think of Guinness as their national beer.

Another growth area in the colonial period was footwear manufacturing, and by far the leading local consumer brand of the time was Bata. In 1932, the British Bata Shoe Company was established in Nigeria as a trading company, before transforming itself into a manufacturing outfit in 1964. The company spearheaded the development and modernisation of shoe manufacturing in Nigeria, and maintained local tanneries for the processing of leather. Bata shoes became one of the most popular household brands in Nigeria, and some of the company's products lived long in the national memory. In particular, the Cortina sandal was for many decades the preferred choice of parents of Nigerian primary and secondary school children.

The activities of these and other European companies combined to generate a rapid growth in external trade in British West Africa in the early post-war years. It has been estimated that between 1948 and 1951 annual exports from Nigeria doubled from £62 million to £128 million, while on a similar trajectory annual imports into Nigeria increased from £41 million to £84 million. Over the same short period the equivalent increases for trade in the Gold Coast were from £56 million to £91 million for exports, and from £30 million to £63 million for imports.

A new, more professional cadre of Europeans had arrived on the West Coast to manage and administer this industrial and commecial expansion. Many of the newcomers were appointed for their expertise only for short term contracts, or on a project-by-project basis. Some of those recruited may have been attracted by the opportunity such jobs gave them to contribute to the economic development of the host countries. But most would have been attracted by the higher financial rewards and other incentives offered to those prepared to work in conditions that were still considered to be treacherous and potentially unsafe.

Government officials in West Africa generally enjoyed a relatively comfortable existence, living a sheltered life in well-equipped houses on purpose-built Government Residential Areas, commonly known as GRAs. If they needed to travel any distance on their official duties, they would be accommodated in relative comfort at Government Rest Houses that had their own catering. Europeans operating in the commercial arena had a less privileged experience and had to put up with much greater levels of hardship. As their presence in the country was normally for only a short term, they also found it difficult to be accepted into the established colonial society of the longer serving government officials. Moreover, anyone working in construction or in extractive industries such as mining, petroleum, or cement, would often be operating in an isolated location. Their accommodation would normally be provided by their companies on gated compounds with all their amenities and services on site. And so, their relationship with the local African community was often superficial and largely confined to the workplace.

Although individually Europeans working in the commercial world may have left the faintest of footprints, collectively they did make a contribution to the development of the local economy. The rulers of the Independent West African nations were able to build their new economies on the foundations of at least a partially developed modern infrastructure, especially in areas such as transport and communications. Nevertheless, in general European commercial enterprise had only served to hold back the level and pace of development in West Africa. For the primary purpose of commercial activity in the colonial era had always been to engineer the supply of food and minerals to countries like Britain and France. Some investment was made in the local economy, but the overriding focus was always on projects that would boost the trade between the colonies and their home countries in Europe.

# 15 THE SILENT WITNESSES

*"We have seen the awakening of national consciousness
in peoples who have for centuries lived in dependence
of some other power…A wind of change is blowing
through this continent, whether we like it or not."*

## The End Of Empire

The Second World War and its aftermath brought about many changes to colonial life in West Africa, both in circumstances and attitudes. There were dramatic improvements in living conditions, as new anti-malaria drugs became readily available and refrigerators became standard government issue. Improved air access also brought Europe and Africa much closer together, making it possible for families to shuttle back and forth more easily. Another positive devopment in the post-war period was the more prominent role taken by women in colonial society. Many chose to become more directly involved in the affairs of their district, and in particular to champion the cause of women in what remained a predominantly male dominated African society. In addition, there emerged a new group of professionally trained women, for whom the colonial service was a natural progression from their war work.

Another major change was that District Officers also found themselves increasingly involved in politics, as various pilot schemes for local democracy and indirect elections were introduced. The older administrators sometimes found it difficult to adapt to the new more egalitarian mood of the time. As a result, a gulf developed between the newer and older generations of administrators. This had already been magnified by a freeze on recruitment that had been imposed for the duration of the war. This meant that younger members of the colonial service were called up for active service, whereas the older generation was required to stay on and serve extended tours of duty. Some were even threatened with imprisonment if they attempted to enlist.

The gap between the generations manifested itself most clearly in a difference of opinion over the value of touring the district to get to know the local community better. The new intake into the colonial service began to spend more of their time getting to know the new educated local elite. They recognised that the country's future development lay in their hands, rather than with the traditional rulers and their advisers. There was also opposition among the older District Officers to any ideas for touring by any means other than on foot. So, if a young Assistant District Officer asked his superior for an advance to buy a car, his request would often be refused. One District Officer in Northern Nigeria bluntly told a subordinate:

*"No, Smith, I will give you an advance for a pair of boots, but not for a car."*

This particular problem was largely resolved by the arrival of the four wheel drive Land Rover, which was to revolutionise the work of administrators in many parts of West Africa.

The immediate post-war period also saw the start of a decline in the independence of the District Office, and a corresponding growth in the power of a Provincial or Central Secretariat. As administrators moved up the ladder of promotion, they tended to gravitate towards the centre of government, which was known as the *'scratch box'* on the Gold Coast. By the end of the colonial era, nearly all officials were required to serve in the Secretariat for a period of time at some stage in their career. But that did not stop an atmosphere of suspicion and mutual contempt developing between those in the field and those in headquarters. The Secretariat officials considered District Officers to be a rough crowd, and not exactly the sharpest pencils in the box. They were thought to be incapable of writing a good letter, let alone of understanding the subtlety of government policy. The District Officer, on the other hand, thought that officials in the Secretariat were remote and detached. They were reckoned to be good only at pushing paper around, and wholly ignorant of the language and culture of the country in which they served.

As the sun set on the British Empire, white administrators also became obsessed with matters of protocol, and inordinately preoccupied with matters of promotion and status. Most importantly, the New Year's Honours List was awaited each year with eager anticipation. The list would be scanned anxiously to see whether a colleague had been awarded a CBE or a Knighthood ahead of the natural pecking order or of a particular individual. The peak of an administrative career was to become a Governor, a position which was graded into four categories. Nigeria and the Gold Coast ranked as a Class 1 Governorship, Sierra Leone was in Class 2, and poor old Gambia merited only Class 3. In the post-war period, these posts were in the gift of one man in the Colonial Office, Denis Garson, whose 'A List' contained the names of those regarded as fit material for governorships.

But, while the colonial officials were contemplating their respective navels, they were soon to have to confront the rather more pressing matter that was exercising the minds and hearts of their colonial subjects, the movement towards Independence. The final chapter in the history of colonialism in Africa was about to begin, and the silent masses were at last about find their voice.

## The Rise Of African Nationalism

The rise of African Nationalism had its roots in the Second World War, which had given West African soldiers a window on what was happening in the rest of the world. In particular they became aware of developments in countries such as India where the independence movement was already well advanced. Thereafter, the question of Independence for West African nations was never really the issue, only the timescale for the handover of power. Even so, at the end of the war very few colonial administrators believed that self-government would happen during their career, even though most agreed that it was inevitable. As late as 1950, only seven years before Ghanaian Independence, recruits to the Colonial Service in London were being assured by Charles Arden-Clarke, the Governor of the Gold Coast, that: *"there would be jobs for us there during our lifetimes and the lifetimes of our sons."*

The main stumbling block to granting Independence was the issue of Africans running their own affairs, and therefore their readiness for self-government. It was argued that there were not enough African civil servants to run the countries on their own. This argument had some justification, since schemes to develop a new force of trained local administrators had to date received little official support. This failure to build up an indigenous core of trained administrators was one of the biggest blunders of the colonial regime in West Africa. In all other institutions, such as the Christian church, *'Africanisation'* was already well advanced.

There had always been some level of cooperation between African and European traders dating back to the slave trade. But the real integration came during the market slump of the 1930s, when the larger West African corporations were obliged to cut their salary bill by scaling down their high wage management teams, and in the process created vacancies in jobs that had previously been reserved for Europeans. Commercial companies also recognised that positions in areas such as sales and marketing, which benefited from local knowledge, would also be better filled by African rather than European employees. The white officials in government service alone believed themselves to be irreplaceable.

However, the Nationalist pressure for self-government became irresistible, and in 1957 the Gold Coast was the first West African colony to win its Independence from Britain, and was renamed as Ghana. Nigeria followed three years later in 1960, Sierra Leone in 1961, and The Gambia in 1965. And so, much sooner than they had anticipated, British colonial administrators in West Africa found themselves redundant, an *"extinct species"* as some put it. Some stayed on for one or more tours after Independence, before they too began to realise that they had become surplus to requirements. As they departed, many still held dear to the conviction that their work had served a useful purpose.

For many colonial officers in the 1960s the return home from West Africa was a depressing experience. They came back to a Britain where the public image of colonialism and the colonial service was quite different from their own perspective. They were especially embittered by their fellow citizens' apparent lack of interest in what had happened in their part of West Africa over the previous fifty years. Their inflated pride in their years of loyal service to the Crown was punctured, and they felt disillusioned that both they and their achievements had seemingly been consigned to the dustbin of history. They were particularly aggrieved at the lack of recognition of the personal sacrifices that they and their predecessors had made working in the hostile and perilous lands that had come to be known as the *'White Man's Grave'.*

Some retired colonial administrators and missionaries put up a spirited defence of colonial rule. A number of advances and improvements were put forward to make their case. The main contention of the administrators was that British rule had put an end to armed conflicts between one African community and another. As a result, from their standpoint, colonial conquest had paved the way for an extended period of law and order. Their own thesis was that this stability had brought with it many benefits and created many opportunities for the indigenous peoples.

The introduction of literacy was held up as the shining example of how the colonisers had transformed the lives of local people. The former missionaries celebrated the fact that their African converts now had access to the Bible in written form, either in English or their local vernacular. The art of reading and writing enabled local people for the first time to communicate with friends and relatives over long distances. The retired administrators would add that the newly literate Africans had the opportunity to understand more fully the workings of white European government. It was futher argued that, as the Education system expanded, it had opened up a number of new professions and new technical skills to an increasing number of local people. In addition, advanced medical techniques and enhanced standards of sanitation had also radically improved the health and welfare of local communities.

Another achievement put forward by defendants of the colonial era was that links to the outside world economy had been broadened. As a result, in the thirty years leading up to the First World War there had been a dramatic increase in production in West Africa. It was claimed that the conquest of large kingdoms, such as the Ashanti, had created markets of unparalleled size, and that internal trade had benefited enormously from the disappearance of tolls and other commercial restraints, as well as from the eradication of various forms of slavery. As a result, internal trade had expanded in an unprecedented and dramatic way, and new products in the local markets had transformed daily lives and working practices, ranging from ploughs and wheelbarrows to sewing machines and bicycles.

The former colonial administrators took pride in their efforts to bring the rule of law to the colonies. They had banned judicial practices which they viewed as primitive or barbaric, such as ordeal by poison or water, and had outlawed super-stitious practices, such as human sacrifice and the murder of twins. British courts had also given protection to adulterous wives and alleged witches. Finally, a vast range of political, administrative, ecclesiastical, and economic institutions had been established, which the retired officials considered to be the greatest and most enduring legacy of colonial rule.

Understandably, Nationalists in West Africa had a different narrative for the period. From their perspective, colonial rule had been a brutal regime that had dislocated local African so-ciety by attempting to impose alien customs and practices on the traditional African way of life. They acknowledged that the creation of the new colonial territories had brought about major social and political change, but challenged how much of it had been beneficial. The very notion of the state as a territorial entity independent of ethnic or kinship ties, oper-ating though impersonal rulers, was an imposition. Colonial conquest meant that traditional rulers were stripped of their powers to declare war, to organise slave raids and military expeditions, and to carry out independent diplomatic negoti-ations. They also had to surrender many of their judicial roles, especially the right to kill or mutilate convicted criminals and dangerous political opponents.

In the Nationalists' view, the colonial administration had worked to a large extent through African intermediaries, which had further reduced the status and prestige of trad-itional rulers. As a result, Africans gradually came to look to the District Officer rather than to their local chief as the ultimate source of authority, and became accustomed to ap-pealing to the District Officer's courts in order to challenge decisions taken in the traditional courts. Moreover, the system of Indirect Rule had meant that District Officers were also able to delegate their more unpopular duties to traditional rulers, such as the implementation of any new regulations and laws, the recruitment of labour and supply of porters for government projects, the collection of taxes, and sometimes even the enforced cultivation of specific crops. Increasingly traditional rulers had come to be looked on as mere agents of colonial government, and traditional obligations to the chief and the village community had been eroded.

Nationalists argued that colonisation had disturbed the traditional local economy by imposing internal administrative controls on the movement of population. These regulations, together with the development of mining and other forms of land use, often upset the traditional balance between land and people. Farming communities that were used to shifting cultivation were made permanent and suffered severe hardship as a result. Because farmers were no longer allowed to move to fresh land, many were forced to leave their villages and settle in towns. The diaspora of the Igbo people across Nigeria was regarded as a particularly tragic by-product of colonial rule.

An additional complaint was that the traditional customs of giving and generosity had been eroded by the new systems and practices involved in a wage labour and cash crop economy. Increasingly it was money that enabled a family to rise to a higher social status, and most importantly to purchase an education for their children. Education in turn brought power and influence in society at the expense of traditional hierarchies. On the other hand, Nationalists readily conceded that it was from the ranks of the this new educated African elite that the rulers of the newly independent states of West Africa would ultimately be drawn.

Nationalists harboured a deep resentment at the colonisers' basic initial assumption of racial superiority, which continued to be expressed in the form of benevolent paternalism. Perhaps the most enduring legacies of the colonial era were a feeling of dislocation and a general sense of impotence. The local African peoples were largely silent witnesses to the events unfolding around them. If any had dared to protest, they were promptly suppressed. If any voice was raised, it was quickly muted. Mercifully, however, for the Nationalists the colonial period proved to be no more than a brief interlude in the broad sweep of West African history. For a fleeting moment, the conquerors may have held the reins of power, but the impact of their rule had been uneven. The vast majority of West Africans continued to live on the land as they had always done, to honour their customs, respect their ties of kinship and speak their own languages. So they thought of themselves on Independence as Yoruba or Fante rather than as black-skinned British or French. Crucially, they now called the shots, and it was their voice and their viewpoint that was paramount. They had been kept silent for long enough.

## Through African Eyes

Even before the colonial period, Europeans had been an object of curiosity to the peoples of the West African coast. The arrival of Portuguese sailors in the fifteenth century caused a sensation. With their pale skin the visitors seemed to fit the local stereotype of supernatural beings. The fact that they had come by sea reinforced this impression, as the ocean was regarded as the home of spirits and of the dead. The sense of mystery increased as the Europeans appeared to vanish as fast as they came, and then after some time miraculously to reappear.

There are sadly no written texts to tell us exactly how the newcomers were perceived by the local inhabitants. However, the arrival of the first ships did have an impact on local art and led to the production of many fine pieces of sculpture, often with a seafaring theme such as sailing vessels, steamers, and anchors. The Portuguese invaders are depicted as soldiers, priests or traders, quite often with an element of caricature.

In early sculptures soldiers are also sometimes portrayed holding a rifle, the most potent symbol and powerful weapon of conquest. A bronze plaque from the royal palace of Benin in Nigeria shows a bearded Portuguese soldier with long hair holding a lance, and another statue represents a soldier in full armour taking aim with an early form of portable firearm called a *'harquebus'*. Other Benin plaques depict a European carrying a walking stick, a trader wearing a pleated coat, and a man wearing the Portuguese Order of Christ.

The influence of the pre-colonial European visitors manifested itself in other less pictorial ways. The Portuguese and the European traders that followed them to the West African coast brought a treasure trove of strange new merchandise, such as metal, silk, furniture, and clothing, which they exchanged for African gold and ivory. Many of these became fashionable items for the local elite. European jointed furniture became a status symbol, and even an everyday object such as an armchair would be embellished with a beaded African cover to become a royal throne. Spectacles surprisingly became power items, and an essential component of a Ghanaian chief's regalia. Often, they did not even have any lenses, as their function was purely ceremonial, to indicate both political wisdom and a cosmopolitan taste.

During the period of colonisation, Europeans came under even more critical scrutiny. Although European settlers lived apart from their African neighbours, Africans observed them closely. The wooden sculptures of white Europeans carved by the Ijebu Yoruba in Nigeria are stylised in a similar way to the Benin bronze plaques, with features such as a long, thin, hooked nose and a calm, almost blank expression to the face. As Independence approached, artistic expression often contained a hidden, satirical message. The Nigerian sculptor, Thomas Ona Odulate, spent his career documenting colonial life in his carvings and providing a tongue-in cheek commentary on the period. One of his more celebrated works shows a European couple with their arms around each other taking their dog for a walk. The artist is poking fun at colonial lifestyle, by alluding to the common African stereotype that Europeans had a greater love for their dogs than for their fellow human beings.

Some other politically inspired forms of art, such as dance-mask portraits, were aimed more directly at an African audience. One early twentieth century Nigerian mask caricatures a typical white colonial officer, by portraying him with a flushed complexion and stained moustache, and in a pith helmet that is too small for his head. Similar comic carvings were produced during the colonial period in French West Africa by the Baule tribe of the Ivory Coast. Their colourful figures depict a series of Africans wearing European costumes in mockery of an imperial cast of characters, from colonial officers and magistrates to dentists and barbers.

The majority of the few African literary works that exist from the early colonial period are slave narratives. In 1789, Olaudah Equiano, an Igbo from Nigeria, published *"The Interesting Narrative of the Life of Olaudah Equiano"*. The story begins in the West African village where he was kidnapped into slavery in 1756 and includes a vivid description of his first encounter with the white man when he reached the West African coast:

*"The first object which saluted my eyes when I arrived on the coast, was the sea, and a slave ship, which was then riding at anchor, and waiting for its cargo. These filled me with astonishment, which was soon converted into terror, when I was carried on board. I was immediately handled, and tossed up to see if I were sound, by some of the crew; and I was now persuaded that I had gotten into a world of bad spirits, and that they were going to kill me. Their complexions, too, differing so much from ours, their long hair, and the language they spoke, (which was very different from any I had ever heard) united to confirm me in this belief. Indeed, such were the horrors*

*of my views and fears at the moment, that, if ten thousand worlds had been my own, I would have freely parted with them all to have exchanged my condition with that of the meanest slave in my own country."*

Equiano then gives a harrowing personal account of the horrors of the Middle Passage and his transportation to a plantation in the Americas, where he was a witness to further torture and abuse. The conclusion he draws from his experiences is that slavery brutalised everyone involved in the terrible trade, not just the slaves themselves, but also the overseers and their wives, and ultimately the whole of society. The autobiography continues with a description of the adventures that brought him to London, where he married into English society and became a leading Abolitionist. His exposure of the infamous slave-ship *'Zong'*, whose 133 slaves were thrown overboard in mid-ocean for the owners to claim insurance money, shocked the nation. Equiano's book proved to be one of the most powerful contributions to the Abolitionist movement, as it vividly illustrated the humanity of Africans as much as the inhumanity of slavery.

African literature in the late colonial period increasingly focused on themes of liberation, independence and, among Africans in the French colonies in West Africa, *'négritude'* or black consciousness. In 1948, one of the leaders of the Négritude movement, Léopold Sédar Senghor, who was later to become President of Senegal, published the first anthology of French language poetry written by an African: *"Anthologie de la Nouvelle Poésie Nègre et Malgache de Langue Française"*. Another influential writer from the colonial era was Joseph Ephraim Casely Hayford of the Gold Coast, who in 1911 wrote *"Ethiopia Unbound: Studies in Race Emancipation"*, which is commonly regarded as the first African novel to be written in English. After Independence, West African literature grew dramatically in quantity and in recognition, with many works appearing in Western academic reading lists and on bestseller lists. In 1986, the Nigerian Wole Soyinka became the first post-Independence African writer to win the Nobel Prize in Literature.

But perhaps the most ground-breaking literary work was the Nigerian Chinua Achebe's English language novel *"Things Fall Apart"*, which was published in 1958. Before its publication, most novels about Africa had been written by Europeans, and they largely portrayed Africans as savages who needed to be enlightened by Europeans. For example, Joseph Conrad's classic tale *"Heart of Darkness"* (1899), one of the most celebrated novels of the early twentieth century, presented Africa as a dark, uncivilised, and barbaric continent. In Joyce Cary's *"Mister Johnson"* (1939), which was hailed as *"the best novel ever written about Africa"*, the main character is a semi-educated, somewhat naive African who on the whole reinforces the colonial racial stereotype. Achebe broke the mould with a novel that viewed European colonisation from an African perspective. The novel chronicles pre-colonial life in the southeastern part of Nigeria and the arrival of Europeans during the late nineteenth century. He wanted his narrative to show the complexity and sophistication of African society before European arrival, and to reveal the deep wounds that the colonial era had inflicted on his own country's social, cultural, and political fabric.

There are three key European characters in *"Things Fall Apart"* who between them summarise the uncompromising and insensitive nature of colonial rule. They provide an insight into how Achebe and his contemporaries viewed their colonial masters. Mr. Brown is the first white missionary to arrive in the fictional Igbo village of Umuofia. He is portrayed as a gentle and kind man who tries to convert the villagers through his preaching and by building a hospital and school. He is a man of peace, and is contrasted with his successor, Reverend Smith. He is a fire and brimstone preacher, who is uncompromising and strict in his methods. He demands that his converts reject all their traditional beliefs, and shows complete disregard for indigenous Igbo customs and culture. Smith represents the common local stereotype of a white colonialist, and his aggressive behaviour epitomises the oppressive nature of the colonial regime.

The third character, an unnamed District Commissioner, is depicted as a pedantic official who follows the colonial rulebook to the letter, and who arrogantly dispenses justice in total ignorance of local circumstances. And yet, he prides himself on being a benevolent leader, as well as an expert on the anthropology of the local area. He fondly believes that he has only the best intentions for pacifying the primitive people in his district and for bringing them into the modern world. The reality is different, as Achebe's central character Okonkwo says:

*"The white man is very clever. He came quietly and peaceably with his religion. We were amused at his foolishness and allowed him to stay. Now he has won our brothers, and our clan can no longer act like one. He has put a knife on the things that held us together and we have fallen apart."*

A somewhat different European viewpoint is offered in the explosion of autobiographical accounts and memoirs written by retired British colonial officers in the years just before and immediately after Independence. Their biased accounts just occasionally provide glimpses of the impression that the colonial regime must have left on the local peoples that they had conquered and ruled for the best part of a century. In Nigeria, one District Officer's summary of touring was that:

*"In a bush village the arrival of a DO was rather like the arrival of a touring music hall"*

Another District Officer wrote that he was looked on as *"well-meaning if slightly comical"*.

These opinions are echoed by a third District Officer's commentary on his Nigerian experience, which perhaps accurately reflects the prevailing view among retired ex-colonials reflecting on their careers:

*"They thought us slightly mad but were glad to take advantage of our sense of fair play and honesty".*

There was a strong initial antipathy between the Western-educated, often mission-schooled African and the colonial District Officer, who was unused to having his decisions questioned or his motives queried. Sadly, it was often the case that the DO commonly snubbed or ignored the educated elite. This attitude only shifted towards the end of the colonial era when *'Africanisation'* became official policy. There followed a frantic rush to find qualified Africans to fill senior government positions in the new administrations. As one District Officer in Nigeria put it, it became easier in the final years of colonial rule:

*"to treat Nigerians as fellow humans rather than just as pleasant people we administered".*

Sadly, there are few written testimonies from the colonial period to give the alternative perspective of what the average African thought of their colonial masters. For an authentic African voice from the period, we must turn to the educated elite and the Nationalist politicians who were at the forefront of the movement to Independence. The memoirs and speeches of Nationalist politicians are not surprisingly peppered with invective towards the European colonial administrators. Nnamdi Azikiwe, a leading Nigerian Nationalist in the 1950s, castigated colonial policy on the grounds that:

*"it seems to be dedicated to "the gospel according to the man on the spot" whose word is law and whose administration often entitles him to be kicked upstairs with a GCMG or a peerage as his reward".*

Chief Obafemi Awolowo, another Nigerian Nationalist figure, expressed similar contempt for the District Officer whom he accused of being:

*"a source of annoyance to the people. He is aloof, suspicious of the educated classes, and treats their political aspirations with con-*

*tempt. The DO is arrogant."*

Along the coast in Sierra Leone, Siaka Stevens, who became the country's first President, recalled how his father would end his family's daily prayers with:

*"And save us, O Lord, from the trouble of the DO".*

But perhaps the most famous quotation of all is the one delivered on Independence Day by the new Prime Minister of Nigeria, Abubakar Tafawa Balewa, which is a more generous and sympathetic appreciation of the role played by the administrators of the colonial era:

*"We are grateful to the British officers whom we have known first as masters and then as leaders and finally as partners, but always as friends."*

It is also perhaps a fitting epitaph for the European adventurers and explorers, traders and missionaries, sailors and soldiers who had trespassed on the coast of West Africa in the preceding five centuries. It is to be hoped that at the end of their careers they would have been able to reflect on their experience with equal humility. Certainly many of their memoirs reveal a growing respect for the lands over which they travelled, and a lingering affection for the peoples they encountered on the way. They had embarked on their journeys to the West African coast for a variety of motives, and not all of them had the best of intentions. But they endured great hardship in pursuit of their goals, were prepared to take great risks with their personal health and safety, and in some cases sadly gave up their lives to reside forever in the *'White Man's Grave'*.

# BIBLIOGRAPHY

**Chapters 1/2/3**
Aitken, J., *John Newton* (2013).
Barbot, J., Jones A./ Law R. (eds.), *Barbot on Guinea: The Writings of Jean Barbot on Guinea 1678-1712* (1999).
Blake J., *European Beginnings in West Africa 1454-1578* (1937).
Bosman W., *A New and Accurate Description of the Coast of Guinea: Divided into the Gold, the Slave, and the Ivory Coasts* (1704).
Christopher E., *Slave Ship Sailors and Their Captive Cargoes 1730-1807* (2006).
Falconbridge A., *An Account of the Slave Trade on the Coast of Africa* (1788).
Falconbridge A., *Narrative of Two Voyages to the River Sierra Leone during the Years 1791-1792-1793* (1794).
Jones A./ Law R. (eds.), *Barbot on Guinea: The Writings of Jean Barbot on Guinea 1678-1712* (1999).
Law R. (ed.), *The English in West Africa: The Local Correspondence of the Royal African Company of England 1681-1699 Parts 1-3* (1997/2001/2006).
Martin B./ M. Spurrell (eds.), *John Newton: The Journal of a Slave Trader 1750-1754* (1962).
Schama S., *Rough Crossings* (2005).
Thomas H., *The Slave Trade: History of the Atlantic Slave Trade, 1440-1870* (2015).
Walvin J., *The Trader, The Owner, The Slave* (2007).


**Chapters 4/5**
Brent P., *Black Nile* (1977).
Hallett R., *Niger Journal of Richard and John Lander* (1965).
Hallett R., *Records of the African Association, 1788-1831* (1964).
Howard C., *West African Explorers* (1951).
Lloyd C., *Search for the Niger* (1973).
Park M., *Travels in the Interior Districts of Africa* (1799).
Park M., *The Journal of a Mission to the Interior of Africa, in the Year 1805* (1815).


**Chapters 6/7**
Baikie W., *Narrative of an Exploring Voyage up the Rivers Kwora and Binue in 1854* (1856).

Baker G., *Trade Winds on the Niger: The Saga of the Royal Niger Company 1830-1971* (1996).
Crowther S., *Journal of an Expedition up the Niger and Tshadda Rivers* (1855).
Dike K., *Trade and Politics in the Niger Delta 1830-1885* (1956).
Kingsley M., *Travels in West Africa* (1897).
Whitford J., *Trading Life in Western and Central Africa* (1877).

**Chapters 8/9**
Ajayi J., *Christian Missions in Nigeria 1841-1891* (1965).
Ayandele E., *Missionary Impact on Modern Nigeria 1842-1914* (1966).
Buchan J., *The Expendable Mary Slessor* (1980).
Groves C., *The Planting of Christianity in Africa Vols. 1-4* (1948-1958).
Hinderer A., *Seventeen Years in Yoruba Country* (1872).
Livingstone W., *Mary Slessor of Calabar: Pioneer Missionary* (1916).
McLennan B., *Mary Slessor: A Life on the Altar of God* (2014).
Schweizer P., *Survivors on the Gold Coast: the Basel Missionaries in Colonial Ghana*, (2001).
Slessor M., *Correspondence of Mary Slessor (1848-1915)*, School of Oriental and African Studies (SOAS) Archives, University of London (1986).

**Chapters 10/11/12**
Brendon P., *The Decline and Fall of the British Empire 1781-1997* (2007).
M. Crowder M., *West Africa Under Colonial Rule* (1968).
N. Ferguson N., *Empire: How Britain Made the Modern World* (2003).
Duignan P./Gann L., *The Rulers of British Africa 1870-1914* (1978).
Flint J., *Sir George Goldie and the Making of Nigeria* (1960).
Geary W., *Nigeria Under British Rule* (1927).
Lugard F., *The Dual Mandate in British Tropical Africa* (1922).
O'Grady R., *The Passionate Imperialists* (2018).
Pakenham T., *The Scramble for Africa* (1991).
Perham M., *Lugard: The Years of Authority, 1848-1945* (1960).
Smith R. (ed.), *Memoirs of Giambattista Scala: Consul of his Italian Majesty in Lagos in Guinea (1862)*, (2000).

**Chapters 13/14**
Allen C. (ed.), *Tales from the Dark Continent* (1979).
Cary J., *Mister Johnson* (1939).
Clayton A./Killingray D., *Khaki and Blue: Military and Police in British Colonial Africa* (1989).
Crown Agents for the Colonies, *The Nigeria Handbook* (1953).
Crozier A., *Practising Colonial Medicine*, (2007).
Fafunwa A., *History of Education in Nigeria* (1974).
Jaekel F., *The History of the Nigerian Railway* (1997).
Kirk-Greene A., *Imperial Administrators 1858-1966* (2000).

Kirk-Greene A., *Symbol of Authority: The British District Officer in Africa* (2006).
McWilliam H., *Development of Education in Ghana* (1975).
Perham M., *Native Administration in Nigeria* (1937)
Saha S., *History of Agriculture in West Africa* (1990).

**Chapter 15**
Achebe C., *Things Fall Apart* (1958).
Brain R., *Art and Society in Africa* (1980).
Equiano O., *The Interesting Narrative of the Life of Olaudah Equiano* (1789).
Senghor L., *Anthologie de la nouvelle poésie nègre et malgache de langue française* (1948).

www.ingramcontent.com/pod-product-compliance
Lightning Source LLC
LaVergne TN
LVHW051541080426
835510LV00020B/2801